Internal Migration from Odisha:
A Reflection on KBK Districts

Internal Migration from Odisha:
A Reflection on KBK Districts

Dr Narendra Kumar Behera

KALPAZ

The Publication of this thesis was financially upheld by ICSSR and the responsibility of the facts stated, opinions expressed or conclusions reached are entirely that of the author and ICSSR accepts no responsibility for them.

ICSSR

First Published, 2017

Published by

Kalpaz Publications
C-30, Satyawati Nagar,
Delhi – 110052
E-mail: kalpaz@hotmail.com
Ph.: 9212142040

Printed at: G. Print Process, Delhi

Cataloging in Publication Data—DK
Courtesy: D.K. Agencies (P) Ltd. <docinfo@dkagencies.com>

Behera, Narendra Kumar, 1960- **author.**
Internal migration from Odisha : a reflection on KBK districts / Dr Narendra Kumar Behera.
pages cm
Includes bibliographical references.
ISBN 9789351282419

1. Labor mobility—India—Odisha. 2. Rural-urban migration—India—Odisha. 3. Unemployment—India—Odisha. I. Title.

HD5820.O35B44 2017 DDC 331.127954133 23

Dedicated
to
My Parents and Teachers

Contents

Tables List

List of Figures

Foreword

I am delighted to write the forward of the book authored by Dr Narendra Kumar Behera who has been associated with me for about one decade. As a scholar he has attempted to portray the socio-economic condition of migrant workers of KBK districts of western Orissa; which was originally an India Council of Social Science Research (ICSSR) New Delhi, funded research project titled, 'Internal Migration: A Case Study in the KBK Districts of West Odisha'. The author expresses his deep sense of gratitude to the authorities of ICSSR for considering the topical importance of the study and for financing the research study.

The undivided districts of Koraput, Bolangir and Kalahandi (popularly known as KBK districts) in 1992-93 were divided into 8 districts; viz., Kalahandi, Nuapada, Bolangir, Sonepur, Koraput, Malkangiri, Nawrangpur and Rayagada. These eight districts comprise of 14 Sub-divisions, 37 Tahsils, 80 Community Development Blocks (CDBs), 1,437 Gram Panchayats (GPs) and 12,293 villages.

Notwithstanding the rich natural resources and amenable setup of aboriginals thedesired economic development is still to take place in KBK, presently the eight districts. A majority of population of KBK region continue to remain under poverty with illiteracy, poor infrastructure, poor connectivity and very poor exposure to rest of the world.They are poor in terms of per capita income, in terms of indices generally used to categorize people Below Poverty Line such as inadequate calorie intake, poor housing and sanitation facilities, very poor access to education, health, electricity, drinking water, transport and communication. Due to high incidence of corruption and leakages of fund meant for the development of the region, the entire system puts limiting factors to the people for accessing the main economic system.

The common determinants of migration in rural areas are abject poverty, persistent unemployment, low and irregular wage conditions, landlessness, poor facilities of education and health which push these people to those areas like urban centres where they identify its possibilities. Thus, these factors become the pull factors for the distressed migrants of the study villages. These migrants may settle permanently in such areas whereas there are migrants who move different places for regular employment and higher wage but do not settle there and again come back to the place of origin. This type of migration can be termed as circular or seasonal migration. This type of migration occurs during the lean agricultural season. It can be termed as distress induced seasonal migration. People move to other states out of distress or due tonatural calamities like flood, draught and famine which are the contributing push factor for migration.

Migration is an integral part in the process of economic development and overall development discourses. Mostly migrants are getting employment opportunities through social networks such as friends and relatives, who are already in the mainstream of workforce at destination. Migration directly increases the income of the recipient and can help smooth household consumption, especially in response to adverse events such as crop failure or health crisis. In most circumstances, migrant's remittances appear to be associated with increased household investments in health education and social status.

Odisha, the poorest state in India, both in terms of socio-economic and demographic characteristics, (Census 2001), with 86 percent of its total population lives in the rural area; mostly depend on agriculture as their prime source of livelihood. But agriculture being a seasonal activity, majority of these rural people migrate (both in interstate and intrastate form of migration) in search of an alternative source of livelihood during the lean season. In rural Odisha, internal migration (Intra and inter states) plays an important role to influence its socio economic and health status of the people.

Migration is often conceived through narratives in which rural inhabitants, mostly men, migrate in response to negative factors such as environmental change, population growth or increasing economic pressure. Though migration has contributed substantially to the poverty stricken households and are found invariably better off economically and socially compared to non-migrant households. Migration is a major coping strategy of the poor. Earlier studies (Tripathy and Das 1997,

Tripathy 2006) revealed that migrants are mainly from the agricultural households, from the backward and scheduled communities, who prefer to migrate to urban centres, and to construction work sites. A lot of the work that migrant workers are engaged in is seasonal, temporary and low paid. Migration across the border is a major cause for the less than rapid decline in poverty in the border and more prosperous states. The continuous influx of migrant population from neighboring states and adjacent countries has not only worsened the unemployment situation but also has changed the socio-cultural fabric of some states.

In the above-context the study conducted by Dr.Behera is justifiable. He has organised the study in six chapters. The first chapter deals with the introduction to the concept of labour migration internal/ external nature and its associated issues, such as definition, typology of internal migration, determinants of migration, history of migration in India, estimates, effects of migration, importance of the study, objective of study, hypothesis and scope of the study. This chapter provides the scheme and brief outlines of the study.

The second chapter is devoted to the analysis of review of literature to the issues of migration. The migration is of several dimensions that is why the review of literature has been carried out from different angles such as external and internal aspects of migration, basis of migration, displacement and migration, circular and seasonal migration, data on internal migration, migration and informal sector, condition of migrants and state action, migration and child labour, effects of migration and prevention of migration. As labour migration is not specific to any particular country or region, it is quite obvious to take notes of literature relating to the studies of international, national and regional levels. In the above sections views of economists, geographers, psychologists, sociologists and other social scientists have been placed with a reference to the present study.

The third chapter covers the regional profile of the study area such as topography, administrative set up, demographic profile and separate sections relating to the profile of each district of the region. It also covers the migration data of the state and region as well. The region under study is considered as underdeveloped, the state has launched several economic measures to uplift the people, and a brief analysis has been made about such state plan and programme for this region.

The fourth chapter deals with a legal provision associated with the issues of internal migration in the country/state. It covers briefly, different Acts in general and the Inter State Migration Workman (Regulation of Employment and Condition of Services) Act, 1979 in particular. The other related Acts such as Bond Labour System (Abolition) Act, 1976 and Child Labour (Prohibition and Regulation) Act, 1986 have been focused in relation to the study of internal migration.

The fifth chapter covers the analysis of data collected from the region for the purpose of study of internal migration. It covers the assessment of socio-economic condition of migratory labour of this region. In this context, data have been presented in tabular form to discuss their caste, education, demographic character, reason for migration, future plan for migration, plight of migrants at destination etc. The land holding status of different categories of migrants has also been analyzed. Apart from push and pull factors, the social network and other factors associated with migration have been analyzed in the context of the primary data.

The last chapter presents summary and conclusions of the study. It highlights the contents of the chapters in the study and general conclusions derived from the analysis of primary data in relation to the issue of internal migration and a policy implication in relation to the study have been provided for the betterment of the migrants of KBK region.

The conclusions and observations drawn by the author are of stimulating interest. No doubt the present volume is a perpetual narrative of the issues and problems under study. The work is undoubtedly beneficial to the researchers on rural development, migration studies, policy makers and the general readers.

I wish all success in his life and hope; he will continue the academic spirit for years to come.

Professor S N Tripathy,

Gokhale Institute Politics Economics,
BMCC Road, Deccan Gymkhana,
PUNE – 411 004
Email: sn_tripathy2004@yahoo.com

References

Tripathy, S.N and Das, C.R. (1997) Migrant Labour in India", Discovery Publishing House, New Delhi

Tripathy, S.N (2006) 'Dynamics of Tribal Migration, Sonali Publication, New Delhi

Preface

India is a developing country and heading to become a develop country in the days to come. Neither all states nor all regions are developed equally, thus there is the presence of inter-state and regional inequality within the state. Odisha, being an under-developed state the presence of regional inequality is more pronounce. This inequality in development leads to population movement. In the age of liberalisation, privatisation, globalisation and urbanisation the study of migration of human population assumes a significant place. Broadly population movement or migration is of two types: external and internal. The former deals with the movement of people beyond the national boundary, to other country, on the other the later deals with movement of the people within the country. Internal migration is of different types such as inter-state, intra-state, rural-urban, urban-rural, daily, oscillating, seasonal, circular, relay, family, individual, female migration etc. Migration of labour from rural to urban areas usually dominates the discussion and it is basically viewed from economic point of view although non-economic factors have a little bearing. Among different factors responsible for rural out migration, lack of employment opportunity in their places of origin dominate other factors. Natural calamities like drought in the under-developed mono-cropping areas squeeze the scope of employment further, whatever that exist in those areas. This acts as a major push factor for internal migration. The pull factors in other states/regions in the form of employment pull these migrant labours.

However, in the context of KBK region in Odisha, the problem of internal migration has drawn special attention of the researchers, media, social workers and national and international circles. The word KBK has been coined as an acronym of the three undivided districts of Odisha namely, Kalahandi, Bolangir and Koraput. Now these three districts have been divided into eight districts. The term KBK has become popular in the national and international scenario for the infamous incident of child selling that took place in 1985. The recurring drought, the starvation deaths, the selling of human beings and the distress migration drew the national and international attention as well. The KBK region could see the visit of three Prime Ministers at quick succession after the infamous incidence of child sale. To over these problems of deep poverty and distress migration, special development programme (KBK plan) has been launched since 1995.

Despite special development programmes for the region, it is still prone to distress seasonal internal migration. These migrants are called 'dadan' who generally work in the brick kilns of south India states of Andhra Pradesh, Tamil Nadu, Telengana, Karnataka etc. after the kharif crop every year. Unofficially it is estimated that 3,46,471 and 2,78,641 migrant labours from Kalahandi and Bolangir respectively have gone to the southern states during 2008-09. Officially, no systemic data has been prepared so far therefore surrogated data becomes the main source of information. The chief characteristic of this distress internal migrants/dadans is that they are recruited through agents, contractors or dalals and sent to different states to work mainly in brick kilns. These dadans are subject to exploitation and cheating at the hands of agents, contractors and employers at different point of time. The nature of exploitation varies in many ways from physical, sexual to financial. In 2013, the palms of two dadan labourers from Kalahandi were chopped up by the contractors and they became handicapped forever.

The study of internal migration from KBK region of Odisha need to be considered in the light of prevailing conditions of rural poverty, growing landlessness, inequality, unemployment and the failure of government programmes due to leakages of funds and other factors. The working of MGNREGA, the largest rural employment generation programme has failed to check distress migration from this region. Thus, the problem of distress migration from the KBK district assumes a significant study in the context of internal migration taking place in the country. There is dearth of detail study relating to the whole of KBK region, therefore the present study may be claimed to be the first such attempt to study the problem of distress migration. In general, the study provides a regional analysis and a base for further research into the socio-economic problems relating to internal migration and the measure to overcome such problem. It is my humble endeavour to highlight the process of labour migration from KBK region to other parts of the country, their socio-economic condition, method of recruitment, problems at destination and income generation during migration etc. It will certainly open new avenues of research on internal migration and policy formulation for the betterment of these poor migrants engaged in the process of development of the country in varied manner.

Dr Narendra Kumar Behera

Acknowledgements

The present work originally, being an ICSSR sponsored project, I sincerely express my deep sense of gratitude to the authorities of the institution for their consideration to allow me to carry out research on this important economic and social issue of KBK region. The author gratefully acknowledged the help and cooperation, great or small whatsoever it might have received from different quarters/section of people at different point of time to carry out the work. I must express my gratefulness to the host of migrant respondents who have extended their cooperation in answering the questions in the schedule. Their work in the enhancement of national income is duly acknowledged for the development of the nation. I am thankful to the assistance render by Narendra, Ganesh, Chaudhury, Prasanta and Priya Ranjan and other field assistants for their hard work undertaken to collect the field data from a host of population in the KBK districts. Mr Rahul Si, Field Investigator, NSSO Sambalpur deserves thanks for his assistance in the preparation of the schedule questionnaire. Dr Rajendra Gartia, and Mr Mohan deserves a special thanks for assisting in data analysis. Mr Sushanta Kumar Mishra, deserves a special thanks for his careful checking of the manuscript.

I am thankful to DLOs of KBK districts for their cooperation from time to time. Mr P.K. Bhoi, DLO, Bhawanipatna deserves a special thank for his friendly cooperation and suggestion at different point of time. Mr Kshetrabasi Naik, the young writer, Mr. Saroj Mohanty, social activist deserve thank for their friendly discussion and suggestions on the issue. Mr Abani Mohan Panigrahi, President Lokadristi, Rajkhariar deserves a special thank for his valuable cooperation and suggestion from time to time. Sri S.K. Singh deserves special thank for his timely typing of the manuscript. Sri Satyabrata Behera also deserves thank for his assistance.

The librarians of IIAS, Shimla, ICSSR, New Delhi, National Library, Kolkata, NKCDS, Bhubaneshwar, deserve thanks for their cooperation at different point of time. I must express my heartfelt thanks to my wife Tarabati, daughter Sasmita and son Manas for their inspiration, silence and patience tolerance of inconveniences and neglect caused by me in course of this work. Finally, I express my thankfulness to Kalpaz Publications, Delhi for taking effort in the publication of the work.

Dr Narendra Kumar Behera

Abbreviation

BDO	–	Block Development Officer
BPL	–	Below Poverty Line
BRGF	–	Backward Region Grant Fund
CARE	–	Cooperative American Relief Everywhere
CPI (M)	–	Communist Party of India (Marxist)
CRD	–	Centre for Rural Development
DFID	–	Department for International Development
DLO	–	District Labour Officer
DRDA	–	District Rural Development Agency
DTDP	–	Dispersed Tribal Development Programme
GDP	–	Gross Domestic Product
GGY	–	Gopabandhu Gramin Yojana
HDI	–	Human Development Index
IAP	–	Integrated Action Plan
ILO	–	International Labour Organisation
IS	–	Informal Sector
ISMW	–	Inter-State Migrant Workers
ITDA	–	Integrated Tribal Development Agency
ITDP	–	Integrated Tribal Development Project
KBK	–	Kalahandi, Bolangir and Koraput
LTAP	–	Long Term Action Plan
MADA	–	Modified Area Development Approach
MDGs	–	Millennium Development Goals
MGNREGA	–	Mahatma Gandhi National Rural Employment Guarantee Act
MPC	–	Marginal Propensity to Consume
MPCE	–	Monthly Per Capita Consumption Expenditure

MPS	–	Marginal Propensity to Save
MoU	–	Memorandum of Understanding
NCRL	–	National Commission on Rural Labour
NGO	–	Non-Government Organisation
NREGA	–	National Rural Employment Guarantee Act
NHRC	–	National Human Right Commission
NRLM	–	National Rural Livelihood Mission
NSS	–	National Sample Survey
NSSO	–	National Sample Survey Office
OBC	–	Other Backward Classes
OTELP	–	Odisha Tribal Employment and Livelihood Programme
PTGs	–	Primitive Tribal Groups
PVTGs	–	Particularly Vulnerable Tribal Groups
PUCL	–	People's Union for Civil Liberty
RA	–	Rehabilitation Assistance
RIEC	–	Regional Imbalance Enquiry Commission
RLTAP	–	Revised Long Term Action Plan
RNFS	–	Rural Non Farm Sector
RTE	–	Right To Education
SC	–	Scheduled Caste
ST	–	Scheduled Tribe
TSP	–	Tribal Sub-Plan
UEE	–	Universal Elementary Education
UP	–	Uttar Pradesh
UNESCO	–	United Nations Educational Scientific and Cultural Organisation
UNICEF	–	United Nations International Children's Emergency Fund
UPA	–	United Progressive Alliance
UPR	–	Usual Place of Residence
WODC	–	Western Odisha Development Council
WORLP	–	Western Odisha Rural Livelihood Programme
WRP	–	Work Rate Participation

Chapter - 1

Introduction

1.1 The Background

Population movement from one place to another place, temporarily or permanently and its settlement is an age old phenomenon of human civilisation. Among the terms used for population movement, the most frequently used are three Ms: - Movement, Mobility and Migration. Movement of population does not involve a permanent change of residence. Mobility is perhaps the most general concept in migration literature. It covers all kinds of territorial movements, both temporary and permanent, over different distances. Mobility might be considered as the facility of being mobile, which enables people to move from one place to another. Mobility may be restricted by different conditions such as economic, geographical barriers and physical disability. Migration on the other hand may assume a character of temporary or permanent nature. Substantial literatures have come up since Ravenstein's formulation of 'migration laws' in 1885 along with the spatial movement of population. "It is one hundred years since E.G. Ravenstein's first paper on the laws of migration was published in the *Geographical Magazine*; his later but better known articles appeared in the *Statistical Journal* in 1885 and 1889. His work laid the foundation for the subsequent research on migration, and indeed one recent authority has written that "while there have been literally thousands of migration studies in the meantime, few additional generalisations have been advanced."[1] The scholars of nineteenth century emphasised the social, cultural, and economic factors behind population migration. Professor W. Arthur Lewis (1954) developed a theory of economic development with unlimited supplies of labour. In a capitalist economy movement of workers takes place from subsistence sector to capitalist sector. Based on Ravenstein's law, Lee (1966) divided the forces exerting an influence on migration perceptions into 'push' and 'pull' factors. John C.H. Fei and Gustav Ranis (1961), Sjaatad (1962) improved Lewis's model and emphasised sectoral relocation of labour for improvement in productivity and wage equalisation between sectors. Professor J.R. Harris and M.P. Todaro (1970) based on the experience of tropical Africa facing the problem of rural-urban migration and unemployment expressed labour migration in terms of rural-urban differences in average expected wages. Thus, in different models of economic development, labour migration have been discussed in respect of sectoral movement. In an undeveloped economy, labour movement takes place from agriculture to industry or from backward region to forward region within the country. Growing urbanisation and newly created development centres have added further impetuous to population movement.

1.2 The "laws" of Migration

Ravenstein's "laws" of migration (1885-1889) may be restated as follows:

(i) The majority of migrants go only a short distance.

(ii) Migration proceeds step by step.

(iii) Migrants going long distances generally go by preference to none of the great centres of commerce or industry.

(iv) Each current of migration produces a compensating counter current.

(v) The natives of towns are less migratory than those of rural areas.

(vi) Females are more migratory than males within the Kingdom of their birth, but males more frequently venture beyond.

(vii) Most migrants are adults: families rarely migrate out of their country of birth.

(viii) Large towns grow more by migration than natural increase.

(ix) Migration increases in volume as industries and commerce develop and transport improves.

(x) The major direction of migration is from the agricultural areas to the centre of industries and commerce.

(xi) The major causes of migration are economic.

Thus, the laws broadly states different causes and nature of migration but subsequently there is addition of new concepts to these laws.[2]

1.3 Defining Migration

The word migration has been derived from the Latin word 'migrate' meaning change of one's residence. But it is difficult to define the concepts relating to migration, precisely since it envelops different aspects on the basis of 3 D's such as distance, duration and direction. Migration is studied on quantified statistical methods. Migration, whatever the type may be it is the product singularly or in combination of economic, social, political, physical and cultural circumstances.

The NSS 64th round states, mobility is an integral part of human existence. However, all types of human mobility are not migration. In NSS surveys, those movements which resulted in change of the Usual Place of Residence (UPR) of the individuals were treated as migration and a household member whose last UPR was different from the present place of enumeration was considered a migrant. Though social, cultural, political, personal and natural forces have a bearing on migration, viewing it as an economic phenomenon which receives special attention. People may be motivated to change their place of residence because of lack of employment opportunities in the area where they are residing or with the hope of finding better opportunities elsewhere.

An operational definition of migration needs to cover both temporal and location criteria. The operational definition depends on the nature and type of research carried out and its structure of data availability. A migrant is a person who moves from one administrative unit to another, with an intention to settle permanently in a different region or a country. The minimum time frame for a migrant may be for a period of six months or one year. Thus, at any point of time the total population can be divided into migrants and non-migrants or movers and non-movers. This indicates the mobility status of the population relating to a particular area/region. The terminologies of in-migration and out-migration are often used in the context of internal migration which takes place within the country, while migration outside the country is associated with the terms of immigrant and emigrant. Immigrant refers to a person who has come to live permanently in a country, other than his own. On the other hand emigrant is a person who leaves his country to leave in another country permanently. Migration takes place from one area of origin to another area called destination and the group of people moving from origin to destination is termed as migration stream.

The internal migration of seasonal character involves greatest number of people is also termed as distress migration, circular migration or oscillatory migration. It has a special bearing as a means of livelihood for the poor people in underdeveloped regions. This seasonal migration is a phenomenon of rural India can be further categorised into (i) 'subsistence' equilibrating seasonal migration (ii) Innovation induced 'subsistence' seasonal migration and (iii) The 'survival' seasonal migration.

The subsistence equilibrating seasonal migration is a form of equilibration, which tends to balance between the supply of labour and demand for labour. This type of migration is largely associated with paddy crop in irrigation endowed and agriculturally more developed regions. For example, labour migration to Hirakud Command Areas of Bargarh district in Odisha takes place from the dry area of the same district or neighbouring districts. This is inter-regional (locality) migration from dry to wet areas.

The second categories of seasonal migration induced by introduction of a new crop which may necessitate certain new skills or introduction of an 'old crop' in new area which may propel along with the crop migration of labour to the new areas. For example, in Andhra Pradesh, tobacco cultivation was introduced in early 1905 in Guntur district and by 1930 the district became the homeland of tobacco. Migrant peasants from Guntur-Krishna districts took tobacco to West Godavari, Khammam, Karimnagar in Andhra Pradesh and Hassan, Shimoga, Chitradurga in Karnataka.

The third category of seasonal migration is of 'survival in nature which takes place from dry and draught prone region of the state. It may take place in the form of (1) contract labour to projects and public works (ii) Individual or family migration to urban areas for casual work and (iii) migration in search of agricultural work in the neighbouring districts of the states.[3]

To add to the above three categories, a fourth category of labour migration is seen in the form of contract labour on advance payment known as '*dadan*' from underdeveloped districts of West Odisha particularly Bolangir, Bargarh, Nuapada, Kalahandi, and Sonepur usually moves to the neighbouring states of Andhra Pradesh, Telengana, Tamil Nadu, Karnataka etc. to work in the brick kilns. So also the Bihari labour move to West Bengal to work in brick kilns or for self employment in informal sector. Migration of this seasonal character sometime becomes demonstration induced, particularly for the young generation who are motivated by the modern style of living in the age of mobile and internet.

The phenomenon of rural-labour migration is an age old problem. Since time immemorial people have been migrating, from one place to the other in search of pastoral land, livelihood, business and employment. In the context of neo-liberalised economy too, migration continues unabated in spite of developmental activities undertaken in all parts of the country. But the persuasion of in-equitable development and planning has generated lands of developed region or urban pockets which act as pull zone for the potential migrants of the rural areas. In view of this situation most of the urban township and metropolitan cities found a substantial growth only due to the addition of migrant population.

Sometime the event of migration to urban areas may deviate. As it happened in case of Chennai in the early part of twentieth century, it experienced an outflow of population and continued up to 1941. But after independence Chennai started growing through population migration as a direct result of industrialisation and urbanisation in the State. This type of situation was experienced in a town of the study area of KBK districts. The princely state township of Sonepur experienced a situation of declining population. In 1941, the population of Sonepur was 9,065 while in 1957 and 1961 the figures decreased to 7,356 and 7108 respectively. It was termed as a deserted town during those decades.[4] Earlier, it had been observed that the economic plight put them, (in the context of people of undivided Balangir district) almost in the point of starvation leading to pledge their services to the Gountias (village landlord).[5]

There are reliable reports with regard to the mass migration of labours to the neighbouring State due to long spell of drought in the poverty stricken districts of Kalahandi during the year 1990. In the district of Kalahandi there happened a large scale migration in some villages.[6]

The shift of employment from a non-mortised-agriculture economy to mortised-non-agricultural economy through the spread of education and transformation of general socio-economic characteristics of the population followed by a drastic change in the aspiration of the people to lead a comfortable life in urban areas rural-urban migration has become a common phenomenon. The percentage of urban population was only 11 per cent in 1901 in 1,627 towns increased to 27.8 per cent in 2001 with 5,166 towns. It is expected that by 2021 the urban population may touch 40 per cent of the total population in the country. The growth of urban population has another significant aspect in term of occupational distribution. The occupation under primary sector declined from 72 per cent in 1951 to 56.7 per cent in 2000 whereas the occupation in secondary sector and tertiary sector shown an increase from 10.6 per cent and 17.3 per cent in 1951 to 17.5 per cent and 25.8 per cent respectively in 2000. This shows that growing urbanisation (mainly through migration) leads to transformation of jobs from agricultural to non-agricultural sectors.

1.4 A General Typology of Internal-Migration

Internal migrant is a person residing in a place other than his/her place of birth or one who has changed his/her usual place of residence to another place or those who move within national boundaries are several times more significant in terms of numbers involved compared to those who move across countries, but fail to receive the attention that international migration receives from the researchers, international organisations and funding agencies. According to UNDP Human Development Report 2009, the number of those who moved across the major zonal demarcations within their countries was nearly four times larger (740 million) than those moved internationally (214 million).[7]

Broadly, migration can be divided into two categories namely, internal and external migration. Internal migration takes place within the boundary of a country from one region/state to another or from one place to another which has socio-economic and other reasons. Internal migration has four streams; rural-urban, rural-rural, urban-urban and urban-rural. Out of these four streams rural-urban migration is the usual demographic movement. On the other, urban to rural (turn-back) migration has not yet started in India. Voluntary internal migration in modern India has taken place to urban and industrial centres and developed regions. Internal migration can also be classified into inter-state and intra-state. The movement of people between states is known as inter-state, while intra-state migration refers to movements within the state. People have migrated in large scale to big cities/industrial centres such as Delhi, Mumbai, Chennai, Bangalore, Ahmedabad, Surat etc. in search of employment. The volume of these streams varied from state to state depending upon their historicity and level of economic development.

Migration may be positive and negative. Opportunities for economic improvement attract migrants as a positive factor whereas lack of economic opportunities distract people from their place of living to other places. Migration may be permanent or temporary. Permanent in migration leads to settlement of migrant permanently. On the other hand, a migrant goes to another place during natural calamities like flood, cyclone, drought etc. for a temporary period and comes back to his original place of residence after the calamity is over.

Basically, unequal economic development causes short duration internal migration in the form of inter-state, inter-district or intra-district migration. Among the migrants in both rural and urban areas nearly 99 per cent of the migrants were internal migrants. Out of which 91 per cent migrated from the rural areas and eight per cent constitute migration from urban areas.

Millions of people were displaced by the projects of India's modernisation. The construction of large dams, in particular, made unwilling migrants of the whole communities. Their livelihoods were ruined, their communities broken, and they received little or no monetary compensation.[8]

"It's happened in India, where in the period 1951-90, over 21.6 million people suffered precisely that fate—displaced by just dams and canals alone. Add mining that has dispossessed 2.1 million people and you have the population of Canada. Further, industries, thermal plants, sanctuaries and defense installations have thrown at least 2.4 million human beings out of their houses. That's around twenty-six million Indians."[9] Without adequate resettlement and rehabilitation measures this huge displaced people have become a potential source of migration as a by-product of development projects. They are thrown to the space of landlessness and joblessness which is termed as involuntary or forced migration.

There are many cases of involuntary or forced migration within India such as migration of people from Pakistan to India after its partition in 1947. This is the greatest displacement or forced migration due to political reason. The Bengalis moving from Assam due to tension there, the Kashmiri Pandits from Kashmir due to terrorism 1988-89 are now living in different parts of India. Following the Indo-Pak war of 1971, the Hindu population migrated from Bangladesh have been resettled in Dandakaranya area of Malkangiri district of Odisha. The displaced people of different development projects have migrated to various parts of the country for example the displaced people of Hirakud dam project in Odisha have migrated to the neighbouring state of Chhattisgarh, and other districts of the state. So also the displaced people of Bhakra dam have migrated to Rajasthan for livelihood. Search for means of livelihood and unavailability of adequate means of livelihood in the place of origin is believed to push the people to other regions where livelihood is arranged, these acts as the pull of the migrant to such regions. Migration in India has shown that resource poor people participate extensively in migration. It may be permanent/semi-permanent shifts of population between underdeveloped and developed regions and between rural and urban areas, mostly being absorbed in the informal and unorganised sector of the economy.

The concept of circular migration may be defined as a temporary move from, followed by return to the original/normal place of origin/residence for the purpose of employment during the lean seasons of agricultural activities. The dualistic model (Lewis, 1954; Fie and Ranis, 1961) explains the trend of labour migration from subsistence sector to the modern sector of the economy. It is the movement of labour from subsistence sector where labour's marginal productivity is low and thereby prevail low wage, to modern sector where labour's marginal productivity is high along with high wage rates. In practice circular/

seasonal migration originates due to lack of sufficient local employment (both farm and non-farm), landlessness, marginal and small holdings, fragmentation and sub-division of land holding pushes the people to the areas of better employment opportunities in higher productive and growth sector. The common destinations of these migrants which pull them include: command areas of different large irrigation projects, industrial belts, cities/urban localities, brick kilns, constructions sector, transport sector such as rickshaw pulling, auto-rickshaw driving, street vendor, railway coolies, and other informal sector where the jobs are available with a higher wage in comparison to the place of their origins.

Migration turns into circular when the employment is of a limited duration. A marked example of circulation is that of the seasonal workers who leave their villages often accompanied by wives and children, to escape the off-season in the agrarian cycle by working as care-cutters or brick makers. Seasonal and circular (also known as cyclical, oscillatory) migration has long been part of the livelihood of poor people across India.[10]

In India, people are still primarily migrating for survival, as a survival strategy to somehow make two ends meet. The focus is on eking out an existence despite miserable living conditions in far-flung destinations. Extreme poverty and the constant burden of debt riddled penury are the main push factors responsible for migration. For many of the people in rural areas, migration is an alternative to seeking a living outside the village. However, migration has wide-ranging implications for the economy and society.[11]

Migration is also associated with precarious employment. Precarious employment is a contributing factor to global poverty as it is accompanied by unpredictable sources of livelihoods, inadequate earnings and difficult working conditions. The link between precarious employment and poverty is evident in India, where about 92 per cent of workforce of 457 million estimated to be in the unorganised sector.[12]

Poor people do migrate, but it is not necessary that the poorest of the poor only migrate from rural to urban places. Public work programmes have little impact to check circular migration in the KBK districts. Circular migration has become the way of life and livelihood strategy for the poor and backward class of people in the districts of

Bolangir, Nuapada, Kalahandi, but to a lesser degree in Koraput, Malkangiri, Nabarangpur and Rayagada of KBK region of south-west Odisha.

Developing countries have found development progressively more difficult. Continuing high population growth has increased the work force but has done nothing to create jobs. In 1960, the ratio of annual labour force growth in the developing countries compared with the industrialised countries was 4:1, in 1990s, the ratio has increased to 12:1. In this situation migration is an attractive option.[13] Under these conditions different types of temporary short-term internal migrations have been phrased in the study of migration, these are as follows.

1.4.1 Oscillating Migration:- 'Oscillating' migration, in contrast to seasonal migration, may not be tied to seasonal employment availability but can take place at any point of time, and occurs strictly due to economic factors. It consists of out migration for shorter duration of one day to three months and occurs on a repeated basis.

1.4.2 Seasonal Migration:- According to Kundu (2007), persons who have gone to any other place for 60 days or more during the last six months from the date of survey and returned may be termed as seasonal or short-duration migrants. Circular/seasonal migration includes a wide variety of movements usually short-term, repetitive or cyclical in nature, but all having in common the lack of any declared intention of permanent or long-lasting change in residence (Hugo, 1982).[14] Seasonal migration is seen in a region where production of one or two agricultural output takes place with varying labour requirements over the course of the year, which thereby force the local labour force to search for jobs elsewhere at regular intervals. It may also emerge in urban economics which is dominated by certain activities like tourism which depends on local climatic conditions and may not engage permanent labourers. According to Haan and Rogaly (2002), Seasonal migration has drawn the interest of the scholars in recent times. Migration, particularly of poor, is seasonal, temporary and most of which remains within rural areas. Though, the daily earnings of the migrants at the destination may be only marginally higher, migrants undertake this migratory work to maintain or slightly improve their situation at home.[15] Seasonal labour migration is an increasingly important aspect of rural livelihood in underdeveloped regions of

Odisha, Bihar, Jharkhand, Chhattisgarh, Madhya Pradesh, Andhra Pradesh.

1.4.3 Circular/Return Migration:- Short-term migrants are more likely to return to the place of origin where there is some stake in the form of house, property or family ties. Return migration is often practised for the purpose of making sufficient money to invest in land or business in the place of origin to lead a comfortable life after retirement.

1.3.4 Relay Migration:- Relay migration is another variant of short term movement, as the term suggests, it involves more than one individual. Relay migration generally consists of decanting different family members to external labour markets at different points of life cycles. In this case the fathers move first followed by their children or brothers in older age.

1.4.5 Individual Migration:- In this case one member of the family migrates whereas the rest of the family members stay back in the place of origin.

1.4.6 Family Migration:- When families either move as complete unit or as is often the case in successive stages, with one member moving to an area ahead of others in order to find work and shelter. In case of seasonal migration family migration is a usual practice for the migrants.[16]

1.4.7 Female Migration:- Female migration usually takes place in large scale following their marriage. In India, most of rural-rural migration of women is associated with marriage. Female migration is also associated with family seasonal migration, which is a also common form of migration.

Mike Parnwell (1993) divides internal and external migration in spatial term in the form of distance and direction. Distance relates to international, local, intra-district, inter-district, intra-provincial, inter-provincial, inter-regional, and international: third world-third world, and third world-first-world. On the other hand direction of migration relates to rural-rural, rural-urban, urban-rural, periphery-core, core-periphery, traditional-modern sphere, step migration, migration stream and counter-migration.

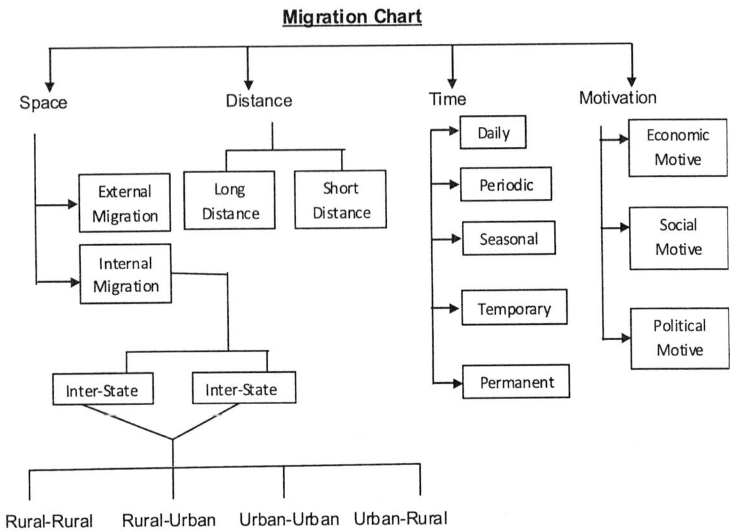

Source:-Verma, A.K., Labour Migration in Agriculture Sector, 2011, p. 5.

Figure 1.1

Figure 1.1 indicates different type of migration on the basis of space, distance, time and motive. External or international migration relates to population movement from one country to another across the international boundary. It may be voluntary or involuntary. Voluntary migration arising out of 'brain-drain' situation from developing countries to developed countries. The case of India Diaspora in the USA and UK is an example of external migration of voluntary in nature. On the other hand involuntary or compulsory international migration arises due to political factors like partition of British India into two nations i.e. India and Pakistan. Millions of people were forced to migrate from one nation to other and vice versa. Migration may also take place to one nation where the refugees of a nation get legal protection in another nation. As it is the case with Tibetan refugees in India. India has experienced large scale immigration from its neighbouring countries particularly from Bangladesh and Nepal. Although India's population is considered as one of the least mobile population of the world, still it has experienced both types of migration. Internal migration is said to exist when people move within the territorial jurisdiction of the country. Internal migration may take place within the state (Intra-state) and outside the state (Inter-state). It may also take place on an inter-regional basis within a state. Internal migration of labour takes place from rural to urban, rural to rural, urban to urban and urban to rural. Among all these form of migration rural to urban migration find a prominent place in the demographic study of migration. Urban to rural migration has not assumed any significant dimension in the country. Migration becomes permanent when they settled in a place permanently and it mostly happens in case of urban settlement. The migrants from the study area KBK districts have settled permanently in the irrigated area and perusing different petty business, agricultural activities, rickshaw pulling and have become a source of labour class for different works. It is observed in the place working of the researchers (Bangal district of West Odisha) that mostly they have come from the KBK region and settled in rural and urban areas as well.

1.5 Decision to Migrate

Migration takes place when an individual decides that it is preferable to move rather than to stay where the difficulties of moving seem to be more than offset by the expected rewards (L.A. Kosinski and R.M Prothero (eds.) 1975).[17]

The decision to migrate may be taken by an individual himself; by the family members as a unit, by a class or caste or a group as a whole. A common interest or common suffering may lead to a decision as a whole of the group to migrate. Social oppression and discrimination also lead to migration of a family or a group of families. But economic reason dominates in case of seasonal or circular migration prevailing in developing countries. The decision to migrate is influenced by earlier migrants, agents and middlemen. The attraction of higher wage along with regular employment and better economic condition leads to the decision to migrate.

Migration decisions are made in the contexts of men and women having different access to critical resources such as migrant network. Money paid in lump sum as advance for maintenance during an occasion by the agent leads to the decision to migrate. The migrant recruitment agencies that funnel migrants into jobs influence a great deal to the decision of the potential migrants.

Each person is constantly exposed to factors at a place of residence some of which inhibit movement and others which encourage it. By the same token, there are numerous positive and negative impulses coming from different potential destinations. The decision to move or not to move results from the evaluation of all these factors.

1.6 Determinants of Migration

There is little agreement about the immediate determinants of migration within or away from rural areas. There are three different approaches to the materialistic basis of migration. While the neo-classical traditional writers tend to view migration as a kind of 'profit maximisation' activity, researchers interested in circulation have tended to emphasise 'risk minimisation' and argue that migration is often a way of diversifying economic options. Researchers who take structural perspective usually interpret migration as a 'survival strategy'......... The dominant model of migration determinants for past three decades is generally referred to as Harris-Todaro approach.[18]

Factors like high population growth and lack of livelihood, unemployment push for migration. Development of transport and communication has facilitated migration to the areas of industrial growth and trade centres. Development of social sectors like health, education, housing etc. and changing social structures act as social factors which influence migration. The increased importance to nuclear families and decline in joint family is one of the major social reasons for migration. Change in occupational structure primarily from agricultural sector to non-agricultural sector promotes migration in the recent trend of migration. Physical factors like new agricultural land and irrigation facilities attract migration. It has happened in case the migration of farmers from Andhra Pradesh to Bargarh and Sambalpur districts of Odisha in the early phase of construction of Hirakud dam across the river Mahanadi during 1950s. Natural or physical factors such as draughts, flood, cyclone etc. may push migration. The political factors like war, ethnic violence are also behind population migration. The situation set during partition of India led to large scale migration between the newly created nations. The negative factors at the source act as 'push' factor whereas the positive factors act as 'pull' factor for and some time both 'push-pull' factor acts jointly for migration.

The overwhelming conclusion of almost all migration studies, both descriptive and econometric, is that people migrate primarily for economic reasons. The greater the difference in economic opportunities between urban and rural regions, the greater is the flow of migrants from rural to urban areas. While distance is usually a significant intervening obstacle, its negative influence can largely offset by sizable income differentials, especially for the more educated migrants. [Barnum and Sabot, 1975b; Schultz 1975; Lipton 1976).[19]

Neo-classical equilibrium theories while differing slightly in their micro and macro formulations focus on migration as the product of labour market disequilibrium between regions. In contrast, structural theories, whether they highlight labour markets or world systems, emphasise that migration is a structural feature of global capitalism. In our view, the historical theory that runs through most structural accounts gives them a significant edge over neo-classical counter-parts. They at least provide some explanation as to why mobility is on the rise, linking into structural transformation of the global economy during the past four decades.[20]

Migration as a process is usually decided by taking into consideration the advantages and disadvantages of such migration. The flow of migrants occurs as a group from underdeveloped region to developed regions where jobs during lean seasons are available. Thus, a 'push' factor appears in the area of origin to pull them into the area of employment. This labour market operates through dalals, sardars or agents who play a vital role in the process.

Migration may thus be seen as people 'voting with their feet' by moving away from depressed regions and seeking to gain access to the opportunities and rewards which they perceive to be available in the core region. In this way migration can be viewed as a response to the unevenness of the development process.[21]

The NSS data pertain that only one per cent of households' moves to the rural areas and three per cent of the households to the urban areas during the last 365 days. Among all these reasons of migration, employment related reason dominates the migration scenario. In urban areas 67 per cent of migrant households and nearly 55 per cent of rural migrants' households migrate for employment related purpose. The table below presents a detail determinants and reason for migration in India. Social factor like caste system in the village community some time promotes migration. Once they are migrated, the caste structure gets diluted and they enjoy a life of common men.

Table 1.1: Distribution of (per 1000) Households by Reason for Migration (2007-08)

Sl. No.	*Reason for migration*	*Present place of residence*		
		Rural	*Urban*	*Anywhere in India*
1	2	3	4	5
1.	In search of employment	168	202	185
2.	In search of better employment	175	169	172
3.	Business	43	48	45
4.	To take employment/better employment	106	128	117
5.	Transfer of service/contract	48	105	77
6.	Proximity to place of work	12	13	12
7.	Sub-total (Sl. No. 1 to 6)	552	665	608
8.	Studies	267	210	238
Forced migration				
9.	Natural disaster	13	2	7
10.	Social/political problem	7	2	5
11.	Displacement by Development Project	4	15	10
12.	Sub-total (Sl. No. 9 to 11)	24	19	22
Others				
13.	Acquisition of own house/flat	24	30	27
14.	Housing problems	30	16	23
15.	Healthcare	4	9	7
16.	Post retirement	5	4	5
17.	Marriage	29	13	21
18.	Others	53	34	44
19.	Sub-total (Sl. No. 13 to 18)	145	106	127
20.	All (including n.r.)	1000	1000	1000

Source:-NSS Report No. 533, Migration in India 2007-08.[22]

The seasonal or temporary migration is usually dominated by single most important reason of employment only. In mono-cropping area the potential migrants don't find regular job during the lean agricultural season, that is why they are motivated or tempted to go in search of their livelihood for a short duration of six months and return to their usual place of residence before the agricultural activities begin in the monsoon (i.e. June). Table 1.1 shows the NSS data and it finds that search for employment is the dominant determinant of migration in India.

1.7 The Micro-level Perspectives and Volume of Migration

The Micro-level dimension of why people move includes factors in the places of origin and destination which influence people to take decision for migration. People move for what reasons and to which directions are provided by the model developed by Evertt Lee in the mid-1960s. He drew inspiration from the 'Laws of Migration' which were suggested by E.G. Ravenstein during the later part of nineteenth century, which influence the decisions to migrate. The model helps to know the importance of micro-level influences on the migration decision-making process.

No matter how short or how long, how easy or how difficult, every act of migration involves an origin, a destination, and an intervening set of obstacles. Among the set of intervening obstacles we include the distance of the move as one that is always present.[23]

The factors that influence in the process of migration are (i) factors associated with the area of origin (ii) factors associated with the area of destination (iii) intervening obstacles and (iv) personal factors.

The factors that hold and attract or repeal people are precisely understood neither by the social scientist nor by the persons directly affected. Like Bentham's calculus of pleasure and pain, the calculus of +s and –s at origin and destination is always inexact.[24]

Taking into account of these factors the volume of migration within a given territory varies with the degree of diversity of area within the territory, diversity of people, difficulties of surmounting the intervening obstacles, fluctuation of the economy, checks and imposition of restrictions and the state of progress of the origin and destination areas.

The decision to migrate is governed by a set of prevailing factors both in the migrant's place of origin and destination. Lee has identified, these factors as being positive (+), negative (-) or neutral (0). The negative factors at the place of origin influence the migrants' decision

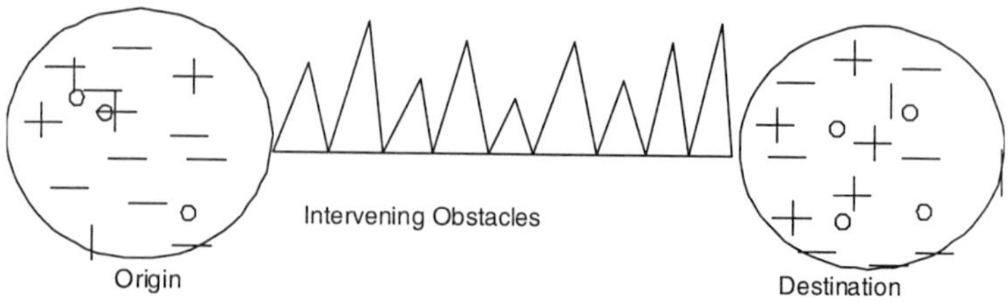

(Evertt S Lee, (1966) A Theory of Migration Demography 3, p. 50)

Figure 1.2: Everett Lee's Model of Migration.

to migrate. These factors may also be termed as 'push' factors. The positive factors at the destination attract the migrants that can be termed as 'pull' factors. The push, pull or push-pull factors result in the volume of migration from the place of origin to the place of destination. The repulsive factors push the migrants from the origin and the attractive forces pull them to the place of destination. A relative balance between positive and negative factors, acts as a powerful factor on the occurrence of migration, its direction and destination areas. It also influences the period of stay and return for the migrants. The prevailing positive and negative factors may not affect all the people of origin equally and the decision to migrate is solely depend on the individual's decision. In the recent past, researchers on migration have set its importance on non-permanent form of movement within the context of total demographic mobility. Researchers have focused on the migration at short distance for short periods of which there is a considerable occurrence (Skeldon, 1985; Hugo, 1983).

Lee further puts that the decision to migrate is also influenced by the information from secondary sources such as the media or from the returned migrants. But these sources of information may not be complete and fully reliable. In case of seasonal labour migration the agents and returned migrants play a crucial role in influencing the potential migrants. To adopt migration as a means of livelihood in case of short-term seasonal migration is often decided by a group or number of families either by themselves or through the agents. This type of migration usually involves group movement to a particular area either within the state or outside the state.

In Lee's model there are various intervening obstacles on the way of migration. These barriers to migration are cost of travel, family attachments, personal anxiety, government restriction, cultural and social restriction etc. Those who overcome these intervening obstacles are able to migrate. The prevailing seasonal migration in the study area of KBK districts, payment of '*baina*' or cash advances forms the basis of '*dadan*' migration in luring the migrants to adopt internal migration to the neighbouring southern states during the lean seasons of agricultural activities. This type of migration is occurring in massive scale and which is of distress in nature, can be termed as 'distress seasonal circular migration'.

Successful migrants are able to persuade relatives and friends to migrate (chain migration). While unsuccessful migrants return and dissuade potential future migrants from trying their luck.[25]

Capitalist way of farming displaces agricultural labour directly which pushes labour for migration. Although the pace of such displacement may be slow, still it acts as a factor towards migration. The buildings of mega dam projects displace large number of agriculturists without adequate arrangement of their livelihood has become a major factor of migration in the developing countries. Several studies on displacement due to development projects suggest that the displaced people have not been resettled and rehabilitated properly (Cernea, 1999; Mahapatra, 2000; Pandey, 1998 and Behera, 2012).

Landlessness and marginalisation result from long-term process of structural inequality, which creates deprivation and denies basic entitlements required for minimum subsistence to certain sections of society. It is primarily the denial of ownership and control over productive resources, hierarchical structures, and unequal power relations that marginalise and impoverish the deprived and disadvantaged prevail in the underdeveloped district of Kalahandi of west Odisha.[26]

1.8 Characteristics of Migrants

The general characteristics of seasonal/circular migrants reveal that these people are coming from the bottom rank of the social and economic strata. In the study area of KBK districts the internal migrants largely belong to schedule caste, schedule tribe and other backward caste. It is hardly noticed that people of higher caste with better economic background do adopt seasonal/circular migration of the nature prevailing in the area. In the contract labour system of *dadan* the labourer used to move along with his family and enjoy little freedom to work elsewhere. They are one type of tied labour through a chain of debt and agents for a period of at least six to eight months. The agents may either be a registered or unregistered who play a role of linkage between labour and owner.

The characteristics of migrants can be noticed from the migrant themselves. Migration is selective; migration responding primarily to plus factors at the destination tends to be positively selective. Migrants responding mainly to the minus factors at the origin tend to be negatively selected or where the minus factors are overwhelming to entire population groups, they may not be selected at all. Selection tends to be bimodal by taking all migrants together. The degree of positive selection increases with the difficulty of the intervening obstacles. The heightened propensity to migrate at certain stages of the life-cycle is important on the selection of migrants and the characteristics of migrants tend to be intermediate between the characteristics of the population at origin and the population at destination.[27]

1.9 Migration during British Period

If we look into the history of pre-independence India it reveals a number of cases of internal and external migration to different directions and volume in different periods. These incidences of migration had occurred either involuntarily or voluntarily. The adoption of tea plantation in Assam led to large scale internal migration particularly from Bihar, West Bengal and Odisha (by that time it was one state). These migrants have more or less settled permanently and a unique mixed society has developed. The growing plantation of tea gardens in north-east region of India encouraged low caste, landless labourers from Andhra Pradesh, Rajasthan, Odisha, Bihar etc. to travel over the country as manual labourers. They were organised by labour sardars (Bosses) out of these states to cities as casual labours, rickshaw pullers or construction workers. These migrations ultimately became family migration. It is also seen during those days that migration to Andaman Islands took place to meet the need of the prisoners on various counts. The indentured labour migration to other colonies was promoted through state promotion.

The British land revenue policy resulted landless poverty stricken agricultural labourers who began to migrate to various cities even to British colonies like British Guinea, West Indies and Mauritius. In fact, there was acute shortage of labour in the British colonies. Therefore, it was the Indian labour who were sought to be introduced in the plantation of their colonies. Poverty stricken Indian labourers were exported to such colonies. Thus, the emigrant Indian labour was another victim of brutal colonial exploitation. In 1830s and 1840s the recruiting ground was mainly the tribal area. Most of emigrants were so called "hill coolies" who were recruited from Chhotanagpur division, Sahabad, Bankura, Birbhum and Bardhan districts of Bengal Presidency.[28]

In a study of a village, Oghani in between Azamgarh and Varanasi in Eastern Uttar Pradesh it was found that at least one person from each family emigrated either to Bombay or to Singapore, during the British Empire. These migrants from Uttar Pradesh living in Singapore, Kualalumpur, Bangkok joined the voluntary army of Subash Chandra Bose for 'blood and money' to overthrow the British Raj in India. During that period the British Government had encouraged and facilitated people to migrate, in order to ease the pressure of local movement. Incentive in the form of transportation and cash were provided to the people to migrate to different South Asian and African countries.[29]

In the British Empire migration in large scale was confined to three major destinations: Burma, Cylon, and Malaya. After a briefgap in the 1910s, migration resumed to an even greater peak in the 1920s; 1927 was the single greatest year of migration. That year, nearly 300,000 people joined from India to Burma and Malaya, well over half a million Chinese travelled to Southeast Asia, and a close to one million to Manchuria. Almost everywhere, the economic depression of the 1930s saw this trend reversed.[30]

The treatment to indenture labour from India was harsh. To dwell a bet more on the harsh and rather abusive practices in the indenturing process of Labour from India, which was run mostly on a private basis by agents on India till 1842, and later by the British appointed officials and agents, on observes the prevalence of considerable ill-treatment faced by the indentured.[31]

Information available from different sources in the study area, it is said that the Britishers discovered *tea leaf* in Assam by 1832 although much earlier they were aware of it from the local adivasi. In 1834, they constituted Tea Committee and started tea plantation by1837. During 1850-55, tea production started on commercial basis. For tea plantation thousand and thousand acre of land were provided to companies free of cost. But labour problem arise, because of least population and malaria infested areas. To overcome labour shortage intentionally a particular caste people (one section of weaver community) were declared criminal type and were imprisoned. The 1866 famine and reservation of forest in 1878 created huge crisis of food and employment. These situations helped British government to adopt human trafficking to tea plantations in Assam through labour agents or sardars from Balangir, Barpali, Loisingha, Dungripali areas of the erstwhile Sambalput district.

1.10 Sources of Migration Data (A Brief History)

Census of India is the single largest source of data on migration characteristics for the people of India. Various surveys conducted by the NSSO are also the important sources of migration data. To assess the volume and structure of migration in India, NSSO starting with the 9th round (May-August, 1955), conducted a number of surveys to collect data on migration as part of its employment and unemployment enquires. In the 9th, 11th (August 1956 to January, 1957) and 12th round (March-August, 1957) of survey, migration particulars were collected for the labour force population only. From the 13th round (September, 1957 to May, 1958) onwards, more detailed information on migration has been collected. In the 18th round, survey on migration was conducted on a much larger scale. In the NSS 28th round (October, 1973 – June, 1974) survey on birth, death, morbidity and disability, migration particulars of the usual members of the sample households were also collected. In the 38th round (January–December,1983) collection of migration data was integrated with the regular quinquennial survey on employment and unemployment. The same approach was followed during the 43rd round (July, 1987–June, 1988). Data on migration was collected during the 49th round (January-June, 1993) which had a comprehensive coverage including inter-alia, housing condition and migration in India. In the sixth quinquennial survey on employment and unemployment during NSS 55th round (July, 1999–June, 2000) information on migration particulars was collected for each household member of the sample household through employment-unemployment schedule.[32]

There is no direct data on interstate seasonal migrants either in the Census or the NSS. One has, therefore, to rely on surrogate information to arrive at the magnitude and selectivity of seasonal migration. As seasonal migration is mostly promoted by the 'push' factors, the migrants suffer from disadvantages of poor control over their migration process with respect to direction, activity, terms of employment and other working conditions. The miseries of migrant labour start from the place of origin and shadow them till they come back. The channel of information flow to the potential migrant is very weak due to which they are prone to be exploited by the middlemen and employers.[33]

In the recent years the state department of labour is Odisha has initiated a process to collect data on such seasonal migrants through Anganwadis and Panchayats. But there is the lack of complete record of such data with the state Department of Labour.

1.11 Estimate and Magnitude of Migration

Official data on migration of permanent nature are covered where as it grossly underestimates the seasonal and circular migration. There are two major official agencies namely, National Sample Survey Office (NSSO) and Census of India to provide the trend and pattern of migration. But these agencies provide inadequate information about circular migration. The information about external migration is usually recorded in both migrating and immigrating countries. Information relating to external migration is available from the Ministry of External Affairs/Directorate of Immigration, Government of India.

The Census of India has started collecting data on migration since 1971 and the 55th round (1999-2000) of NSSO collected data on temporary migrant workers and shows that nearly one per cent of the people come under such category of migration. The 2001 census figures 307 million as internal migrants on the basis of definition who live in a place that is different from their place of birth or last residence. The census does differentiate internal migration within districts, between districts, in the same State and across the State but does not provide information on circular, seasonal migration. As with the census, temporary, seasonal and circular migrants are difficult to estimate through the NSS data, and the survey's estimates of seasonal migrants are far below those other analysis.

In China, according to 2000 census, between 1995 and 2000, 144 million people changed their place of residence (township, town and community) regardless of whether they changed their hokov (Household registration system). The one per cent population sample survey in 2005, show 147 million internal migrants in that same category, an increase of three million. As planned migrants account for only a small percentage of this number, it is clear that the majority are internal rural-urban migrants.[34]

The NSS counted 15 million short-term migrant, but other estimates have placed the number at 100 millions. (Abbas and Varma; 2014). Seasonal migration for agricultural work most often over short distance, and involving more women than men. This sort of migration was constant over the period and involved greatest number of people. It is the least likely to be counted in the censuses of official statistics.[35]

The findings of several studies have shown that there is an increasing trend of short-term/circular migration which has not been estimated properly. The National Commission of Rural Labour (NCRL) puts the number of circular migrants into 10 million (including roughly 4.5 million inter-state migrants and 6 million intra-state migrants.

The construction sector is the largest employer of 40 million migrant workers, followed by 20 million as domestic workers, 11 million in textile industries, 10 million in brick-kilns and many more in transportation, mines, quarries and agriculture. Workers in construction are seasonal migrants and their number has increased by 26.5 million in the decade 2000-2010.[36]

So far as migration in India is concerned, it has been evidenced, throughout its history, that India has received migrants from various parts of the world and has absorbed them into its culture, language, economic and social status. According to the Census of India, 2001, there were about 5.1 million migrants who had penetrated the international boarder especially that with Bangladesh, in search of prosperity. About 97 per cent of these immigrants were from the eight neighbouring countries. Though immigration to India has slowed down in the recent past, emigration from India has increased considerably. India is the second largest migrants sending country after China. The Indian diaspora, estimated at some 20 millions, spread across a hundred and ten countries.[37]

While the socio-economic factors associated with international (cross-border) migration dynamics have been well documented, processes of internal migration, within developing countries, in particular are not well understood. In India, internal migration has been accorded very low priority by the government, partly on account of a serious knowledge gap on its extent, nature and magnitude. As per the 2001 census, the total number of internal migrants was 309 million or nearly 30 per cent of the total population. However, due to empirical and conceptual difficulties in measurement, migration flows are often grossly underestimated.[38]

The census does not collect data on the temporary and seasonal migration separately. Serious doubts have been raised regarding the definition and estimates of temporary, seasonal and circular migration used in National Sample Surveys. Although there has been some improvement in the measurement of seasonal and temporary migration over the NSS rounds, it remains inadequate.[39]

In the context of internal migration of poor labour class from the backward regions of India like Eastern Uttar Pradesh, Bihar, Chhattisgarh, Jharkhand and Odisha has been a matter of great concern for social scientists and development planners alike. There are six states from where labour migration is highly in favour of male. Bihar recorded highest sex ratio of inter-state male migrants with 1,388 male for every 1000 female migrants, followed by Uttar Pradesh (1153), Manipur (1080), Kerala (1068), Mizoram (1059), Tripura (1037) and Odisha (1022). Out migration from Odisha preferred Gujarat and Maharashtra as the destination even when these states were not nearby or bordering areas.[40]

There has been a steady increase in the country's internal migration. An attempt has been made to present the migration data both internal and external for the period 1971 to 2001 in the Table 1.2.

Table 1.2: Internal and External Migration in India, 1971–2001

Census	*Total Population (in millions)*	*Internal Migration (in millions)*	*External Migration (in millions)*	*Total Migration percentage*
1	*2*	*3*	*4*	*5*
1971	548.1	159.6 (29.2)	8.1 (1.4)	30.6
1981	659.3	200.5 (30.4)	6.0 (0.9)	31.3
1991	814.3	220.7 (27.1)	5.9 (0.72)	27.8
2001	1028.6	307.2 (29.9)	5.1 (0.5)	30.4

Source:-Census of India, 1971-2001 (Figures in the parenthesis indicate percentage of migrants to total population, internal and external).

The Table 1.2 reveals that the percentage of internal migration ranges between 27 to 30 per cent during 1971-2001. By generalisation, we can state roughly 30 per cent of people in the country adopt internal migration for livelihood purposes. The census 2001 shows 307.2 million people have reported as migrants by place of birth. The internal migration may be classified into rural to rural (53.3 million) rural to urban (20.5 million) urban to rural (6.4 million) and urban to urban.

Table 1.3 shows the inter-state migration based on the census data of 1991 and 2001 and has projected the migration figures for all the states and union territories of Indian union. States like Maharashtra, Punjab, Delhi, Gujarat, and Haryana show high in-migrants on the other hand, States like Bihar, Odisha, Rajasthan, Uttar Pradesh show high out-migrants population. The net in-migrant states are considered as developed states, whereas the out-migration states are considered less developed states in term of demographic movement. But it does not mean that people of less developed states do not move to other less developed states or from developed states to developed states. For example, we find large number of migrants from Bihar and Andhra Pradesh in Western Odisha. Our field studies show that, large scale of population from Coastal and souther districts of Odisha have migrated to western Odisha, the Bihari migrants are working in different informal sectors like selling of *gupcup* or *panipuri, jhal muri, chana* and working in construction, business sector. On the other hand, the migrants from Andhra Pradesh have settled in large scale in the command area of

Table 1.3: Population Census 1991 &2001 on Inter-state Migration, Based on last Residence.

Rate of population–States/Union Territories (0-9), migration rate and growth

Sl No.	*States/Union Territories*	*Population (1991)*	*In-migrants from other states (2001)*	*Out-migrants (2001)*	*From other countries (2001)*	*Net In-migrants (2001)*	*Migration rate (per 100) 1991-2001*	*Population (2011)*	*Projected Migration 2011*
	India	**846387888**	**16826879**	**16826879**	**740867**	**740867**	**0.09**	**1210193422**	**1089174**
1	A&N Islands	280661	29538	8011	728	22255	7.9	380581	30178
2	Andhra Pradesh	66508008	421989	637360	6292	-209079	-0.3	84580777	-265894
3	Arunachal Pradesh	864558	71789	12507	2931	62213	7.2	1383727	99572
4	Assam	22414322	121803	281510	5053	-154654	-0.7	31205576	-215312
5	Bihar	64530554	460782	2241413	57724	-1722907	-2.7	104099452	-2779361
6	Chandigarh	642015	239263	106734	5108	137637	21.4	1055450	226270
7	Chhattisgarh	17614928	338793	444679	2615	-103271	-0.6	25545198	-149764
8	Dadra & Nagar Haveli	138477	47649	3440	964	45173	32.6	343709	112122
9	Daman & Diu	101586	48362	5401	1835	44796	44.1	243247	107264
10	Delhi	9420644	2172760	457919	49281	1764122	18.7	16787941	3143732
11	Goa	1169793	120824	32578	4775	93021	8.0	1458545	115982
12	Gujarat	41309582	1125818	451458	14800	689160	1.7	60439692	1008304
13	Haryana	16463648	1231480	588001	26639	670118	4.1	25351462	1031878
14	Himachal Pradesh	5170877	188223	165776	28276	50723	1.0	6864602	67337
15	Jammu & Kashmir	7718700	86768	122175	2938	-32469	-0.4	12541302	-52755
16	Jharkhand	21843911	502764	616160	2309	-111087	-0.5	32988134	-167761
17	Karnataka	44977201	879106	769111	20533	130528	0.3	61095297	177304
18	Kerala	29098518	235087	431821	32077	-164657	-0.6	33406061	-189032
19	Lakshadweep	51707	4444	1149	17	3312	6.4	64473	4130

(Cond...)

20	Madhya Pradesh	48566242	814670	842937	6939	-21328	0.0	72626809	-31894
21	Maharashtra	78937187	3231612	896988	48394	2383018	3.0	112374333	3392445
22	Manipur	1837149	4529	30867	182	-26156	-1.4	2570390	-36595
23	Meghalaya	1774778	33710	20436	1154	14430	0.8	2966889	24123
24	Mizoram	689756	22599	31739	8436	-704	-0.1	1097206	-1120
25	Nagaland	1209546	33594	51857	1752	-16511	-1.4	1978502	-27008
26	Odisha	31659736	229687	440893	3931	-207275	-0.7	41974218	-274803
27	Pondicherry	807785	105208	35755	1426	70879	8.8	1247953	109501
28	Punjab	20281969	811060	501285	26861	336636	1.7	27743338	460478
29	Rajasthan	44005990	723639	997196	11873	-261684	-0.6	68548437	-407627
30	Sikkim	406457	22519	6238	7655	23936	5.9	610577	35956
31	Tamil Nadu	55858946	270473	674304	25671	-378160	-0.7	72147030	-488429
32	Tripura	2757205	40262	23538	11246	27970	1.0	3673917	37269
33	Uttar Pradesh	132061653	1079055	3810701	32110	-2699536	-2.0	199812341	-4084461
34	Uttaranchal	7050634	352496	354718	29138	26916	0.4	10086292	38505
35	West Bengal	68077965	724524	730226	259204	253502	0.4	91276115	339885

Note: 1. Projected Migration 2011 arrived on the basis of Migration Rate of 1991-2001.

2. The figure has been arrived keeping in view the growth rate and other factors remain constant.

Source: Census of India, 2001, Govt. of India.

Hirakud dam projects since 1950s. The figure for Odisha projects a net out-migration of 2,74,803 people to other states. At the all India level Uttar Pradesh has the highest out-migrant population of 40,84,461 people followed by Chhattisgarh with 27,79,361 people. Thus the data reveals the picture of out-migration from less developed States to more developed States as the trend of internal migration. The construction of mega dam project like Hirakud involves large number of migrant labour from south Indian state and southern district of Odisha. On completion of the project large number of them settled in the periphery towns like Burl and Hirakud permanently and other went back to their place of origin.

The net in-migration states have the advantage of strong pull factors. These states generally attract population from all parts of the country. On the other hand most of the remaining states are net out-migrating but not are all underdeveloped states; Kerala is one of the major out-migration states to the gulf countries. Migrants from Bihar relocate to the destination of Maharashtra, Delhi, West Bengal, Haryana, Gujarat and other north and central states but with the highest numbers to Delhi and West Bengal. Other major migrant sending states are Rajasthan, Madhya Pradesh, Andhra Pradesh, Chhattisgarh, Jharkhand and Odisha. Predictably, all of the major migrant-sending states are characterised by low social and development indices.[41]

Studies on the draught-prone area of West Bengal by Rogaly et al (2002) observe that over 500,000 tribal, Muslims and lower-caste people migrate seasonally to the rice-growing areas of the State. Madhya Pradesh shows similar high levels of out-migration from both draught-prone and forested tribal areas.[42]

In this context, the circular or short-term migrants from KBK districts have been witnessed in large scale to the neighbouring states of Andhra Pradesh, Telengana, Tamil Nadu and Karnataka in general and particularly to the districts of Rangareddy, Nalgonda and Visakhapatnam every year to work in brick kilns. Although the trend of migration has set in since the drought of 1960s, but it has seen a phenomenon increased during the last 30 years or more precisely after adoption of new economic policy, 1991. The boon in the construction sector has demanded huge labour force for brick industries and the brick kiln owners find it easy to get labour from KBK districts of

Western Odisha. The improvement in railway connectivity has added a new feather to their demand for labour from this region. According to an estimate, 3,46,471 and 2,78,641 labourers from Kalahandi and Bolangir respectively had gone to Andhra Pradesh as brick kiln workers in 2008-09. The other districts namely, Nuapada and Sonepur have also sent sizable migrant labourers to Andhra Pradesh. But official figure pertaining to that period for such migrants is estimated to barely one lakh only. However, except for the main worker who is the male head of the family, none of the worker is registered. Non-registered migrants outnumber the registered migrants as registration is not mandatory for people adopting internal migration. This type of migration usually involves family migration. The women work with her male counterpart and the children assist their parents but they are not in the pay roll of the employers.

Reports from different field studies by NGOs say family labour and engagement of children aged between 10-14 producing unbaked bricks. Most children engaged at kilns do not go to school and have never attended regularly. This questions the attainment of universal primary education for all by, 2015.

A study of Bolangir district in Odisha estimates that nearly 60,000 people migrated during the draught year of 2001 from this district alone. Bolangir is one of the three infamous KBK (Kalahandi-Bolangir-Koraput) districts in Odisha with low level of agricultural production and persistently high level of poverty. Although there is inaccuracy in the data of internal migration from across different states in general and KBK region in particular, we can safely conclude that there is the presence of large scale seasonal/circular migration in the region.

1.12 Effects of Migration

Migration as a demographic study reveals that it does potentially contribute towards the development of different sectors of the economy. Migration significantly contributes to the productive activity and there is no doubt in it. The migrant labours from Jharkhand, Andhra Pradesh and South Odisha could help in the building of a mega dam project like Hirakud in the 1950s. It provides employment to unemployed and thereby leading to increasing in income and livelihood. An increase in income beyond subsistence level can help saving and capital formation in the economy. The remittance to the source areas helps the left behind members of the family to lead good life. In the case of external migration remittance is considered as a boon to the economy.

The inflow of labour to urban centres/places of work (rural or semi-urban areas) enables to overcome the problem of labour shortage in a rapidly prospering area. The unemployed migrants prior to leaving their sources get employment leading to a fall in the rate of unemployment in the labour out-migrating zone. Provision of employment enables them to overcome the problem of search for employment. The labour sending areas also gain economically through remittance of the migrants. Thereby a wage balancing mechanism operates between the source and destination areas of the migrants. But the surge of population in the urban centres creates serious troubles in the form of civil amenities, particularly in less developed countries. The out-migration areas suffer from labour shortage and thereby productive activities suffer. But it is not so in case of migration of students for higher studies in cities.

The demographic effects created through migration from rural areas to urban areas reduce the size of rural population and increases urban population thus bring about a change in the composition of population in the country. This change in the composition of population is asserted by the demographer as positive result of development process. The net social effects of migration lead to breaking of caste barriers in the urban environment.

Migration has to a greater extent solved the problem of unemployment among women, as all migrant women have been able to seek job. Migration has increased the annual earnings of all migrants. The burden of debt has increased among the low income groups.[43] Migration itself may affect gender relations as both men and women, whether they migrate or not, are exposed to new socio-economic and cultural forces that moderate or restructure the patriarchal system.[44]

But migration is not always followed by positive results in all cases. The migrants have to face the poor living condition, harassment in the form of physical, sexual and financial in the hands of the employers and agents. Unemployment may prevail in the event of retrenchment and completion of the project. Thus, the picture of migrant labour is not always rosy.

1.13 Importance of Study

The population movement in a country is often regarded as an index of its economic development. This is based on the historical phenomenon related to the fact that the very process of industrialisation in the presently developed countries brought in its wake concentration of people in the urban industrial centres. However, the link between urbanisation and economic development could be different in the developing countries compared to the developed countries.[45]

One major failure of development about poverty removal is that the poor are modeled as passive recipients of hand-outs rather than active agents who can do things to get themselves out of poverty. Thus, poverty removal programmes focus on redistributive mechanism such as development assistance from the rich countries to the poor countries or even within the poor countries themselves, such redistribution is always bigger in ambition than in actual transfers and is often appropriated by the not-so-poor who control the transmission channels of the aid. We need to look instead at how the poor can get themselves out of poverty.

It has been recognised for some time by migration experts that internal short-term population movements ranging from daily commuting to seasonal migration have become widespread all over Asia. India is one such country where internal migration is more important than international migration in terms of the numbers of people involved and possibly even the volume of remittances. Besides, temporary internal migration is more likely to involve the poor, lower caste and less educated and thus has large implications for poverty reduction and meeting the Millennium Development Goals (MDGs). India is now crises-crossed all over by thousands of circular migratory routes between villages within the same district, across districts and across states and sometimes at the opposite ends of the country.[46]

Historically, migration has played a very important role in poverty removal. During the nineteenth century, one-third of Europe's population moved to North America or Antipoles. People moved from India and China to South East Asia, to East and South Africa and to the Americas. During much of the twentieth century, the option was much more restricted, and basically applied to internal migration. One task of MDG promoters is to facilitate international migration on a global scale. It is not easy but it is a way of taking people out of poverty, if not immediately than at least by the next generation.

In the process of development of any country, the study of internal migration assumes special significance. The movement of people across smaller units within the country is related to a process of change taking place within the economic, social and political system. The study of internal migration assumes two aspects namely, quantitative and qualitative. The quantitative aspects deal with the number and characteristics of the migrants and their role in the population distribution and density over a period of time. On the other hand qualitative aspects relates to their development of human quality with the transition and transformation of the migrants in their place of settlement.

The studies on migration of people have received wide attraction by the researchers cutting across discipline and have become a study of multidisciplinary in many respects. It has a historical prospect, geographical linkages, social and cultural dimension, political linkages and above all a dominant economic role for the migrant both external and internal nature. Economists have developed various theories of labour migration and relates to the concept of migration to prospective development. Their interest in the study of migration also relates to volume, growth and changes in their economic condition due to their movement in the economy.

The present study relates to an area known for its poverty, under development and backwardness. Distress, seasonal, circular migration has become a common occurrence in this area. It is necessary to know the reasons for such migration in the area in spite of special development programmes undertaken by the state during the last four decades. The study will enable to highlight the economic condition of these migrants during pre-and post-migration periods. It will look into the process of recruitment and their movement and problem at different stages of such migration. Above all little has been studied over this issue of the area.

1.14 Statement of the Problem

In the recent years many studies have come up to understand the issues of migration particularly, internal migration. Most of these studies deal with the problems of urbanisation and its evils. A little is evident about the nature and determinants of rural out-migration which is characterised by seasonal, circular or oscillatory in nature. Since very little study is available on internal migration which is of seasonal/ circular in nature pertaining to the KBK districts of Western Odisha, a survey has been undertaken in these districts to study the ground reality of internal migration prevailing in this region.

1.15 The Study Area

The present study of internal migration covers eight districts of South-western part of Odisha. These districts are popularly known as KBK i.e. Kalahandi, Bolangir and Koraput. After the reorganisation of districts in Odisha during 1992-93 these three KBK districts have been reorganised into eight districts:-Kalahandi (Kalahandi and Nuapada), Bolangir (Bolangir and Sonepur), and Koraput (Koraput, Rayagada, Nabarangpur and Malkangiri). The erstwhile undivided Kalahandi and Bolangir comes under the western part and Koraput comes under southern part of Odisha. So from practical point of view the present study of internal migration covers all the eight districts of former KBK districts.

1.16 Objectives of the Study

1. To find out reason for internal migration in the KBK districts of Odisha.
2. To find out the land holding and occupational pattern of migrants.
3. To know the process of recruitment of migrant labour and their destinations.
4. To know the provision and pattern of employment at the destination.
5. To determine migrants' standard of living of in the pre-and post-migration.
6. To know the problems faced by the migrants during transit and destination.
7. To know the role of state towards the betterment of the migrants.
8. To know the conditions of the left behind members of the migrant families.

9. To know the bane or benefits of migration in their socio-economic conditions.
10. To know the amount of remittance by the migrants to the rest of the family members stayed at home/place of origin.

1.17 Hypotheses

The following hypotheses have been formulated for the study:

Null Hypothesis (H_0): Migration does not have significant impact on increase in the level of income of the migrants.

Alternative Hypothesis (H_1): Migration has significant impact on increase in the level of income of the migrants.

1.18 Scope of the Study

The scope of the study relates to the rural out-migration which is characterised as seasonal/circular internal migration. Within this purview, the study has covered the rural out-migration prevailing in KBK districts, which seems to be distress/seasonal/circular in nature. The detail characteristics of migrant households have been analysed by taking household survey from the out-migrating areas. Various causes of migration have been analysed to find out the important factor for migration. The net effects of migration on the migrants in terms of income, employment, asset creation and standard of living have been focused. The problems expressed by the migrants at different stages; from source to destination and back to the place of origin have been documented. Based on the field study a few measures have been suggested for the betterment of migrants of the study area.

1.19 Methodology of Study

The study of internal migration in KBK districts is based on the following methodology:

(a) ***Reference period:***-The period of study is conducted during 2013-14 for collection of primary data and compilation of report is done in the 1st quarter of 2015.

(b) ***Sources of data:***-The study is based on primary and secondary data as well. The primary data have been collected by direct personal interview method with the help of a household interview schedule and village profile schedule. The primary data have been collected by different groups of enumerators/

investigators engaged in different districts of the areas of study. The study is also based on number of secondary sources of data. These secondary sources are books, journals, newspaper, media reports, government offices particularly the state department of labour and employment and District Rural Development Agency (DRDA).

Sampling Design:- The study has been carried out on the basis of primary data collected from different districts of KBK region. In this regard, the method of simple stratified random sampling technique has been applied to collect data from the universe of population. A total of 773 samples have been collected from eight districts. A multi-stage random sample basis the migrant households of different villages have taken as samples from each district. The Table 1.4 shows the sample design for data collection in the study area. While collecting data the head of the family has been taken as the usual respondent to the schedule questionnaire. The questionnaire covers around 50 open ended questions to collect information from the respondents directly.

Table 1.4: Sample Design for Data Collection in the Study Area

Sl. No.	*Name of the District*	*No. of Villages/ Hamlets*	*No. of Sample Households*
1.	Kalahandi	04	104
2.	Nuapada	04	100
3.	Bolangir	02	100
4.	Sonepur	04	106
5.	Koraput	09	107
6.	Nabarangapur	06	74
7.	Rayagada	12	120
8.	Malkangiri	02	62
	Total	**43**	**773**

(c) ***Statistical Tools***:- To determine various results in a precise manner and bird's eye view, the study has used different statistical tools to determine its accuracy. Statistical tools such as tables, diagram, averages, percentage, circulation, student 't'-test etc. have been used in this study of internal migration.

1.20 Limitation of the Study

In view of paucity of time, fund and energy, the study is subject to certain limitations. The study does not cover the entire gamut of migration and its related issues. It is confined to the study of internal migration relating seasonal-circular nature. It has studied the different aspects relating to distress migration which is being adopted as a means of livelihood by the migrants. The data collected from the respondents are mostly based on his/her personal memory power which he/she has expressed to the investigators. Due to illiteracy respondents might not have been able to express their information properly, which serves as a great limitation to the subject. However, care has been taken to overcome such problems by taking the assistance of his/her fellow migrants or neighbours. Necessary care has been taken by the researcher to collect reliable data from the migrants. It limits to the area of study only, nevertheless it provides reasonable information over the issue of internal migration of the area and has its implication of the problem in general.

1.21 Chapterisation of the Study

The entire study has been designed as per the standard set for the preparation of report. Accordingly, it is divided into six chapters:

I. The first chapter covers introduction to the subject matter, definition, estimate of migration, statement of the problem, objectives, scope, methodology, limitation and chapterisation of the study.

II. The second chapter deals with review of literature relating to the topic of research from different angles conducted by previous studies and researches.

III. The third chapter covers the regional and socio-economic profile of the study area and different development programme and poverty alleviation measures.

IV. The fourth chapter deals with the legal provisions and state intervening measures to deal with the problems arising out of internal migration.

V. The fifth chapter deals with the analysis of data collected from the study area and testing of hypothesis.

VI. The sixth chapter deals with the summary of the study, findings, conclusion and suggestions in line with the field study.

1.22 Conclusion

The introduction on the study of internal migration in the KBK districts of south-west Odisha covers a range of points with regard to definition, general typology, factors governing migration, characteristic of migrants, effects of migration etc. A general picture of internal and external migration prevailing in the country has been presented to show its presence in demographic study. The chapter covers the importance of study, sample design, methodology, study area and limitation of the study.

Notes

1. **Usual Place of Residence**: UPR of a person was defined as a place (village/ town) where the person had stayed continuously for a period of six months or more.
2. **Baina**: It is a term used in Western Odisha to connote payment of cash advance to the debtor by the creditor.
3. **Dadan**: The recipient of baina or cash advance in turn becomes indenture labour to work under a brick kiln owner or any other work provided by the owner. The system of labour contract is carried out through a chain of agents in the area. Such an indenture labour is locally called a dadan.

References

1. Grigg, D.B. (1977). *E.G. Ravenstein and the "laws of migration"* Journal of Historical Geography, 3, 1(1977) 41-45.
2. Ibid., pp. 43-44.
3. Reddy, N. (2009), *Rural Migrant Labour in Andhra Pradesh,* In K. Gopal Iyer (2009)(Ed.) Distress Migrant Labour in India, Key Human Rights Issues. Kanishka Publishers and Distributors, New Delhi, pp. 186-89.
4. Senapati, N.K. (1968). *Odisha Gazetteers, Bolangir*, pp. 495-96.
5. Ibid., pp. 466.
6. Tripathy, S.N. (2005). *Tribal Migration*, Sonali Publications, New Delhi, p. 7.
7. UNESCO (2013). *Social Inclusion of Internal Migrants in India*, UNESCO, New Delhi, p. 3.
8. Amrith, S. (2011). *Migration and Diaspora in Modern Asia,* Cambridge University Press, New, Delhi, p. 130.

9. Sainath, P. (1996). *Everybody Loves a Good Draught, Stories from India's Poorest Districts.* Penguin Books, New Delhi, p. 71.
10. Ghosh, R. (2004). *Brick Kiln Workers, A Study of Migration, Labour Process and Employment.* V.V. Giri National Labour Institute, Noida, p. 4.
11. Roy, A. (2011). *Distress Migration and 'Left Behind' Women*, Rawat Publication, Jaipur, p. 37.
12. Camelo, (2014). *Migration and Precariousness: Two Sides of the Contract Labour Coin,* Economic and Political Weekly, Sept., 6, Vol. XLIX, No. 36. pp. 39-47.
13. Singh, Sudama (2001). *Migration in the Third World,* Radha Publications, New Delhi, p. 39.
14. Korra, V. (2011). *Short-duration Migration in India,* In S.I. Rajan (Ed.) Migration, Identity and Conflict Indian Migration Report 2011, Routledge, New Delhi, p. 55.
15. Samal, K. C. (2008). *Informal Sector, Concept, Dynamics, Linkages and Migration,* Concept Publishing Company, New Delhi, p. 122.
16. Sylvia Chant and S. A. Radcliffe (1992). *Migration and Development the Importance of Gender.* In Syliva Chant (1992) (Eds.) Gender and Migration in Developing Countries, Belhaven Press, London, pp. 1-29.
17. Parnwell, M. (1993). *Population Movements in the Third World,* Routledge, London.
18. Samal, K. C. (2008). *Informal Sector, Concept, Dynamics, Linkages and Migration,* Concept Publishing Company, New Delhi, p. 140.
19. Todaro, M.P. (1980). *Internal Migration in Developing Countries: A Survey,* In R.A. Easterlin (ed) Population and Economic Change in Developing Countries, Unversity of Chicago Press, p. 337.

    Access through, http://www.org/chapters/c9668
20. Mark Ellis, Dennis Conway and Adrier J. Bailey (2000). *The Circular Migration of Puerto Rican Women towards Gendered Explanation,* In Gender and Migration Edited by Katie Willis and B. Yeak, Also in International Migration Quarterly Review XXXIV (1) pp. 32-62.
21. Parnwell, M. (1993). *Population Movements in the Third World,* Routledge, London, p. 74.
22. NSS 64th Round (2010). *Migration in India (2007-08),* Ministry of Statistics and Programme Implementation, Govt. of India, p. 19.
23. Lee, E. (1969). *A Theory of Migration*, In Jackson, J.A. (1969) (ed.) Migration Cambridge University Press, Cambridge, p. 255.
24. *Ibid,* p. 286.
25. Connel, J. B., Dasgupta, R. Laishley and M. Lipton (1976). *Migration from Rural Areas,* The Evidence from Village Studies, Oxford University Press, Delhi, p. 7.

26. Mohanty, M., S. Ray, G.N. Trivedi and N. Sukumar (2011). *Landlessness and the marginalised : A study of Kalahandi, Bhojpur and Chittoor*, in M. Mohanty (ed.) India Social Development Report 2010, Council for Social Development, Oxford University Press, New Delhi, p. 224.
27. Lee, E. (1969). *A Theory of Migration*, In Jackson, J.A. (1969) (ed.) Migration Cambridge University Press, Cambridge, pp. 295-96.
28. Saha, Panchanan (1970). *Emigration of Indian Labour (1834-1900),* Peoples Publishing House, Private Ltd. New Delhi, p. 29.
29. Mishra, P. (2012). *Migration and Mobility in an Eastern U.P. Village,* in Brij Raj Chauhan and A. Satyanarayan (Eds.) Changing Village in India. Rawat Publication, Jaipur, p. 31.
30. Amrith, S. (2011). *Migration and Diaspora in Modern Asia,* Cambridge University Press, New, Delhi, p. 31.
31. Sen, Sunanda ni (2016) Indentured Labour from India in the Age of Empire, Social Sientist, Vol. 44/No. 1-2 January-February, p. 46.
32. NSS 64th Round (2010). *Migration in India (2007-08),* Ministry of Statistics and Programme Implementation, Govt. of India, p. 1-2.
33. Ram, K. (2009). *Inter-State Circular Migration Labour in India,* in K. Gopal Iyer (2009) (Ed) Distress Migrant Labour in India, Key Human Rights Issues. Kanishka Publishers and Distributors, New Delhi, pp. 292 and 307.
34. Cai Fang and Wang Dewen (2008). *Impact of Internal Migration on Economic Growth and Urban Development in China.* In J. De. Wind and J. Holdaway (eds) Migration and Development within an Across Boarders! Research and Policy Perspectives on Internal and International Migration, The Social Science Research Council, New York. p. 250.
35. Amrith, S. (2011). *Migration and Diaspora in Modern Asia,* Cambridge University Press, New Delhi. p. 3.
36. Kalkoti, Gopal (2014). *Status of Rural Migration-Need for Development Initiatives,* Kurukshetra, Vol. 62, No. 11, September, p. 15.
37. Sharma, J. C. (2002). *Inaugural Address in Indian Diaspora, First International Conference on 'Indian Diasporic Experience: History, Culture and Identity'* Organised by Centre for India Diaspora and Cultural Studies, Himachandracharya North Gujarat University, Patna. During January 22-24, available on line http://www.ngu.ac.in/centre/dias/index.htm.
38. Bhagat, R.M. (2011). *Internal Migration in India: Are the Underclass More Mobile?* in S.I. Rajan (Ed) Migration, Identity and Conflict, India Migration Report 2011, Routledge, New Delhi, p. 22.
39. *Ibid.,* p. 5.
40. Roy, A. (2011). *Distress Migration and 'Left Behind' Women*, Rawat Publication, Jaipur. p. 31.
41. Abbas, R and D. Varma (2014). *Internal Labour Migration in India Raises Integration challenges for Migrants.* The Online Journal: Migration Policy Institute, March 3.

42. Deshingkar, P. (2008). *Circular Internal Migration and Development in India.* In Wind, J. De and J. Holdaway (eds) Migration and Development within and Across Boarders : Research and Policy Perspectives on Internal and International Migration, The Social Science Research Council, New York. Fang, Cai and W. Dewen (2008) Impacts of Internal Migration on Economic Growth and Urban Development in China. p. 162.
43. Sundari, S. (2007). *Migrant Women and Urban Labour Market Concepts and Case Studies of Problems, Gains and Losses,* Deep and Deep Publications Pvt. Ltd., New Delhi. p. 398.
44. Halfacree, K.H. (1995). *Household Migration and the Structuration of Patriarchy, Evidence from USA,* Progress in Human Geography 19 (2) 159-182.
45. Rale, J.R. (1969). *Trends and Significance of Internal Migration in India,* Sankhya: The Indian Journal of Statistics, Series B(1960-2000), Vol. 31, No. 3/4 December, 1969, p. 504.
46. Deshingkar, P. (2008). *Circular Internal Migration and Development in India.* In Wind, J. De and J. Holdaway (eds) Migration and Development within and Across Boarders : Research and Policy Perspectives on Internal and International Migration, The Social Science Research Council, New York. Fang, Cai and W. Dewen (2008) Impacts of Internal Migration on Economic Growth and urban Development in China. p. 101 and 161.

Chapter - 2

Review of Literature

2.1 Introduction

The migration of people from one place to another both internal and external is a complex phenomenon. It has multiple dimensions and it varies according to class and social strata of the migrants. The process of migration has undergone a structural change in the changed economic and social condition, particularly after the adoption of neo-liberal economic policy. In a dualistic economy like India, the dimension and characteristic of internal migration, has largely been influenced by the development in some pockets of the state and other states, thereby promoting internal migration of inter-region/inter-state character within the country. Different studies have been made on the issue of migration in the country but little has been studied in the present area of KBK districts in south-west Odisha. The micro-studies on migration in India emphasises such factors like inadequate development of agriculture and industry, lack of employment opportunities, inequality in land ownership, poverty and backwardness act as push factors for internal migration. The present chapter on review of literature tries to focus on the findings of selected studies on various issues associated with migration. Attempt has been made to review the selected literature out of different studies on migration. It is too difficult review the literature exclusively on a particular point basis because issues of migration are often inter-related.

Although migration is emerging as an important phenomenon from economic, political and public health points of views, migration research finds low priority among Indian demographers. This is due to a shift in the emphasis to the issue of reproductive health whereas the case of internal migration dwindled. That is why the studies on India's internal migration, its causes and consequences are limited in nature.[1]

According to Ravenstein (1855), the processes of migration in its first stage people move from village to smaller town of neighbourhood and thereafter they move to cities. Every migratory current is usually compensated by a counter-current.

Godrich (1936) states that areas of low level living tends to be areas of net out-migration, while areas of high level living tends to be areas of net immigration.

Lee points out that Mr Ravenstein had spoken of "Laws of Migration"; he had not formulated them in such a categorical order that they could be criticised. Nevertheless, Ravenstein's papers have stood the test of time and remain the starting point for migration theory (1969: p. 282) [On the Ravenstein's celebrated paper on the laws of migration before the Royal Statistical Society on 17th March, 1885]. Lee further points out that except for Dudley Kirk, Ravenstein seems to have been the last person to make a detailed comparison of the volume of internal migration on the characteristics of migrants within a good number of nations.[2]

While discussing the classical and Keynesian ideas on internal migration in Britain, Lind (1969) points out that classical economists have simplified the proposition of migration by assuming homogeneity among the labour and a perfect mobility of labour within the country in the long-run. The supply of labour like capital is ready to meet a demand initiated exogenously. Accordingly, the demand for labour was independent variable whereas the supply of labour was dependent variable.[3]

Lewis (1954) in his theory of Economic Development with Unlimited Supplies of Labour says in underdeveloped countries the marginal productivity of labour is negligible or even zero and characterised by overpopulation, and unlimited labour supplies expansion/and establishment of industries is possible by drawing labour from this subsistence sector. He argues skilled labour can be made by providing training to the unskilled workers.[4]

Fie and Ranis (1961) went one step ahead of Lewis and say development is possible by reallocation of surplus agricultural workers, whose contribution to output is zero or negligible, can become productive workers at equal wage with industrial sector.[5]

On the other hand, the Keynesian analysis has seen the multiplier effects on total income in the area due to changes in investment and migration. The movement of capital takes place in the same direction as the labour. This could lead to change in the size of market, a greater availability of skilled labour and a change in the climate of investment in contrast to a depressed market situation. Thus, there is no harm in the process of labour migration for a very long time.

2.2 External Migration

History took another turn with the emergence of powerful migrant companies, right from the fifteenth century onwards, especially in Europe whose very survival and further expansion was dependent upon the free mobility of traders. ————Slave trade was followed by an increased urbanisation in the wake of Industrial Revolution of the last quarter of the eighteenth century. Between the beginning of trade in human beings as such and ultimately restricting it to the buying and selling of their labour power in capital which rendered the worker a free floating seller of productive capacities. Most of the existing literature on migration is an attempt to understand this massive redistribution of human resources in response to the capitalist labour market.[6]

Various studies highlighted the nature and causes of migration of indentured labour to other countries and internal migration to tea plantation and other industries. The indentured labourers were sent to Mauritius, British Guinea, Trinidad, Namibia and other places where sugar plantations had grown on a large scale.[7]

Hassankhan (2013) stating on the historical aspects of migration says, the abolition of slavery system was followed by system of indentured labour in the tropical plantation colonies of the British Empire. In all the colonies taken together, more than one million indentured emigrants arrived during 1834-1916. They were generally employed in the sugarcane plantation. Most of them were young male migrants, leaving their families/relatives to earn more and to come back after the expiration of their indenture. The indenture period was very hard for them and different from expectation when signed the contract in India. The number of indenture migrants varies from colony to colony. Mauritius received the highest migrants of 453,000 immigrants, followed by Guyana 238,000, Natal 152,184, Thailand 143,930, Fiji 60,965, Jamaica 36,4000, Suriname 34,300 etc.

Sharma (2011) on the issue of Tamil migrant labour in Ceylon's coffee, tea and rubber plantation was the need for the society at a particular point of time. But later on became an anachronism and a contentious issue because of divides between the Sinhalese and the Tamils settlers. This long-term settlement of such migrants leads to various disputed issues and ultimately civil war between these two settlers.

Mishra (2012) in his study of a village Oghari located in eastern Uttar Pradesh between Azamgarh and Varanasi found a unique composition that at least one person from each family emigrated to Bombay or to Singapore, during British rule. In order to overcome the local movement against the British Government, the government had itself facilitated their movement to Singapore, Kualalumpur, and Bangkok through transportation and monetary incentives. Migrants from these areas joined the voluntary army being inspired by the call of Subash Chandra Bose, to fight against British Raj in India. His findings on the village highlighted that money was not merely a natural medium of communication, but combined with other factors like education, it generated new conditions for social development.

In the context of international migration during British rule in India and external migration Amrith (2011) points out that the Indian migrants largely continue to migrate to three major destinations namely, Burma, Ceylon and Malaya. During 1920 to 1927, nearly 300,000 people moved from India to Burma and Malaya, well over half million Chinese travelled to Southeast Asia and close to one million to Manchuria. The economic depression of the 1930s saw this trend reversed with net reduction in migration, mobility became more difficult.

Estevez (2012) on international migration says, the dynamics of globalisation has led to unprecedented population movement. Around 200 million people are living in different countries other than their place of birth. In 2005, 34 per cent of those migrants accounts for

Europe, 23 per cent for North America and three per cent in Oceania. So also millions of refugees and asylum seekers had to leave their home countries due to natural disasters and civil war. In addition to these thousands of seasonal workers works under the control of their employers and remain subdued with the violation of their rights.[8]

Poros (2011) in the context of migrants from Gujarat to other parts of the globe says that the surplus labour force of India was used for expansionist purpose of the British Empire in its other colonies. For instance, there was debt bondage and labour migration from India to Trinidad, Fiji, Guyana, East Africa, and other parts of the Empire from the 1800s into the early 1990s.[9] The Indian workers worked in railways to civil servants and petty traders and professionals, would voluntarily or involuntarily migrated to United Kingdom after Kenya, Tanzania and Uganda, gained independence from the British in the early 1960s. Today the situation has changed and most Indian migrants even the poorest ones board airplanes for at least part of their journey to a new land. The preferred destinations are the US, the UK, Australia, Canada and the Middle East.[10]

Gurung (2012) says the Nepalese have been used by the Britishers in consolidating the frontier region. They came here for a living and subsequently to settle down. In this process the Nepalese have contributed significantly towards the political consolidation and socio-economic development of the region.

Migration in the context of Bangladesh, Mahamood (1992) points out, more than 600,000 Bangladeshi nationals have migrated to the middle-east and North African countries only for employment. Ninety five per cent of these migrants have concentrated their gross outflow to Bahrain, Iran, Kuwait, Libya, Oman, Qatar and UAE. Most of these migrants were unskilled or semiskilled labourers. Recently there is a significant change in those migrants from Bangladesh in terms of number and destination, due to change in socio-economic and political conditions of those destinations. The factors like fall in oil revenues, long Iran-Iraq War and growing Arabinisation of these economies have forced the change in the trend in labour migration to these destinations and it has lost its earlier momentum.[11]

Nair (1992) on the context of migration from Kerala highlights the steps taken by State Government along with the support from the

Central Government to mitigate the problems of migrants. The State has submitted a plan of 7,500 million rupees to the Government of India for the rehabilitation of return migrants. The Central Government has supported the proposal and introduced several schemes for the returned migrants in the form of insurance against accidents and death while at work abroad.[12]

Indian migrant workers are seen globally. In the recent trend it is observed that large scale migration takes place from Kerala to Gulf countries. The Gujarati and Sikh people are known for their enterprising skills and migration to European countries and America. Since 2003, every year on 9th January the Prabasi Bharat Divas or Non Resident Indian Day is celebrated to mark the contribution of the overseas Indian community to the development of India. In Fiji, the Indian migrant population is more than forty per cent of the total population and they could form government there. People from coastal Odisha are moving to different countries to work in different sectors. Liberalisation in the policy of international migration has helped people to adopt external migration easily.

2.3 Internal Migration

Floger (1953) laid two principles, first if two areas are in different economic regions, the relationship between distance and the number of migrants may be different from the relationship within an economically integrated area and secondly rate of net migration between two areas tend to be directly proportional to differences in the level of living and inversely proportional to the distance between them.[13]

Gosal and Krishna (1974) quoting Davis (1951) says despite immense economic, social and political significance, the study on internal migration in India has not received the due attention, although people were allowed to move freely from one princely State to another, to British, to non-British India, and even from other countries. Zacharia (1960, 1964) made a detailed investigation into the problem of internal migration in the Indian sub-continent during 1941-51 and 1901-31.

Oberai *et al.* (1987) in their study on migration from Bihar, Kerala and Uttar Pradesh find that 96 to 97.5 per cent of unemployed migrants became employed and capable of earning their livelihood. The migrant students from Uttar Pradesh have become part of labour force after migration. Around 14 per cent of Bihar and 25 per cent of Kerala migrants are working in housekeeping activities. Thus, migration has helped a lot of migrants from these States in seeking employment in cities.

Rawat (1993) in his study in the rural Garwal region finds that there is a change in the traditional activities of women from the normal agricultural operation and house chores to non-familial economic occupations which were traditionally prohibited for them. Women have now assumed a new role in the changing socio-economic conditions.

Amrith (2011) in the context of internal migration, points out that the Bhilai Steel Plant, one of the largest in the world symbolising India's future industrialisation attracted thousands of workers from different parts of the country. In 1961, out of 18,000 workforces, 60 per cent of male workers were from other States, and 78 per cent of population was in the age group of 15-35. A vast army of unskilled migrant workers mainly from dalit communities from Odisha, Andhra Pradesh, and Bihar joined the workforce of the newly established steel city. The Rourkela steel city in Odisha represents a city of migrants mainly coming from coastal Odisha, West Bengal, Bihar etc. The local tribals were displaced and are being marginalised in the development of the city.

Lam (2011) emphasises the role of migration in the determination of livelihood for poor people. In spite of this important aspect of livelihood for a larger section of the society in the context of social change little attention is paid to migration. The pattern of livelihood has become increasingly multidimensional and individualisation has lead to break up of households in the age of liberalisation. Poor people are now moving to multiple activities and multiple areas as well. (This view has also been expressed by other writers, like Caney, 1999; Ellis Zoo, Scones, 1998; De Haan and Zoomers, 2003).[14]

Mukherjee and Phadke (2011) say the adoption of capital and technology has increased labour productivity; thereby job availability in urban locality has become a difficult proposition. This has induced to a "jobless growth" which tends to connect a short run problem of resource imbalances into a long-run problem of chronic and rising urban surplus labour. This is further worsening due to the inflow of rural migrants to urban areas.[15]

Kalra (2000) in the context of migration and social change points out that the reasons given by Lord Salisbury for migration from the area were to supplement the meager income from the sale of ghee (clarified butter) and husbandry. To get immediate cash by mortgaging land is a difficult task by the zamindars. The only option before them was to go into debt and to actually purchase land outright from mahajans or money lenders. As a way out of this situation migration into cities seemed to be the better option.

Bhutalia (2007) in the context of India's partition and migration says, partition was one of terrible violence and fear. Their choice was between death and sexual violence–death at the hands of their 'own' men and sexual assault at the hand of others. These would be 'migrants' therefore faced death, and many families were guilty of their own women, ostensibly in order to escape from rapes, conversion and/or impregnated. Thus, this was a situation of migration arising out of political division of a country into two parts.

On the study of demographic changes of a region, Mishra pointed out birth rate and death rate are more associated with cultural, social and biological factors, although economic forces too have a significant role to play in their determination. However birth rate and death rate do not generally, exhibit by sensitive response to changes in economic parameters in the short-run. Hence, when the period under study does not involve in a long-run, migration becomes the most accountable factor in determining the rate of increment in the size of population in the region.[16]

Mandal (1981) on the study of migration from Ranchi says that a greater part of the labour demand from Assamese tea garden and Hoogly side industrial complex is met by migrants from Ranchi. Bihari migrant labourers are seen in most of the states of the country.

Chattopadhyaya (1987) with regards to the inter-provincial migration till 1931, says the movement was between Bengal, on the one hand and Assam, Bihar, British-Burma, U.P., Punjab, Rajputana, Central Provinces and Berar, Bombay and Madras, on the other. While Bengal sent out labourers into Assam, Bihar, British Burma, Bengal received labourers from Bihar, Odisha and U.P.[17]

A salient feature of the migration between Bengal and the sister provinces was that migrants from Bengal into Assam, Bihar and Burma were mostly labourers. While the majority of Bengali migrants into Orissa, UP, Madras, Bombay, Punjab, Central Province and Rajputna comprised were white coloured persons such as teachers, lawyers, clerks and other service holders, medical men and pilgrims. On the other hand migrants into Bengal from Orissa, Bihar, U.P. belonged mostly to working classes, unskilled and skilled.[18] To corroborate the findings of Chattopadhyaya, the auther found in his present place of work in a rural college, namely Larambha College in Bargarh district western Odisha which was established in the 1960s by an eminent educationist named Braja Mohan Panda, who was educated in Calcutta, recruited most of the teachers from Bengal and they served here for more than 30 years. The providers of medical services during those days were also from Bengal.

Chaudhuri (1993) on the study of migration and remittance relating to the steel city of Durgapur, finds that while making the physical planning of a town the component of migration into the city is not taken into account and therefore research emphasises the need to allocate space and government allocation of funds from the beginning of the development of town in order to control the unplanned growth of squatters.[19]

Singh (2001) while analysing the pattern of development in the developing countries finds that the continuing high population growth has increased the workforce but has failed to create adequate job opportunities to match the growing population. In 1960s and 1990s the annual labour force growth rate of developing countries as compared to industrialised countries were 4:1 and 6:1 respectively. Under this situation migration is the only option left behind before the growing workforce.[20]

Zachavial *et al.* (2003) in the context of migration in Kerala says during 1901-31 the then State of Travancore-Cochin was consistently an area of in-migration, the volume of net migration increasing from 10,000 to 67,000. But during and after the Second World War this net in-migration state became a state of net out-migration. The factors such as large scale Malaylis for war related jobs, formation of separate Kerala State (Nov. 1956), integration and opened up wide opportunities to Malaylis people in military and civil services in a rapidly expanding government in Delhi. The demographic expansion followed by rapid progress made in the field of education largely facilitated out-migration in large scale. For them Gulf countries became a preferred destination of external migration.[21]

In the context of partition and migration Ghosh (2007) points out that by December 1951, roughly 6,597,000 refugees had moved from India to West Pakistan and 794,127 to East Pakistan. Of those headed for Pakistan between 1947-48, 95.9 per cent of the migrants from Assam, West Bengal and Bihar moved to East Pakistan and 3.2 per cent to Karachi. According to the 1951 Pakistan census, 66.69 per cent of the migrants in East Pakistan were from West Bengal, 14.50 per cent from Bihar, 11.84 per cent from Assam and 6.79 per cent from other parts of India. By contrast, around 60 per cent of 464,000 Muhajirs from U.P. settled in Sindh. (p. 11-12).

Barik (1994) says most of the Odia migrants to Surat, came from Ahmadabad and Bombay and not from Odisha directly. The newly established companies in Ahmadabad recruited cheap Odia labours who were previously working at different companies of Calcutta. Most of the Odia labourers migrated from Bombay to Surat were working as gardeners, cooks, and care-takers, who shifted along with their masters. Till today Odias are known for the derogatory expression "Malibhai," gardener locally. By 1994, when the study was conducted it was estimated that more than 60,000 Odia migrants were living in various slum areas in Surat were from Ganjam district of South Odisha.[23]

Giege (1999) says chain migration was introduced in the population studies in the 1950s to describe the phenomenon that established migrants help their relatives or friends to migrate the same destination (Macdonald and Macdonald, 1964) chain migration generally said to be helpful for easy and quicker setting at the destination.[24]

Bookman (2002) discusses the concept of migration in relation to the proposed Hirschman micro-level framework for analysing individual choice in order to explain behaviour. When an institution/ organisation fails to meet people's expectation, people exit in the form of stop buying or through protest. This framework can also be applied to migration. Accordingly an individual will adopt migration if the residence area fails to provide to live up to its economic, social or political expectations.[25]

The push factor for migration arises in a region, when it fails to meet the economic expectation of potential migrants in terms of employment and income. On the other hand economic expectation pertaining to opportunities in the host region exerts a pull factor on the migrants. Potential migrants calculate gain out of migration. Economists like Hicks, Lewis, Ranis and Fei, Harris and Todaro, and Todaro have focused on these economic considerations in their analysis of migration.

Espinosa and Massey in their study on undocumented migration and the quantity and quality of social capital point out that the concept of social capital introduced by Glenn Loury in 1977 has undergone considerable elaboration and refinement. Social capital is referred to a set of intangible resources in families and communities that promote cognitive growth and social development among young people. The goal set by Loury was beyond individual level and expressed concern over the poor performance of youth in schools and labour force. Over a period of time migration has become self perpetuating because each act of migration creates additional social capital to promote and sustain more movements. The expansion of social capital through expansion of network changes the distribution of costs, benefits, risk and rewards among the migrants social environment. The future decision for migration is largely influenced by feedback received by them is particularly very strong in the case of undocumented migration.[26]

Bhagat (2011) says the features of new economic policy tend towards greater role of private sector and reduced governmental expenditures would increase internal migration. The supports of liberal policy believe that new impetus would boost economy and job opportunities, which will create large, pull factors favourable for greater rural-to-urban migration. On the other hand the opponents held the view that economic reforms would impoverish the rural economy thereby leading to increased rural-urban migration.

2.4 Basis of Migration

Though, there is controversy about the push and pull factors, both the factors have been responsible for massive migration. The 'push' and 'pull' are simply evidence of wider socio-economic condition and structural transformation in the society. The push factors rather than pull factors, as a prime cause of migration from rural areas were observed in five class-I towns of the state.[27]

Given the diversity of the nature of migration in India, the causes are similarly varied in terms of space and time. Migration in India reflects household subsistence strategies in the face of social, cultural, demographic and other constraints. It is also influenced by the demand for migrant workers and development patterns (NCRL, 1991). The National Commission on Rural Labour, (NCRL) focusing on seasonal migration, concluded that uneven development was the main cause of seasonal migration. In the tribal region intrusion of outsiders, settlements in tribal areas, displacement and deforestation have also contributed significantly to the seasonal out migration of tribals.[28]

Connell, et al (1976) says migration is indeed the child of inequality. It is from the village where land is distributed in the most unequal manner. Migration however is also the father of inequality. It confers cumulative gains upon the richer migrants family, including access to further probable migration, for the poorer migrants, migration is increasingly a wandering search for work, and even if the search for work succeeds it is unlikely to do more for his family than prevent a decline into defer poverty.[29]

Pryor (1979) discusses the pattern of internal migration affected in part as a cost of covering distance, and the regional differences and changes in the natural environment. The preference of the migrants regarding migration depends on the range of options available in the changing perceptions and learning adaptation through time. Influence of social changes is also reflected in the attitude of migration.

Chadha (2007) states in the post-liberal phase the urban employment grows continuously faster than the rural employment, and employment setbacks are prominent in rural areas than urban areas leading to movement of people from rural to urban areas.

Abraham Maslow (1954) a psychologist explains the theory of Hierarchy of Needs. In the pyramid of needs, at the bottom there is the physiological need for existence. The government programmes for the poor do not take care beyond basic needs. Minimum wage does not fulfill all components of human needs. There is growing expectation of all people in all fronts, which may not be fulfilled in their place of living. Hence there arises the need of migration.

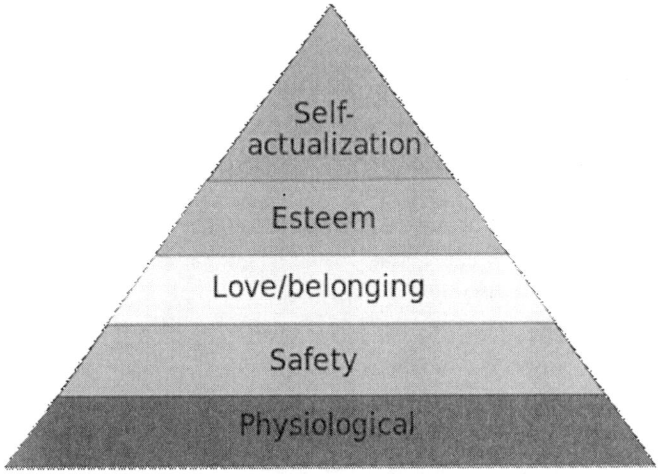

(Maslow's hierarchy of needs, reprcsented as a pyramid with the more basic needs at the bottom)

Figure 2.1: Maslow Theory of Hierarchy Need Pyramid. [30]

Desai (2007) says the development programmes directed for the removal of poverty consider that the poor only act as passive recipients. The redistribution mechanism is often appropriated by the not-so-poor who control the transaction channels of aid. Historically, migration has played a very crucial role in the removal of poverty and unemployment. One task of Millennium Development Goals (MDG) is to promote international migration on a global scale to reduce poverty in use.

Shrestha (1996) says the land reform measures followed by mechanisation of agriculture enticed landlords to withdraw their land from the renting and share cropping market and cultivated it themselves by using machines and seasonally hired labour. This type of development reduced land accessibility on the part of landless or near landless tenants and thus diminished their position in the agrarian related production. The decline in their socio-economic conditions forced them to join the ranks of migrants as the only economic option before them.

The incidence of out-migration from rural Bihar is greater than anywhere else in India. It is the result of natural and societal forces, which compels a family member to think of a basic survival strategy. The migration of people from draught and flood affected areas of Bihar is age old. But the closure of industries and law and order problems has added another dimension to the incidence of circular migration since 1990's.[31]

Shah (2009) on his study of brick kiln workers from Jharkhand quoting the survey of a University Professor states that majority of migrants working in different brick kilns left home to escape from a fight at home, to explore a new country, or for an amorous relationship. These findings were opposed by his colleagues and friends protesting against brick kiln migration.[32]

Korra (2011) in his field work on labour migration from Mahabubnagar in Andhra Pradesh indicates that large numbers of households depend on migration as a strategy for their livelihood and their selection of destination is influenced by accessibility of information of past experience and social networks. The STs and SCs section of population are the usual migrants because these communities are economically deprived due to landlessness, inadequate farm land and other assets.

Pandey (2013) says the uneven nature of economic development among states results in a heavy shift of population from backward States like Uttar Pradesh and Bihar to developed States like Maharashtra, Gujarat and Delhi etc. The migration literature in India suggests the main cause of female migration is still either marriages of associational migration i.e. migration with earning member of the family and the role of the female migrants on economic development is less compared to male.[33]

Mandal (1981) says migration helps in exchanging population between two regions and hence population migration is an open phenomenon. It is easy to distinguish between population at origin and population of destination. In case of nuptiability the corresponding migration between male and female is possible, but with a small number of women.

Jayaraj (2013) finds in his study on family migration in India that irrespective of migrants' place of origin, had reported deteriorating livelihood conditions in the place of origin as the major reason for rural urban migration. These migrants generally live in the urban slums. But the micro level studies limited amount of evidence towards push factor as a major element of push element to induce movement. However, family migration in India suggests push, pull and pull-push factors behind migration.[34]

2.5 Migration due to Displacement

"It happens in India, where in the period 1951-90, over 21.6 million people suffered precisely that fat-displaced by just dams and canals alone. Add mining that has dispossessed 2.1 million people and you have the population of Canada. Further, industries, thermal plants, sanctuaries and defense installations have thrown at least 2.4 million human beings out of their houses. That's around twenty-six million Indians."[35]

Malhotra (2013) points out five factors behind their decision to migrate. There are failure of agriculture, lower economic state of development, natural calamities, socio-economic discrimination and displacement of backward classes. The Gadaba tribe of Chikapor village has been displaced three times due to the establishment of Hindustan Aeronautics Ltd. (HAL), upper Kolab Multi-purpose project and Naval Ammunitions Depot. The land grabbed by the State in all three occasions belonged to the same villagers. This involuntary displacement has forced them to migrate to the neighbouring district/State. Thus development projects have accelerated the process of migration.[36]

Behera (2011) on Hirakud Dam Project finds that a sizable section of displaced people have migrated to Raipur and Raigarh in Chhattisgarh to escape from starvation due to disruption of livelihood. There they are working as rickshaw puller and causal labour. The incidence of internal migration due to displacement is a common occurrence in the Indian pattern of development adopted since 1950s.[37]

2.6 Circular/Seasonal Migration

The idea of population movement as circulation was first conceptualised in Wilson's study (1968:42) in the African town Kabwe (Broken Hill). The concept was later implicated by Mitchell (1969: 175) "where local opportunities for earning do not exist or are generally inadequate, people migrate to satisfy their basic needs. However, sooner or later these migrants come back to their places of origin. Again in due course of time because of local economic inadequacies, they once again feel the necessity to try to find employment opportunities elsewhere. Under these circumstances migrants circulate between places of employment and their native villages.

Mc Gee (1982: 59) declares "———the volume and importance of circulatory migration, is invariably underestimated in the Asian context". The extensive research of Hugo (1980) leads to the same conclusion regarding Indonesia. In Latin America circulation may be not as typical as permanent movement, but in this continent we can also find many examples of the phenomenon (C.f. Conaway, 1976 and Lomritz, 1977).

About 10 million were estimated to be seasonal/temporary migrants out of whom 1.7 million located in Utter Pradesh, 1.5 million in Madhya Pradesh and one million each in Maharashtra, Andhra Pradesh and Bihar. The seasonal and temporary migration is an important livelihood strategy of India's poor who are mainly located in the tribal and forested tracts of mid-India.[38]

Rapid internal migration in general was thought to be a desirable process by which surplus rural labour was withdrawn from traditional agriculture to provide cheap manpower to fuel a growing modern industrial complex (Lewis, 1954; Fei and Ranis, 1961) the process was deemed socially beneficial (at least on the basis of historical evidence, Kuznets, 1964, 1971), since human resources were being shifted from locations where their marginal social products were often assumed to be zero to places where these marginal products were not only positive but also rapidly growing as a result of capital accumulation and technological progress.[39]

Fritz Selier and Pefer Nientied (1986) on their pilot study on circular migration in Karachi point out that evidence indicates that temporary movements, the concept of circular migration is often used are quite common in less developed countries and are becoming increasingly prevalent (C.f Goldstein and Goldstein, 1981; Hugs, 1983). However in migration literature, no consistency is found as to what is to be regarded exactly as permanent or temporary or circulation.[40]

Seasonal migrants were able to supplement their income by short-term "circular" migration in accordance with seasonal variations in labour requirement. (Elkan, 1960, 1967). If real wages imbalance occurs between two locations, the neo-classical price-adjustment model dictated that in-migration would work to re-establish the balance by raising rural average incomes and lowering urban wages.

Kasap (1992) in his study of seasonal migration of agricultural labours in Pune region finds the presence of 'push' factor as a prominent factor rather than 'pull' factor in the determination of seasonal migration. The agricultural labourer moves out in the lean season because of lack of livelihood opportunities in the place of their origin. High wage, fall in local demand for labour and labour surplus lead to intra-regional and inter-regional seasonal migration. Mukodam the intermediary between sugarcane factory and migrant labour plays a vital role and the factory is not directly involved in employing migrant labour.[41]

Reddy (2007) in his study of rural migrant labour in Andhra Pradesh classified seasonal migration into three categories namely, subsistence equilibrating, innovation induced subsistence and survival seasonal migration. Subsistence equilibrating is inter-regional migration which takes place from dry areas to wet areas. Innovative induced subsistence seasonal migration takes place when an old crop is replaced by a new crop and requires skilled workers which may propel along with the crop migration of labour to the new area. The survival seasonal migration takes place from dry and draught prone area in the farm contact labour to different project works, migration for casual work and migration to neighbouring districts to work as agricultural labour.[42]

Lesher (2005) in the context of Millennium Development Goals and Migration points out that internal and external migration have continued to rise and more people are affected by migration in different manners. "In international migration one of the most significant trends is the rise of transactional migration". Instead of being unidirectional and permanent, migration has become increasingly temporary, seasonal and circular. New information and communication technologies facilitate contacts between migrants and those they have left behind, and significant advances in international transport have made travelling cheaper and easier.[43]

Chatterji, Joya (2010) supporting the expression of MDG for migration points out that following improved networking migrants are seen to maintain and deploy these networks to circulate between locations, rather than permanently to settle in one. Scholars have coined it 'hybridity' in contrast to traditional life style. Studies regard the practice of 'hybridity' as challenging and unsettling the logic of modernity and its vehicle, the nation State.[44]

Deshingkar and Farrington (2009) studies on circular migration points out that it is done in the labour market through intermediaries, who pay in advance to the migrants or their families. This type of arrangement can be linked to debt-bondage and it is difficult to distinguish migration from bonded labour. People also adopt migration to escape from social discrimination or political persecution at the place of origin; hence it is also difficult to distinguish migrants from internally displaced people. It is further pointed out that the strong pressure from urban middle class, government takes a negative and often inaccurate, view of migration and terms it as distress phenomenon and is doing little for the betterment of the migrants at destination and providing support of certain livelihood measures at the destination.[45]

Koteshwar (2004) in the study of seasonal migration in Mahaboobnagar district of Andhra Pradesh finds that most of the seasonal migrants are young and in the age group of 26-45 years and a majority of them belong to backward castes (84 per cent) and illiterate. In the post-migration situation it is seen that majority of them have failed to learn any new skill.

Ram (2009) says seasonal migration is mostly promoted by 'push' factors where the migrants suffer from disadvantages of poor control over other migration process with respect to direction, activity, in terms of employment and other working conditions. The miseries of migrant labour start from the place of origin and shadow them till they return. The channel of information flowing to the potential migrants is very weak due to which they are prone to be exploited by the middlemen and employers.[46]

In India, the importance and impact of return migration on rural life has not been studied in detail. In most of the Indian studies on migration, only passing references are made to return migration, presumably because of the insignificant number of returnees. Many studies have been conducted in Kerala dealing with various aspects of migration to Middle-East.[47]

Bellak, C et. al. (2014) in their study of short-term labour migration from Armenia to Russia find that short-term labour migration is a potentially repeated act, it quantifies the income gap arising from migration for the Armenia-Russian migration corridor, which is likely representative for other Central Asian and Caucasian countries and it quantifies the impact of the income gap on the decision to migrate, while controlling for a broad range of other potential determinants in line with migration theory.[48]

Ray *et. al.* (2004) find that out-migration in an area may occur in the adjacent area which is directly influenced by development projects such as irrigation scheme. Due to limited land resource and increasing population, there is considerable amount of out-migration from irrigated as well as non-irrigated areas. The decrease in out-migration from rural areas can be possible only through the creation of jobs in non-agricultural sectors.

Roy (2011) says it is difficult to check migration completely. Short-term and long-term measures like micro-enterprise, SHG activities, and infrastructure development such as irrigation facilities, transportation, roads, health and education are to be implemented without delay. The left behind women, in the absence of their husbands suffer from mental stress. The condition of left behind women of migrant labour has not been given due attention.[49]

Tripathy (2013) in his study of KBK districts in Odisha says, the cycle of poverty originates from the sordid reality of crop failure, unemployment, food insecurity, vulnerability to health hazards and ultimately debt trap. The vicious cycle continues unabated for decades in these districts. He asserts corruption and leakages of funds for different development programme as the principal reasons for the low state the development and benefits of government programmes are not percolating to the poor.

Jaiswal (2013) has drawn an exception among the out-migration in case of Kerala. Kerala is a socially and educationally developed state in India. Yet a large percentage of state's population migrates to Gulf countries and also in-migrates to other states of India. He further asserts that those negative effects of migration is least related to rich people migration, but with the poor people who migrates to other states.

Migration will exist, but for luxury not for dire necessity. Therefore the development of the country needs to be expedited. The income equality among states is necessary, population control, least corruption and effective implementation of government programme are necessary to check migration.

In course of field visit it is noticed that a voluntary inter-state seasonal migration is taking place from Chhattisgarh to Bargarh town for the last 25-30 years. These migrants are basically farmers who grow organic vegetables in the river bed of Zeera. They get a ready market in Bargarh for the products and earn a better means of livelihood during their stay at Bargarh.

2.7 Data on Internal Migration

Data on family migration was collected only in the 38th, 49th, 58th and 64th rounds of the National Sample Survey Office (NSSO) for the year 1983, 1993, 2002 and 2007-08 respectively (such data were collected as a part of: (1) The employment and unemployment survey of 1983 and 2007-08, and (2) the surveys on Household Amenities and other characteristics for 1993 and 2002). It needs to be noted that the subject of migration continues to be treated as a secondary subject of the surveys on employment and unemployment and on household amenities and other characteristics. No attempt has been made to conduct a specially designed survey on migration.[50]

During the impressive growth period of the economy, migration of families in search of livelihood had gone up. The increase was from around 1.7 lakhs in 1993 to 3.5 lakhs in 2007-08. This suggests that assessment of the economy based on the overall growth of the economy may be misleading. The impact of such growth to provide secure livelihood options to families needs to be taken on board in assessing the overall performance of the economy.[51]

Data on internal migration in India is usually drawn from two main sources–the population census and the quinquennial migration surveys carried out by National Sample Survey Office (NSSO). One of the main lacunae of both the census and NSS surveys is their failure to adequately capture seasonal and/or short-term circular migration, and their coverage is best for permanent migrants and reasonably adequate for semi-permanent migrants.

Despite improvement in coverage of seasonal/circular migrants, NSS estimates are still inadequate for such migrants for two major resources. First, in May, the seasonal/circular migration cycle is longer than six months. Second, quite often, entire households and not individuals participate in seasonal migration. Census data show that inter-State migration has grown 12.02 per cent in 1981 to 13.31 per cent in 2001 (Srivastava, 2011a) NSS data, specifically in the rural-urban stream also show that the percentage of inter-state migrants has gone up from 19.6 per cent in 1999-2000 to 25.2 per cent in 2007-2008.[52]

Migration in India is predominantly limited to short distances, with around two-thirds of migrants changing their residence within the district of enumeration, and over one-fifth within the State of enumeration, with the reminder moving across State boundaries. There is another category of poor and destitute migrants who have virtually no assets in the areas of origin, and have lost all contact with their origin. Thus, not all poor migrants would fall within the category of seasonal/short-term migrants. But, as stated earlier, for one reason or another, all these categories are likely to be underestimated. In terms of the direction of migration, Census of India estimates that only 7.07 million, or 3.04 per cent of the migrants were short-term migrants (less than one year), with 1.37 million migrating for economic reason.[53]

The districts of Bolangir, Sonepur, Nuapada, Kalahandi, Nabarangapur, and Rayagada, in KBK region are prone to seasonal migration for the last 30-40 years. But due to inefficiency and unwilling character of the administration no data base has been prepared till date. Considering the gravity of the problem, in 1997 the Supreme Court of India had directed the state government to conduct a survey in that direction. But that survey report remains in the red tape.

Khan (1986) points out that in spite of greater socio-economic importance rural migration in the country, lack statistical information about this problem. Indian census provides information about immigration but little information is provided about out-migration. Migration studies have normally dealt migrants in the places of destinations and rarely have the migrants been studied in the places of origin, where decision on migration takes place.

Ghosh (2004) says migration becomes circular when the employment is for limited period. The migrants leave their villages accompanied by wives and children to escape the off-season in the agrarian cycle to work as brick-makers. In India, seasonal and circular/ cyclical/oscillatory migration has long been a part of livelihood of the poor people across the country. The circular migrants in rural areas are around 10 million, including roughly 4.5 million inter-State migrants and 6 million intra-State migrants.[54]

Ram, 2007; Korra, 2011, comment over the non-availability of data on inter-state seasonal migrants either in census or the NSS has its relevancy. Therefore, researchers have to mostly depend on surrogate information to arrive at the magnitude and selectivity of seasonal migration taking in different parts of the country.

Contract/dadan labour from Nuapada district of the study area moves to neighbouring states in an unspecified number every year. As per one government estimate 6000 families (20,000-30,000 People) move as migrant labour to other states. Out of these labours around 5000 constitute child labour. Block-wise Nuapada, Komna, Khadial, Boden and Sinpali share of migrant families are 995, 2289, 1072,678, and 966 respectively.[55]

Debadutta Club an NGO finds in its survey in the Gaisilet Block of Bargarh district that 47,205 number of labourers had out-migrated from 18 villages during 2012-13. Out of them 59.03 per cent belong to OBC, 22.3 per cent ST, 17.47 per cent SC and 5.47 per cent children. 54.15 per cent of these labourers used to migrate every year. Most of them have their destination to Chennai, Erode, Perindry, Tripur, and Vanur districts of Tamil Nadu, Anathpalli, Hyderabad, Tirupati, Visakhapattanam of Andhra Pradesh. A few of them also move to the state of Chhattisgarh, Uttar Pradesh and Maharashtra.[56]

It has been pointed out in the District Level Dadan Labour Meet at Bolangir, Odisha that there is no end to the problem of dadan in western Odisha. In spite of wide coverage in media about the dadan problem, it has not become an effective political issue till date. It shows the unwillingness of political parties and administration. Each year 1-1.5 lakh people from Bolangir district alone move as migrant labour to other states and work there in sub-human condition.[57]

2.8 Migration and Rural Informal Sector

Samal (2008) in his studies of Informal Sector (IS) finds that there is a confirm linkage of rural-to-urban migration in Odisha between urban informal sector and rural to urban migration and found push factors, in general, as more important determinant than pull factors in the migration of rural people to urban areas. But in case of newly established industrial sectors pull factors are prominent for informal sector entrepreneurs and in coal mine region for most of the informal workers. He finds that rural-to-urban migration as one of the tools to alleviate rural poverty may not be easily ruled out, in the age of liberalisation, when large numbers of workers are joining informal sectors being driven out from formal sectors of private and public sector as well. The growth of rural non-formal sector (RNFS) is necessary to alleviate rural poverty and unemployment.

Samal *et al.* (2012) finds that rural non-farm sector (particularly informal component of it) is seen as a promising sector for creating of sustainable employment and as a solution to the problem of poverty in rural areas since agricultural sector is oversaturated. The growth of rural informal sector is possible with public intervention in social sectors like education and health. The migration of rural people to urban informal sector is a sign of development, since migration improves their level of living. After all, the diversion of rural population to urban centres is a progressive phenomenon.

Mariappan (2013) points out that there is a strong evidence that 90 per cent of rural migrants have found employment in urban areas through informal job networks viz., friends/acquaints, relatives, direct approaches and former migrants in the Indian labour market of the unorganised sector. His study further finds that about 63 per cent of them have found employment in urban based informal sector.

2.9 Condition of Migrants and State Action

That migration takes place due to pull and push factors. Migration arising out of push factors is a matter of great concern, because it violates the economic and social rights enshrined in the Directive Principles and right to life as a fundamental right granted by the Indian Constitution. They are deprived up a decent living condition and subject to various kinds of exploitation at destination. Although there are number of laws to deal with the problem of inter-state migration, bonded labour, child labour, the conditions of such labour still remain poor in many respects.

Migrants are mostly employed in the informal economy, often working as construction workers, agricultural labourers, hawkers and vendors, domestic servants, rickshaw pullers, electricians, plumbers, masons and security personnel. Devoid of social security and legal protection, they work in poor conditions and face labour market discrimination. Minimum wages are often flouted and employers bear no responsibility for health, shelter and other requirements of migrants.[58]

Imbanathan (1988) studied the lower caste Tamil migrants in Delhi and finds that, introduction of power loom in their places of origin made the handloom wives unemployed and pushed them to migrate to Delhi. During their initial settlement, they stayed in squatter settlements and were prepared to be evicted at any time. However, in these squatter areas they lived amidst their own caste fellows drawn from their native districts.

Sivamurugan (2013) points out that seasonal migrant labours have enormous contribution to national economy through their involvement in major sectors such as construction, textiles, brick-making, stone quarries, mining, fish and prawn processing etc. But migrants remain on the periphery of society, with few citizen rights and absence of political voice to redress their problems. He finds that there is a significant improvement in the income of the migrants after migration. Their possession of assets has increased after migration and in most of the cases the level of savings has also increased. Thus, his findings have shown a positive sign of the migrants.

Khandelwal, Gilbert and Gantt (2009) point out that majority of tribal migrants from Rajasthan lack skills, little information and virtually no support service. As a result they are poorly paid and engaged in exploitative jobs, without any protection in farm or factory labour.

Ansari (2004) finds that Bihari tribal migrant to Hoshiarpur, Punjab were tortured in a number of ways. They were locked by the employers at night to avoid sharing of feelings with other employees. Payment of wages was held up for months together to force them to stay back. The agent and the musclemen of the employers pick up the migrants from railway stations only on false promises. The agents in the origin i.e. tribal areas of Bihar send large hoards of tribal migrant workers to the contracted agents in Punjab. Thus, the seasonal migrants from Bihar to Punjab suffer at the destination.

Ghosh (2004) in the case of circular migrants working in brick kilns the male head is the principal workers whereas the females and children work as a part of family, work to supplement the income. In her study she finds that there is considerable number of children involved in brick kilns. But children are not under the pay roll of the employers, because brick-making involve piece-rate of work. The Inter-State Migrant Workmen(Regulation of Employment and Conditions of Service Act), 1979 lacks proper implementation. To this the non-cooperation of migrant workers in the brick kilns is the biggest lacuna. She further finds that there is practically no enforcement of any of the provision of this law in state like Uttar Pradesh.

Papola (2011) quoting the study of Rodgers *et al* 2009 : chapter-6 on ILO points out that ILO has tried to ensure decent work and emphasised four constant objectives namely, right to work, employment, social protection and social dialogue.

Abbas and Varma (2014) in their study on internal migration points out that the response of government to the problems of internal migration is limited. Whatever little legislation that exists for worker's right is seldom enforced. It is the response of the civil society or non-governmental organisation, which count more towards the welfare of the internal migrants in the field of education, health etc, that are not taken up by the Government the provisions under India's Inter-State migrant (Regulation of Employment and Conditions of Service/Act 1979) is overwhelmingly ignored by State Governments.

Comelo (2014) in his study of migration and precariousness employment conditions says, under the current haphazard, paper based mode of operation of the governmental bureaucracy, it is highly unrealistic to expect the enforcement of the Inter-State Migrant Workmen Act, which requires constant communication and coordination between Labour Commissions of the concerned State (Goa) and other States to verify compliance under certain provisions of the law. Besides, this law is meant to protect workers in situation that does not understand to the reality of labour migration associated with security industry.[59]

A horrible incidence of chopping off palms of two migrant workers by the labour contractor took place on 15th December 2013 in the district of Kalahandi Odisha. The local media reported the news of Nilambar Dhangdamajhi and Dialu Nial's palms being chopped off by some labour *dalals* and subsequently, the electronic media showed the visuals of bandaged stumps, the hands without palms, of the two lying on the hospital beds. Following the media report the Supreme Court of India took a cognizance of the report and sou moto ordered for an inquiry into the incidence. This shows the plight of the contact labour in the country.[60]

Mishra and Rao (1992) say, the 1980s have brought Kalahandi into national mainstream. The recurring drought, the starvation deaths, the selling of human beings and the distress migration drew the country's attention.[61]

Even if India has the Interstate Migration Workmen Act 1979, it does not help migrants because of the lack of proper implementation and monitoring. Migration policies should be stringent for internal migration in India.[62]

In view of inter-state migration in the KBK region it is estimated that more than twelve thousand voters from one block only will be deprived of their voting right in the general election of 2014. These migrant eligible voters belong to Khaprakhol block of Bolangir district. Out of 68,000 voters from 18 panchayat-132 villages of Khaprakhol block 12000 have migrated as dedan. But the number of unregistered dadan will be more than the stated data.[63]

Taking notes to the plight of the migrant labour dadan, a local young writer Kshtrabasi Nayak, has written a book in Odia entitled *'Dadan'* (2012) and received the Kendra Sahitya Academy award for the young writers. His book has unfolded the sufferings and miseries of migrants through stories.[64]

2.10 Migration and Child Labour

Chubayanger (2013) points out that the National Commission on Labour, 1969 shows the evidence that employment of migrant children is non-existence in case of organised sector. But it persists in varying degree in unorganised sectors such as small plantation, restaurants and hotels, carpet weaving, stone breaking, brick kiln, handicraft and road construction. Employment of such child labour continuing in far-off places and in rural areas, where statutory provisions are rarely implemented.

The ILO report on child labour 2004 expresses concern over the employment of children both boys and girls in various dangerous work. They are subject to different type exploitation not only in underdeveloped countries but also in developing countries.

Sharma (2006) says children in India experience other forms of oppressive realities. These exploitative occupations in India are lock making, gem polishing and carpet weaving. Children facing migration are no exception to such exploitations.

The nature of inter-state seasonal migration means family migration. The male head usually takes female and children along with him to work in different kinds of piece work such as brick making. In that case the female and children have to work with the male head to earn their livelihood. Thereby the children are deprived of their schooling and childhood.

2.11 Effects of Migration

Breaking the myth that internal migration is burdening the cities, a new study says migrants are in fact contributing largely to the Gross Domestic Product (GDP) and proving to be a subsidy. A UNESO report on Social Inclusion of Internal Migrations are looked upon as "outsiders" and considered a burden, but the fact is that internal migrants contribute cheap labour for manufacturing and service and in doing so contribute to national GDP.[65]

Garip (2012) in his study of migration from Mexico to the US during 1970 to 2000 finds that the Mexican migrants consisted mainly male household leads were largely from rural areas with poor educational background and few assets in possession move to the US for increasing their earnings. This type of migration from less developed to developed country is labeled as income maximisers and remained a dominant migrant when the US wages were at their highest level in the early 1970, and slowly declined in number as wages decline in real value.[66]

Oberai and Singh (1983) on the study of internal migration in the Indian Punjab points out that rural-urban migration can be viewed as a factor causing uneven development. The out-migration region is deprived of innovative human resources by diverting cheap productive labour force to the urban growth centres which have advantages of capital investments. This is the concomitant of uneven economic development which generates inequality in the distribution of income and wealth between urban areas on the one hand and rural or village areas on the other. But to a large extent the migrant labour can generate a kind of push factor for economic growth of the country at large. A large scale inflow of rural migrants to urban area deteriorates urban life in the form of slums and squatter settlements.[67]

Sjaastad (2002) treats migration as a means of promoting allocation of resources in an efficient manner because migration is an activity which needs resources. In US, internal migration takes place substantively in narrowing geographic income differentials. In spite of substantive internal migration there persist large income differences in that country. He further states that there exists no information with regard to the expenses incurred by the migrants in the course of moving. The estimates available for such cost may be of conservative in nature. The non-monetary cost for migration is definitely insignificant.[68]

Patnaik and Sekhar (2004) say different studies on the wage rate of migrants provide divergent views. Citing the study of Ansari on migrants from Muzaffarpur district in Bihar finds an increase in the real wage whereas the study made by Jha for Purnea district of North Bihar, shows no such increase in real wage. But both the studies have however shown an increase in the employment rate in the countryside due to migration. Kerala is an exception, where an impressive social achievement and high standard of living as well have been maintained through inflow of remittances.[69]

Deshingkar *et al* (2004) on their study of circular migration in Andhra Pradesh find that migration is on the rise from 19 per cent in 2000 to 54 per cent in 2006-07 in their sample areas. Migration has provided many poor household to eat more regularly, repayment of debt, increase investment in health and education and helps in raising standard of living. It has helped in acquiring skill but acquisition of skill by ST, SC and women acquire fewer skills because of their social disadvantage.[70]

Sundari (2007) in her study on migrant women finds that migration has provided an opportunity to overcome unemployment among migrant job seeker women. There is a shift from agricultural to non-agricultural activities and migration has increased annual earnings of all migrants. As a result saving position has also improved.[71]

Tripathy (2011) on the notes to the issue of migration from Bihar says, Bihari migrants are visible from Kerala to Ladakh and Surat to Nagaland and Manipur. The studies in Bihari migrants have been sliced of time and space for varying reasons related to its impact on development of the state, but no one has tried to estimate the total amounts of remittance to the state. Further, he says as a larger part of labour force migrates; work in the village becomes more lucrative due to labour shortage. But it is not the picture of well being of the people who run, migrate out of despair.[72]

Mukherji (2013) points out that migration-restriction can never be a desirable option or strategy. It will be the most undesirable and undemocratic act. Before the migrants, there is limited choice between early deaths in the villages or slow starvation in the stinking urban slums, the only escape from rural poverty is migration. If migration is not allowed, most of the poverty stricken people will perish in their villages. Migration is also an escape from the tyranny of caste-ridden village society and resultant oppression of the upper castes and the rich on the poor and downtrodden. Therefore, migration needs to be encouraged and migrants must be protected from exploitation and lordship at their place of work that is the destination.

Pandey (2013) in his study finds that regression result shows there exist a positive relationship between Inter-State rural to urban male migration and indicators of economic development like per capita income, per worker Net Value Added in the industrial sector and composite India of infrastructure because all the coefficients of explanatory variables have a positive sign.

Thapa (2013) on the issue of electoral of the migrants in Ludhiana on the post green revolution period finds that, owning to the relatively better economic conditions, the numerical presence in the city have emerged as a distinct and separate stratum. The migrants have emerged as a large segment of voters and have been forced to play an active role in the politics of the city. A number of migrants have contested Assembly Election in 2012 as candidates from different political parties. These migrants have enriched the economy of the city.

2.12 To Reduce/Prevent Out-Migration

Oberai *et al* (1989) suggest, other thing remaining same, out-migration flows from rural areas will be low due to economic development and high infrastructural development, in this situation family migration will be still lower. Young people dominate the migration flows because the return on investment in human capital declines with age. Older people also tend to develop stronger attachments to their property and family.[73]

Mishra and Rao (1992) on the issue of migration from Kalahandi find the lack of access to resources is the main reason, which is not recognised by the mainstream approach. So there is the need to access them with land, water and forest as an alternative to check migration and hunger for food.

Desai (1994) in her study on migrants' slum dwellers in Bombay says there is a balance stay of migrants from within and outside the state in the slum areas of the city. Most of these internal migrants tended to have come from an agricultural background and largely migrated into more closely-knit communities. Her study further finds that those from an agricultural background were better educated and those internal migrants were more likely to be skilled and possibility of entering into the formal sector jobs.

Pranwell (1993) in his study on population movements in the third world presents a typology of migration such as negative, aggressive policy to prevent migrants, accommodative, measures to take care for their accommodation in the cities, manipulative, accepting migration as inevitable and adopting suitable measures for land settlement, colonisation for their settlement and preventive measures taken to prevent movement of people from rural areas to urban centre in the form of rural infrastructure, rural job creation etc.[74]

The people of the Third World is that they may expect to continue to gain access to economic and other opportunities through migration, but that in the process they may continue to undermine the prospects for a self-reliant improvement in conditions and opportunities in their house areas in the longer term. Market forces and not government policy, will continue to determine who is able to move, who benefits, and who suffers as a result of migration.[75]

2.13 Conclusion

The review of literature finds that migration prevails mainly in the form of external and internal in nature. Internal migration are of different categories such as seasonal, circular, oscillatory, relay, family/individual, short duration, in nature. Internal migration in India shows that it takes place mainly due to lack of employment opportunities in the agriculturally backward regions. The poor and economically disadvantaged groups of people resort to seasonal/circular migration as a means of livelihood during the lean agricultural season. The presence of push, pull and push-pull factors are acting in such a way that internal migration which is seasonal in character takes place regularly. Studies show a mix result of migrants' improvement in terms of economic conditions. In spite of physical torture and financial loss, there will be no end to migration in the country. The state laws are not operating properly for the safeguard of the inter-state migrants, who often move on contract basis after receiving a sum from the labour contractors/agents to work in brick kilns and other informal sectors. Internal migrations do contribute to the development of the nation but studies show that it has not yet been properly assessed. Preventive measures can be adopted to check seasonal migration but it may not act successfully.

References

1. Bhagat (2011). *Internal Migration India: Are the Underclass more Mobile,* in S.J. Rajan (ed.) Migration, Identity and Concept, India Migration Report, 2011, Routledge, New Delhi.
2. Ravenstein, E.G. (1853). Journal of Royal Statistical Society, Vol. XLVIII, 1885,167-235, Lii, 241-305.
3. Lee, Everetts (1969). *A Theory of Migration,* in Robin Cohen (Ed.) Theories of Migration (the International Library of Studies on Migration) An Elgar Reference Collection, Cheltenham, U.K.
4. Lewis, A. W. (1954) *Economic Development with Unlimited Supplies of Labour,* in Agarwala, A.N. and S.P. Singh (1973) (Eds.) The Economics of Underdevelopment, Oxford University Press, New York.

5. Fie, John and Gustav Ranis (1961). *A Theory of Economic Development,* in M.L. Jhingan (2008) The Economics of Development and Planning, Vrinda Publications, Delhi.
6. Singh, M.(1995). *Uneven Development in Agriculture and Labour Migration,* Indian Institute of Advanced Studies, Shimla.
7. *Ibid.,* p. 30.
8. Estevez, Arianda (2012). *Human Rights, Migration and Social* Conflict *Towards a Decolonised Global Justice*, Palgrave Macmillan, New York.
9. Poros, Martisa, V. (2011). *Modern Migration, Gujurati Indian Network in New York and London*, Stanford University Press, Stanford, California.
10. *Ibid.,* p. 39.
11. Mahamood, R. A. (1992). *Impact of Labour Migration on Households-Bangladesh,* in Godfrey Gunatilleka (Ed) The Impact of Labour Migration on Houscholds: A Comparative Study in Seven Asian Countries, United Nations University Press, Tokyo.
12. Nair (1992). *Impact of Labour Migration on Households-India,* in Godfrey Gunatilleka (Ed) The Impact of Labour Migration on Households: A Comparative Study in Seven Asian Countries, United Nations University Press,Tokyo.
13. Sharma, R. N. P. and Singh, D. P. (1981). *Population of Ranchi (Bihar) on Move,* in R.B. Mandal (Ed) Frontiers in Migration Analysis, Concept Publishing Company, New Delhi.
14. Lam (2011). *Migration and Development,* in Lahiri et al, Migration, Health and Development, Palgrave Macmillan, New York.
15. Mukharjee and Phadke (2011). *Some Facets of Migration to Districts of Maharastra,* in Lahiri et al, Migration, Health and Development, Palgrave Macmillan, New York.
16. Mishra, S.K. (1991). *Factors and Process of Migration in Developing Economy: A Case Study of Madhya Pradesh*, in R.B. Mandal (Ed) Frontiers in Migration Analysis, Concept Publishing Company, New Delhi, p. 227.
17. Chattopadhyaya, Haraprasad (1987). *Internal Migration in India: A Case Study of Bengal,* K.P. Bagchi and Company, Calcutta, p. 541.
18. *Ibid.,* p. 198.
19. Chaudhury, Jayasri Ray (1993). *Migration and Remittances,* Sage Publications, New Delhi.
20. Singh, Sudama (2001). *Migration in the Third World,* Radha Publications, New Delhi.
21. Zachariah, K.C., E.T. Mathew and S. Irudya Rajan (2003). *Dynamics of Migration in Kerala,* Orient Longman, New Delhi.
22. Ghosh, Papiya (2007). *Partition and the South Asian Diaspora*, Routledge, New Delhi, pp. 11-12.

23. Barik, B.C. (1994). *Rural Migrants in Urban Setting,* Classical Publishing Company, New Delhi, p. 11-12.
24. Giege, Karsten (1999). *Pattern of Migration from Zhejiang to Germany,* in Frank N. Pieke and Hein Mahlee (Ed) Internal and International Migration, Chinese Perspectives, Curzon Press, Richmond, U.K.
25. Bookman, Milica, Z. (2002). *Ethnic Groups in Motion,* Frank Cass Publishers, London.
26. Espinosa, Kristin and Douglasa Massey (1977). *Undocumented Migration and the Quantity and Quality of Social Capital,* in Ludger Prices (Ed) Migration and Transnational Social Spaces, Ashgate, Sydney.
27. Samal, K.C. (2008). *Informal Sector Concept, Dynamics Linkages and Migration,* Concept Publishing Company, New Delhi, p. 141.
28. International organisation for Migration (2012) ILO, p. 115.
29. Connell, John, B. Dasgupta, L. Ray and M. Lipton (1976). *Migration From Rural Areas, the Evidence from Village Studies,* Oxford University Press, Delhi, p. 197.
30. Meslow, A. (1954). *Motivation and Personality,* NY: Harper, New York.
31. Deshingkar, P. and *et al.* (2004). The Evolving Pattern of Circular Migration in P. Deshingkar and J. Farrington (Ed) Circular Migration and Multi locational Livelihood strategies in Rural India, p. 139.
32. Shah, A (2009). *Brick Kiln Workers from Jharkhand, the Labour of Love,* in P. Deshingkar and J. Farrington (Ed) Circular Migration, Multi-locational Livelihood Strategies in Rural India, Oxford University Press, New York.
33. Pandey, A. K. (2013). *Changing Dynamics of Rural-Urban Male Migration and Economic Development in India After Economic Reform,* Man Development, March, p. 122. Vol. XXXV, No. 1.
34. Jayaraj, D.(2013). *Family Migration in India,* Economic and Political Weekly, Oct. 19, p. 122, Vol. XLVIII, No. 42.
35. Sainath, P (1996). *Everybody Loves a Good Draught,* Penguin, New Delhi, p. 71.
36. Malhotra, N. (2013) *Inter-State Migration in India. Nature Causes and Consequences.*
37. Behera, N.K. (2011). *Displacement, Resettlement and Rehabilitation,* Abhijeet Publications, Delhi.
38. Bhagat, R.M. (2011), Internal Migration in India: Are the Underclass more Mobile 7 in S.I. Rajan (Ed) Migration Identify and Conflict, India Migration Report, Routledge, ND, p. 22.
39. Todaro, M.P. (1976), *Internal Migration in Developing Countries: A Survey,* ILO, Geneva, p. 9.
40. Selier, Frits and P. Nientied (1986), *Towards Research on Circular Migration: Result of a Pilot Study in Karachi,* in Migration in Pakistan, (Ed) F. Selier and M. S. Karim.

41. Kasap, D. V. (1992), *Economics of Seasonal Migration,* Classical Publishing Company, New Delhi.
42. Reddy, D. N. (2007). *Rural Migrant Labour in Andhra Pradesh*, in K. Gopal Iyer(Ed) Distress Migrant Labour in India, Kanishka Publishers and Distributors, New Delhi.
43. Lesher, (2005). *The Millennium Development Goals and Migration IOM Migration Research Series,* International Organisation for Migration, Geneva, p. 9.
44. Chatterji, Joya (2010). *Migration Myths and the Mechanics of Assimilation: Two Community Histories from Bengal.* IUC for Humanities and Social Sciences, IIAS, Shimla, p. 141.
45. Deshingkar, P. and J. Farrington (2009). *A Framework for Understanding Circular Migration.* in P. Deshingkar and J. Farrington (Ed.) Circular Migration Multi-locational Livelihood Strategies in Rural India, Oxford University Press, New York.
46. Ram, Kewal (2007). *Inter-State Circular Migrant Labour in India*, in K. Gopal Iyer (Ed) Distress Migrant Labour in India, Kanishka Publishers and Distributors, New Delhi.
47. Sekhar, T.V. (1997). *Migration and Social Change,* Rawat Publications, Jaipur, p. 29.
48. Bellak, C., Leibrecht, M. and Libensteiner, M. (2014). *Short-term Labour Migration from the Republic of Armenia to Russian Federation.* The Journal of Development Studies, 2014, Vol. 5, No. 3, 349-367, p. 351.
49. Ray, A.K. (2011). *Distress Migration and 'Left Behind' Women,* Rawat Publications, Jaipur.
50. Jayaraj, D. (2013). *Family Migration in India* Economic and Political Weekly, Oct. 19, Vol. XLVIII, No. 42, p. 47.
51. *Ibid.,* p. 52.
52. UNICEF and UNESCO (2012). *Internal Migration in India Initiative National Workshop on Internal Migration and Human Development in India,* 6-7 Dec., 2011, Workshop Compendium Vol. 1 and Vol. 2, Workshop Papers, Social Inclusion of Internal Migrants in India, New Delhi, p. 344.
53. International Organisation for Migration (2012). *Migration, Development and Poverty Reduction in Asia,* Academic Foundation, New Delhi, pp. 122-113.
54. Ghosh, Ruma (2004). *Brick Kiln Workers: A Study of Migration, Labour Process and Employment,* V.V. Giri National Labour Institute, Noida.
55. Dharitri Odia Daily News Paper, 24th October 2013.
56. *Ibid.,* Odia Daily News Paper, 12th December 2013.
57. *Ibid.,* Odia Daily News Paper, 14th March 2014.
58. UNESCO and UNICEF (2012). *Internal Migration in India Initiative Workshop Compendium*, Vol. 2, UNESCO, New Delhi, p. 19.

59. Comelo, Anibel Ferus (2014). *Migration and Precariousness.* Economic and Political Weekly, Sept. 6, Vol. XLIX, No. 36, p. 43.
60. Dharitri, Odia Daily News Paper, 27th January, 2014.
61. Mishra, D. and R.S. Rao (1992). *Hunger in Kalahandi, Blinkered Understanding,* Economic and Political Weekly, June, 13-20, pp. 1245-46.
62. Rajan, S.I., V. Kora and R.Chyrmang (2011). *Politics of Conflict and Migration* in S.I. Rajan (Ed) Migration, Identity & Conflict, Routledge, New Delhi, p. 100.
63. Dharitri, Odia Daily News Paper, 27th March, 2014.
64. Naik, Kshtrabasi (2011). *Dadan* (in Odia), Nabneeta Publications, Bolangir.
65. Times of India, English Daily News Paper, 18th October 2013.
66. Garip, F. (2012). *Discovering Diverse Mechanism of Migration: the Mexico-US Stream 1970-2000,* Population and Development Review 38(3), 393-433 (Sept.)
67. Oberai, A.S. and H.K.M. Singh (1983) *Causes and Consequences of Internal Migration, A Study in the Indian Punjab,* Oxford University Press, Delhi.
68. Sjaastad, L.A, (2002). *The Costs and Returns of Human Migration,* in K.F. Zimmerman and T. Baner (Ed) the Economics of Migration (Vol. I) An Elgar Reference Collection, Cheltenham, U.K.
69. Patnaik, P. and C.P.C. Sekhar (2004). *A Perspective on Migration,* in K. Gopal Iyer (Ed) Distressed Migrant Labour in India Kanishka Publishers Distributors, New Delhi.
70. Deshingkar, P. *et al.,* (2004). *The Evolving Pattern of Circular Migration* in P. Deshingkar and J. Farrington (Ed.) Circular Migration and Multi-locational Livelihood Strategies in Rural India.
71. Sundari, S. (2007). *Migrant Women and Urban Labour Market,* Deep & Deep Publications Pvt. Ltd. New Delhi.
72. Tripathy, R. (2011). *Migration, Money, Music*, Economic and Political Weekly, November 12, Vol. XLVI, No. 46.
73. Oberai, A.S., Pradhan H. Prasad and M.G. Sardara (1989). *Determinants and Consequences of Internal Migration in India,* Oxford University Press, Delhi.
74. Parnwell, Mike (1993). *Population Movements and the Third World* Routledge, London, p. 145.
75. *Ibid.,* p. 145.

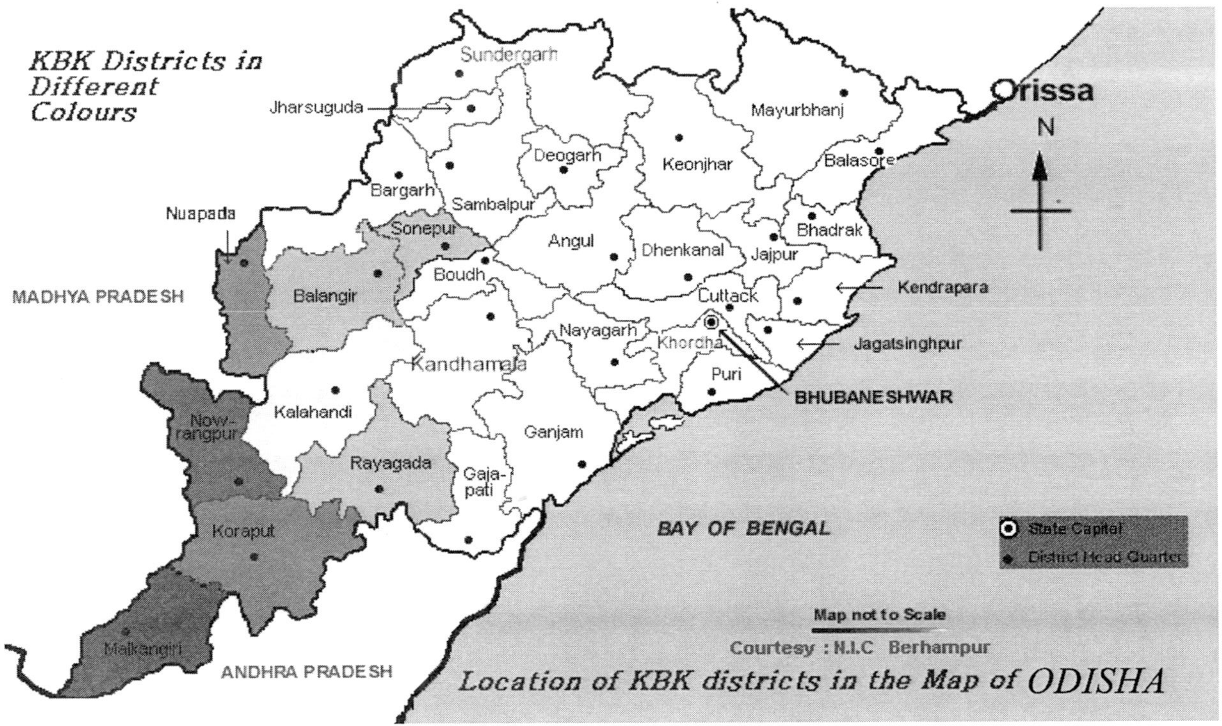

Location of KBK districts in the Map of ODISHA

Chapter - 3

Regional Profile and Field-work Area

3.1 Introduction

The study area of the present work on internal migration covers the KBK districts of south-west Odisha. The name of Odisha has been changed to Odisha in 2013. Some time these two terms are used interchangeably. It remains as one of the most backward states in India. The state per capita income of Rs 40,412 is far below the per capita net national average income of Rs 53,331 at current prices. The monthly per capita consumption expenditure (MPCE) of rural Odisha (Rs 905) was 70 per cent of the average MPCE of rural India (Rs 1287). The MPCE of urban Odisha (Rs 1,830) was 74 per cent of the average MPCE of urban India (Rs 2,477). The Raghu Rajan Committee put Odisha under least developed state in the country on the basis of composite development index (GoI, 2013).[1] The term KBK is an abbreviation of erstwhile undivided districts of Kalahandi, Bolangir and Koraput (KBK). KBK became a popular term during 1980s in the circle of economic and political discussion not only in Odisha but also in the national and international sphere. It came to the lime light not for its prosperity but for its hunger and poverty.

"Amlapali, Nuapada, (part of former Kalahandi district) nine years after Phanas Punji 'sold' her fourteen year old sister-in-law Banita to the nearly blind Bidya Podha for Rs 40 the lives of all the actors in the drama remain largely unchanged. Never mind that sparked of a furious national debate that made Kalahandi a by-product for poverty. Prime Minister Rajiv Gandhi's visit made no different (Mid 1985)...The cover stories on Phanas and Banita in 1985 emphasised the issue of the 'sale of a girl' that touched the nation's conscience and brought some relief to Kalahandi-never mind who cornered the benefits. Yet, the issue of the sale of a girl issue proved a double-edged sword.[2] Thus the picture of Kalahandi came to the lime light of national and international political and economic debate and discussion through the infamous incidence of child sell.

Bolangir, the neighbouring district of Kalahandi is known for its infamous starvation deaths and large scale inter-state migration. The starvation death of Jhintu Bariha, in Gudighat Village, of Khaprakhol block, occurred between September, 2009 and December, 2009, a tribal, created ripple in the politics of Odisha quite for some time, but the State denied any such case of death due to starvation. Whether it is sale of girl child or starvation death, the State administration, irrespective of political party in power never admits these infamous occurrences in these districts.

Phanas Punji got a house on January, 2015 after a long struggle. The Block Development Officer (BDO) of Khadial (Nuapada District) came to Amlapali, under Areda Panchayat and extended the assistance to Phanas Punji. Jagabandhu Punji the son of Phanas has been assured a loan of Rs 40-50 thousand for goat rearing. Her daughter-in-law has also been assured a class 4th job by the BDO. Even after thirty years of this tragic incident and for whom the special KBK scheme started is not cared properly. This tells about programme implementations of the State.[3]

The undivided Koraput district is a part of the tribal belt in Southern Odisha. The district is the homeland of primitive Tribal group like Bonda. The Bondas known among themselves as 'Remo' men are a small tribe of the type now often called Astro-Asiatic. Their country is the wild and mountainous region called Bonda Hills, north-west of the Machhkunda River. They are regarded as the most savage and primitive tribe of Odisha. Other tribes are Marias, Khonds, Bhumias, Paroja, Gonds, Didayis, Sauras, Jatapus, Holuvas, Pentias, Bhottadas and Bagatas live here in complete harmony with nature (Mahalik, 2014, 103). In spite of a number of large scale industries in this mineral and forest rich, erstwhile Koraput district is an underdeveloped and backward district of the state. For government employees this district is considered as a punishment district due to its underdevelopment, whether it is child selling, or starvation death or extreme backwardness. All these negativities were present in these three undivided districts of south-western Odisha. These three highland districts were clubbed together to launch a special development programme in the name of KBK plan and thereafter it is popularly known as KBK districts.

Till 1992, there were 13 districts in the State. Out of these old 13 undivided districts, four coastal districts, namely Cuttack, Puri, Balasore and Ganjam are considered developed districts. The highland districts of Sundargarh and Sambalpur are characterised as semi-developed districts. The other highland undivided districts, namely Kalahandi, Bolangir, Koraput and Phulbani are considered as chronically underdeveloped and backward districts of the State. During 1980-90 the picture of undivided KBK districts were widely discussed for their state of underdevelopment and poverty. These south-western districts are vulnerable to frequent draught and famine like situations which lead to large scale inter-district and inter-state migration of poor and landless people during the lean season of agricultural activities. This trend of distress seasonal/circular migration continues even after 30 years of such special development plan and many more new development programme for the KBK region. Following the reorganisation of districts in the State during 1992-93, now the KBK region consists of eight districts. Kalahandi was divided into Kalahandi and Nuapada, Bolangir into Bolangir and Subarnapur (Sonepur) and Koraput into Koraput, Rayagada, Nabarangapur, and Malkangiri.

3.2 Topography of KBK Region

The undivided 13 districts of Odisha (Orissa) are broadly divided into four geo-climatic regions. These are (i) The coastal plains of Cuttack, Puri, Balasore and Ganjam districts, (ii) The northern plateau, a part of Chhotanagpur Plateau covering three districts, namely Sundargarh, Keonjhar and Mayurbhanj, (iii) The Central Table land covers three undivided districts of Dhenkanal, Sambalpur and Bolangir and (iv) The South-Western Plateau, a part of Deccan plateau and Eastern Ghat mountain ranges cover rest three undivided districts namely Koraput, Kalahandi and Kandhamal. The undivided districts of Koraput, Kalahandi, Phulbani, Sundargarh, Keonjhar and Mayurbhanj are predominantly resided by the tribal population and are declared as scheduled districts and sub-divisions on the basis of

Table – 3.1: Administrative Division of Odisha

Northern Revenue Division, Sambalpur		*Central Revenue Division, Cuttack*		*Southern Revenue Division, Berhampur*	
Districts before 1992	*Present Districts*	*Districts before 1992*	*Present Districts*	*Districts before 1992*	*Present Districts*
1	**2**	**3**	**4**	**5**	**6**
1. Sambalpur	(i) Sambalpur (ii) Bargarh (iii) Jharsuguda (iv) Deogarh	1. Cuttack	(i) Cuttack (ii) Jagatsinghpur (iii) Kendrapada (iv) Jajpur	1. Ganjam	(i) Ganjam (ii) Gajapati
2. Bolangir	(i) Bolangir (ii) Subarnapur (Sonepur)	2. Puri	(i) Puri (ii) Khurda (iii) Nayagarh	2. Koraput	(i) Koraput (ii) Nabarangpur (iii) Rayagada (iv) Malkangiri
3. Sundargarh	(i) Sundargarh	3. Balasore	(i) Balasore (ii) Bhadrak	3. Kalahandi	(i) Kalahandi (ii) Nuapada
4. Dhenkanal	(i) Dhenkanal (ii) Angul	4. Mayurbhanj	(i) Mayurbhanj	4. Phulbani	(i) Phulbani (Kandhamal) (ii) Boudh
5. Keonjhar	(i) Keonjhar				

Table - 3.2: District-wise Percentage of Area to Total Area of the State

Sl. No.	*Name of the District*	*Percentage of area*	*Sl. No.*	*Name of the District*	*percentage of area*	*Sl. No.*	*Name of the District*	*percentage of area*
1.	Sambalpur	4.25	11.	Cuttack	2.53	21.	Ganjam	5.27
2.	Bargarh	3.75	12.	Jagatsinghpur	1.07	22.	Gajapati	2.78
3.	Jharsuguda	1.36	13.	Kendrapara	1.7	23.	Koraput	5.66
4.	Deogarh	1.89	14.	Jajpur	1.86	24.	Nabarangapur	3.4
5.	Bolangir	4.22	15.	Puri	2.23	25.	Rayagada	4.54
6.	Subarnapur	1.15	16.	Khurda	1.81	26.	Malkangiri	3.72
7.	Sundargarh	6.24	17.	Nayagarh	2.5	27.	Kalahandi	5.09
8.	Dhenkanal	2.86	18.	Balasore	2.44	28.	Nuapada	2.47
9.	Angul	4.09	19.	Bhadrak	1.16	29.	Kandhamal	5.15
10	Keonjhar	5.33	20.	Mayurbhanj	6.69	30	Boudh	1.99

Source: Statistical Abstract, 2012.

Table - 3.3: Sub-Division, Tahasil, Blocks, Tribal-Sub-Plan Blocks, Gram Panchayat and Villages in KBK Districts

Sl. No.	*District*	*Nos. of Sub. Division*	*Tahasil*	*Block*	*Tribal Sub Plan Blocks*	*Gram Panchayat*	*Villages*
1	**2**	**3**	**4**	**5**	**6**	**7**	**8**
1.	Kalahandi	2	13	13	2	273	2116
2.	Nuapada	1	5	5	—	108	656
3.	Bolangir	3	11	14	—	285	2468
4.	Sonepur	2	6	6	—	96	856
5.	Koraput	2	14	14	14	226	1941
6.	Nabarangapur	1	10	10	10	169	868
7.	Rayagada	2	4	11	11	171	2667
8.	Malkangiri	1	7	7	7	108	995
	Total	**14**	**70**	**80**	**44**	**1436**	**12,567**

Source: Statistical Abstract, 2012 p. 30.

Table - 3.4: KBK Districts, Location, Area and Population to State Area and Population

Sl. No.	*Name of the District*	*Location*	*Total area in Sq. Km.*	*Per cent of Area to State total Area*	*Per cent area cover under forest*	*Total Popu-lation*	*Per cent to State Popu-lation*	*Total ST Population*	*Per cent of ST Popu-lation*	*Total SC Popu-lation*	*Per cent of SC Population*
1	2	3	4	5	6	7	8	9	10	11	12
1.	Kalahandi	82°31'- 83°47' E 19°8' -20°25' N	7920	5.09	29.93	1576869	3.76	449456	28.5	286580	18.2
2.	Nuapada	82°20'- 82°53' E 20°0' - 21°5' N	3852	2.47	31.91	610382	1.45	206327	33.8	82159	13.5
3.	Bolangir	82°41'- 83°42' E 20°9' - 21°5' N	6575	4.22	14.25	1648997	3.93	347164	21.1	294777	17.9
4.	Sonepur	84°16'- 85°23' E 20°31' - 21°41'N	2337	1.5	13.86	610183	1.45	57192	9.4	156219	25.6
5.	Koraput	82°5'- 83°13' E 18°13' - 19°10'N	8807	5.66	19.23	1379647	3.29	697583	50.6	196540	14.2
6.	Nabarang-apur	81°52'- 82°53' E 19°9' - 20°5'N	5291	3.4	21.58	1220946	2.91	681173	55.8	177384	14.5
7.	Rayagada	82°54'- 84°2' E 19°0' - 19°58'N	7073	4.54	44.05	967911	2.31	541905	56.0	13954	14.4
8.	Malkangiri	81°22'- 82°25' E 17°40' - 18°43'N	5791	3.72	37.75	613192	1.46	354614	57.8	138295	22.6
	KBK		47646	30.6		8628127	20.56	3335414	33.12	1471468	17.9
	Odisha	**81°24'- 87°29' E 17°48' - 22°94'N**	**155707**		**31.41**	**41974218**		**9590756**	**22.8**	**7188463**	**17.1**

Source: Statistical Abstract of Odisha, 2012 and District Statistical Hand Books of Kalahandi, Nuapada, Bolangir, Sonepur,Koraput, Nabarangapur, Rayagada and Malkangiri, 2009. *N.B. Location of these districts is in between East Longitude and North Latitude.*

density of tribal population. From geographical point of view the KBK region is not a perfect homogenous area. But broadly these districts are highland districts having more or less a similarity in linguistic and cultural expressions.

3.3 Administrative Setup of KBK Districts

These 13 undivided districts were divided in 30 districts during 1992-93. The formation of new districts was made more on political consideration and less on economic justification. Even after formation of new districts, the jurisdictions of Revenue Division Commissions remain the same. The newly formed districts such as Koraput, Rayagada, Nabarangpur, Malkangiri, Kalahandi and Nuapada continued to remain in the Southern Division with its head quarters at Berhampur and Bolangir and Subarnapur (Sonepur) remain in the Northern Division with its headquarters at Sambalpur.

The State of Odisha has total area of 1,55,707 Sq. Km. out of this the KBK districts covers 30.66 per cent or nearly one-third of state's geographical area. The percentage of geographical area of each district is presented in Table 3.2.

The eight districts of KBK region comprises 14 sub-divisions, 70 Tahasils, 80 Community Development Blocks, 44 Tribal Sub-Plan Blocks, (TSPB) 1,436 Gram Panchayats and 12,567 villages. In view of significant tribal population in undivided Koraput district all 42 blocks are covered under the special plan of TSP. The other two blocks under TSP are from Kalahandi district. The entire area of Koraput, Malkangiri, Nabarangapur, Rayagada and two blocks of Kalahandi, namely Thuamul Rampur and Lanjigad are under Scheduled areas in Odisha. Under the scheme about 44.70 per cent of Odisha has been notified as scheduled areas. More than 50 per cent of KBK comes under this scheduled area. There are twenty-one Integrated Tribal Development Agencies (ITDAs) in the state to implement various tribal welfare programmes in TSP areas.[4]

3.4 Location and a Glance on Demography of KBK Districts

The longitudinal and latitudinal location of KBK districts along with a few characteristics of demography are presented below. Data have been presented in tabular form to provide a bird's view on certain points of the demography.

The Table 3.4 shows the location of KBK region in terms of Longitude and Latitude of the eight districts. Out of 155707 Sq. Kms. state area, taking together all the eight districts of KBK region represents 30.6 per cent of the state area and with a population of 86,28,127 which accounts for 20.56 per cent of state population. In the demographic features one of the significant things noticed in the KBK districts is that these districts are inhabited by a high percentage of Schedule Tribe (ST) population. The ST population in undivided Koraput district is more than 50 per cent of the district of population. It is lowest in case of Sonepur district with 9.4 per cent only. The other districts also show ST population more than the state average of 22.5 per cent. The SC population is highest in Sonepur district with 25.6 per cent, followed by Malkangiri with 22.6 per cent where-as in the districts of Koraput, Nabarangapur, and Rayagada the SC population is roughly 14.5 per cent. In case of Kalahandi SC population is 18.2 per cent, Nuapada 13.5 and Bolangir 17.9 per cent. On an average, the SC population represents the state average of 17.1 per cent. The table shows that the KBK districts are inhabited by larger percentage of ST (33.12 per cent) and SC (17.9 per cent) population than the average state figures. This implies that a greater percentage of population of these districts is from the lower strata of the societal hierarchy.

Table – 3.5: Percentage of Rural-Urban Population and Population Density in KBK Districts, Census, 2011

Sl. No.	*Name of the District*	*Per cent of Rural Population*	*Per cent of Urban Population*	*Population Density*
1.	Kalahandi	92.26	7.74	199
2.	Nuapada	94.42	5.58	157
3.	Bolangir	88.03	11.97	251
4.	Sonepur	91.82	8.18	279
5.	Koraput	83.61	16.39	156
6.	Nabarangapur	92.82	7.18	230
7.	Rayagada	84.82	15.18	136
8.	Malkangiri	91.92	8.08	106
	Odisha	83.3	16.69	269

Source: Statistical Abstract of Odisha, 2012, p. 43.

Table 3.5 shows the percentage of rural and urban population of the KBK districts. These districts represent 83.61 to 94.5 per cent rural population which is significantly higher than state average of 83.3 per cent rural population. On the other hand, the urban population in all the KBK districts is less than state average of 16.69 per cent. Among all the KBK districts, Koraput represents highest urban population of 16.39 per cent and Nuapada represents the lowest of only 5.58 per cent of urban population. The population density of KBK districts ranges from the lowest of 106 persons in Malkangiri to a highest of 279 persons in Sonepur district. The state average is 269 persons per square km. On the whole, the KBK districts are sparsely populated in comparison the coastal plain districts of the state.

Table 3.6 represents thc work participation rate in the KBK districts. All the districts of KBK region show a higher percentage of work participation in case rural and urban population in comparison to the State average of 43.2 and 34.8 per cent respectively. So also the total work participation of KBK districts is higher than State average of 41.8 per cent. The average percentage of rural and urban male work force of KBK districts is more or less same with State average of 56.5 and 54.1 percentages in rural and urban areas respectively. But one important aspect of this data is that the female work participation in all the KBK districts is significantly higher than State average of 29.7 and 14.1 per cent for rural and urban areas respectively. The female work participation in rural area is as high as 47.3 per cent in Malkangiri district and lowest of 32.9 per cent in Bolangir district. In case of urban female work participation also, Malkangiri has the highest of 20.7 per cent and lowest of 13.6 per cent in case of Bolangir district. Thus, the KBK region represents a high percentage of work participation rate in rural and urban areas and male as well as female workers in comparison to the state work participation rate.

Table 3.7 shows the literacy rate in rural and urban areas of KBK districts. Except Sonepur, rest seven districts of KBK region have less than State literacy rate among male and female in rural and urban areas as well in 2011census. The gaps in literacy rate are higher in all the KBK districts which range from 20.4 to 25.5 in comparison to the literacy gap of 17.6 of state average. This indicates a lower rate of literacy prevailing in the KBK region in comparison to the state average.

Table – 3.6: KBK Districts Work Participation Rate, 2011

Sl. No.	*Name of the districts*	*Person*			*Male*			*Female*		
		Total	***Rural***	***Urban***	***Total***	***Rural***	***Urban***	***Total***	***Rural***	***Urban***
1.	Kalahandi	47.7	48.8	35.0	56.8	57.1	53.5	38.6	40.5	15.5
2.	Nuapada	50.0	50.8	36.9	55.7	55.7	55.2	44.5	46.0	18.2
3.	Bolangir	43.7	45.0	34.1	56.6	57.0	53.6	30.6	32.9	13.6
4.	Sonepur	47.0	47.9	36.9	58.3	58.6	54.9	35.2	36.7	17.9
5.	Koraput	50.3	52.9	36.6	56.6	57.0	54.5	44.1	49.0	18.1
6.	Nabarangapur	50.0	50.9	38.5	56.7	56.8	55.0	43.5	45.2	21.9
7.	Rayagada	48.3	50.4	36.4	54.7	54.8	54.2	42.2	46.3	18.1
8.	Malkangiri	50.7	51.7	38.8	56.2	56.2	55.5	45.3	47.3	20.7
	Odisha	**41.8**	**43.2**	**34.8**	**56.1**	**56.5**	**54.1**	**27.2**	**29.7**	**14.1**

Source: Statistical Abstract of Odisha, 2011, p. 92.

Table – 3.7: Literacy Rate (per cent) in Rural and Urban Areas of KBK Districts, 2011

Sl. No.	*Name of the Districts*	*Rural*			*Urban*			*All Class*			*Gap in Literates Rate*
		Person	*Male*	*Female*	*Person*	*Male*	*Female*	*Person*	*Male*	*Female*	
1	*2*	*3*	*4*	*5*	*6*	*7*	*8*	*9*	*10*	*11*	*12*
1.	Koraput	42.4	54.1	31.3	81.8	88.5	74.9	49.2	60.3	38.6	21.7
2.	Malkangiri	46.1	56.7	36.0	74.5	83.4	64.9	48.5	59.1	38.3	20.8
3.	Rayagada	44.4	56.2	33.5	78.0	85.6	70.4	49.8	61.0	39.2	21.8
4.	Nabarangapur	43.9	55.0	33.0	77.9	84.9	70.7	46.4	57.3	35.8	21.5
5.	Kalahandi	57.3	70.4	44.3	81.6	88.4	74.5	59.2	71.9	46.7	25.2
6.	Nuapada	56.0	69.3	43.2	79.0	86.6	71.3	57.3	70.3	44.8	25.5
7.	Bolangir	62.1	73.8	50.3	83.4	89.8	76.7	64.7	75.8	53.5	22.3
8.	Subarnapur	73.6	83.8	63.1	83.0	90.7	74.9	74.4	84.4	64.0	20.4
	Odisha	70.2	79.6	60.7	85.7	90.7	80.4	72.9	81.6	64.0	17.6

Source: Statistical Abstract of Odisha, 2012, p. 416.

Table 3.8: Families Below Poverty Line (BPL) in KBK Districts

No. Sl.	*Name of the District*	*1997 Census*		*Per cent*
		Total families in Lakh	*BPL families in Lakh*	
1.	Kalahandi	3.08	1.93	62.71
2.	Nuapada	1.27	1.09	85.70
3.	Bolangir	3.30	2.01	61.06
4.	Sonepur	1.10	0.80	73.02
5.	Koraput	2.65	2.22	83.81
6.	Malkangiri	1.09	0.89	81.88
7.	Nabarangapur	2.15	1.59	73.66
8.	Rayagada	1.88	1.36	72.03
	Total in KBK	**16.52**	**11.89**	**71.97**

As per the last poverty estimates provided by the Planning Commission (based on the Tendulkar Committee methodology), Odisha ranked sixth among all Indian states in terms of the percentage of people living below the poverty line-32.59 per cent-in 2011-12. The national average was 21.92 per cent (Bal *et al.,* p 69). The last survey on poverty in the state was conducted in 1997 and the 2012 survey final figure is yet to come up. Table 3.8 reflects the level of people Below Poverty Line (BPL) in the KBK districts of the state during 1997 census. The last BPL survey of 2012 is yet to be finalised by the state. In these eight districts out of a total 16.52 lakhs of families 11.89 families i.e. 71.97 per cent are under BPL category. It is the highest in Nuapada district (85.70 per cent) where the incidence of girl child selling took place in the eighties. It is followed by Koraput with 83.81 per cent and Malkangiri with 81.88 per cent and on an average 72 per cent of people in the KBK districts are BPL category. Although Bolangir represents lowest BPL percentage of 61.06 per cent among the KBK districts, but it is one of the major sources of internal (inter-state) migration. The Kantabanji town of Bolangir is known as migrant 'Dadan' corridor. Kantabanji is well linked with rail network; connecting all major cities of south India, for which it has become easier on the part of the agents to dispatch batches of migrant labour to the neighbouring southern states. Further the Dadan Sardar or labour agents are more active in this district in comparison to other districts of the KBK region.

Mehta and Shah (2003) reported that KBK region of Odisha is one of the poorest regions (including 10 other regions) in India where the poverty incidence is very severe and 34.08 per cent people of rural areas of this region were very poor, 69.02 per cent were poor and the square poverty gap was 6.83 in 1993-94, furthermore, severity of poverty can be expressed in term of hunger and lack of availability of two full meals a day. Hunger is especially severe in rural Orissa, where more than 15 per cent people are unable to access two full meals a day. This is more severe in the southern part of Orissa. Severe poverty and starvation deaths are common in KBK regions.[5]

Haan and Dubey (2005) reported that the trend of poverty reduction in Odisha and KBK region is different from other regions in India. The STs of Odisha experienced the least poverty reduction for the period from 1983-1999 (only 14 per cent) as compared to 23 per cent among other groups and 20 per cent among SC since the STs account for 38 per cent of the total population in KBK region, the poverty reduction trend for KBK was like Orissa.[6]

Table – 3.9: HDI Value and HDI Rank of KBK Districts

Sl. No.	*Name of the District*	*HDI Value*	*HDI Rank*
1.	Kalahandi	0.606	11
2.	Nuapada	0.581	14
3.	Bolangir	0.546	21
4.	Sonepur	0.566	16
5.	Koraput	0.431	27
6.	Nabarangapur	0.436	26
7.	Rayagada	0.443	25
8.	Malkangiri	0.370	30
	Odisha (All India)	**0.579**	**11**

Source: Odisha Human Development Report (2004), pp. 49-50.

Table 3.9 shows the Human Development Index (HDI) of 2004. Among the major states of India, Odisha ranks 11 in term of HDI. The HDI values for the KBK districts are lower than state HDI value. Four districts, namely Koraput, Nabarangapur, Rayagada and Malkangiri represent less than the State HDI value of 0.579. The HDI value of Malkangiri (0.370) represents the lowest in the State as well as among the KBK districts. But strangely the HDI values of Kalahandi and Nuapada districts are higher than the state value. The HDI ranks of all the KBK districts are below the developed districts of the state, which shows the presence of underdevelopment and regional disparities within the state.

A report of the Centre for Rural Development, Bhubaneshwar shows that the extent of migration in five sample blocks, namely Patnagarh and Khaprakhol of Bolangir district, Boden and Komna of Nuapada district and Narla of Kalahandi district is phenomenally high with little difference in pattern between the villages within and outside the watersheds. fifteen per cent of the sample households in the project villages report migration compared to 18 per cent during the year of Western Odisha Rural Live Livelihood Project WORLP base line study. The degree of distress migration is on the decline obviously due to watershed development and other social security measures. Migration is high among the SC and ST groups who are both socially backward and economically disadvantaged.[7]

3.5 Kalahandi

The 1980s have brought Kalahandi into national mainstream. The recurring drought, the starvation deaths, the selling of human beings and the distress migration drew the country's attention.[8] The former undivided Kalahandi is a combine region of plain and hill tracks. A large track of plain area is seen in the area of Bhawanipatna, Nuapada, Junagarh and Dharmagarh whereas hilly area is present in south-western area of Bhawanipatna, Lanjigarh and Nuapada region. There is constant depletion of forest in Kalahandi region due to growing population and urbanisation. The forest of Kalahandi is rich with saal, kendu and teak trees which provide different types of minor forest products as the source of livelihood for the local tribal and common people. The hilly tracts contain huge deposits of minerals of different kinds. The Niyamgiri hill has huge deposit of bauxites. In view of this deposit the Vedanta Sterlite group has established an alumina refinery plant of six million ton capacity at Lanjigarh. The local forest dwellers like Dongaria Kondh of Niyamgiri have protested against the mining at Niyamgiri. Amid protest and objection from different communities, NGOs, and the Supreme Court of India, the company has not yet succeeded to mine the Niyamgiri. Following the direction of the Supreme Court of India, Gram Sabhas were conducted over the issue of bauxite mining in Niyamgiri. And the Gram Sabhas did not allow mining in Niyamgiri. This has hampered the working of the plant.

Drought is always associated with Kalahandi but not uncommon with other district of KBK region. The principal rivers of Kalahandi are Indrabati, Tel and Jonk. These rivers form the major tributaries to the Mahanadi and the Godavari. A major dam across Indrabati at Mukhiguda is the main source of hydropower for the state. The project provides irrigation and has been able to change the agricultural scenario of Kalahandi district.

In the study on the draught situation of Kalahandi (Pradhan, 1993) recognises depletion of cottage industries, like weaving, paddy dehusking, oil extraction etc. depletion of forest, decline in off farm employment and increasing migration. These problems are not unique. Many other parts of the state and neighbouring states have more or less the same type of problems. The good thing that has developed in Kalahandi is that there has been growing consciousness among the common people through different formal and informal organisations in the recent time. The administration has shown willingness to delve in the issues of Kalahandi.[9]

3.6 Bolangir

Bolangir is situated in the western region of Odisha. The north-western part of the district is bounded by Gandhamardan range of hills and forms the boundary for the district. This hill range has two famous pilgrimages one at Harishankar in Bolangir district and the other at Nrusinghanath on the side of Bargarh district. This hill tract has huge deposit of bauxite. The successful protest movement launched by the environmentalists during 1980s could prevent the public sector company, Bharat Aluminium Company to mine in the Gandhamardan. The other minerals such as graphite, manganese and gemstone are also found in the undivided district of Bolangir. The main forest coverage of the district is bordering Nuapada region of undivided Kalahandi district. The district has 21.98 per cent of forest coverage. Poorly distributed rainfall, geological formation resistant to weathering, shallow, sandy and dry nature of land and intensive shifting cultivation are the major factors, which have been responsible for the depletion of forests in the region.[10]

The Indian Ordnance Factory at Saintala is the only large scale industry in the undivided Bolangir district. The canal system from Hirakud dam across the Mahanadi provides irrigation to Binka and

Dungripali blocks of present Sonepur district. These two blocks are economically better up than other blocks. The Hariharjor medium irrigation project provides irrigation facility to Ulunda and Biramaharajpur blocks of Sonepur district. The river Mahanadi flows through central part present Sonepur district. The other major tributaries such as Ong, Jeera, Suktel, Tel etc. joins the Mahanadi. This district is prone to high rate of internal/ seasonal migration for the last three-four decades.

3.7 A Tale on Migration

The report of Vasunddhara (2005) a NGO on the study of a village Jambahal shows that the phenomenon of inter-state migration has been occurring for over 20 years, year after year. The villagers migrate and work hard to develop Hyderabad and not their village or their lands. If agriculture had developed, it would have provided enough employment in the village itself. In that case the villagers would not have been forced into migration. Thus, it is a case of total negligence of agriculture in such villages/districts. Agriculture is dying, and people are migrating. As a result farmers are unable to take care of their lands, which further results in deterioration of agriculture. This is a vicious cycle, which should be broken as soon as possible, or else in another five years time the entire village may be abandoned.[11]

3.8 Koraput

The undivided Koraput was one of the largest districts in India, which is a homeland to many primitive tribes such as Bondas, Kayas, Saoras, Gadabas, Paroja, Roans, Pongania Kondh and Kutia Kondh. The large hilly tract and high plateau ranging from 2000 feet to 3000 feet in the areas of Rayagada, Gunupur, Nabarangapur, Malkangiri and Koraput forms natural barriers as a result the entire undivided Koraput districts remain near isolated from rest of the state for long time. Due to this it has still preserved many of its varied and rich flora and fauna unlike other districts of the state. This is a land of geographical diversities with rich forest and mineral resources. The important minerals such as bauxite, manganese, limestone, china clay, mica etc are found in huge quantity. The Panchmali hill and Niyamgiri hills are famous for huge bauxite deposit. The district is thinly populated and it is estimated that during 1960 around 70 per cent of the area was covered with forest, now it has come down to 35 per cent of the total geographical area. The major rivers are Vansadhara and the Nagavali in the present Rayagada district and the Indrabati, the Kolab and the Machakund are flowing in the present Nabarangapur, Koraput and Malkangiri districts respectively. In view of good climatic condition, in 1870 Britishers had chosen the present Koraput town for better health prospects.

The modern cultural heritage of undivided Koraput district is on the threshold of industrial revolution. Hindustan Aeronautics Ltd., MIG Engine Factory at Sunabeda, Alumina Refinery Complex at Damanjodi, Bellarpur Paper Industries of Jeypore, J.K. Paper Mills at Singpur, Rayagada, Tosali Cement Factory at Ampavalli, Ply Wood Factory at Nabarangapur, Jeypore Sugar Factory, Rare Earth Ltd at Thiruvalli, Ferro Manganese Plant at Damanjodi are some of major large scale industries in the district(s). The majestic water fall Daduma (Machhkund) also known as Matsya Tirtha, comes cascading from a height of 157 meter. A hydro-electric project with its winch developed amidst deep greenery. The other hydro-electric projects is Balimela, where as mentioned in the epic Sri Rama assailed Bali, the hero of monkey across the river Sileru at Chitrokonda. Kolab dam, Indrabati dam and Telingiri dam are the other major projects in the district. The broad panorama of enchanting hills, the rippling streams, spectacular waterfalls, the wonderful caves and traditional hospitality of the tribes, their colourful neckless, head dresses and gesture make the cultural heritage of Koraput wonderful.[12] Koraput is also famous for its coffee plantation. Malkangiri district forms a part of Dandakaranya physiographic region of east-central India. The Dandakaranya includes parts of Chhattisgarh, Odisha and Andhra Pradesh.

'The development of Dandakaranya was undertaken to solve an almost intractable human problem- the rehabilitation of a large number of refugees who were uprooted from their homeland in East Pakistan, victims of a political decision to divide the country in which they were not consulted. ———— By the end of agricultural season 1963-64 about 6286 families had been allotted agricultural land at the rate of 6.5 acre per family and half an acre for home stead and kitchen garden in four widely separated zones of Odisha and Madhya Pradesh (present Chhattisgarh) viz. Pharasgaon, Umerkot, Parlakot and Malkangiri.[13]

'All these development projects have become the principal source of displacement of tribal people in the districts. Inadequate resettlement and rehabilitation of tribal displaced people have forced them to adopt migration as the only means for their livelihood. The Scheduled Tribes constitute about 8.1 per cent of the total population of the country according to 2001 census but they constituted 55.16 per cent of total displaced people which indicates victimisation of the tribes.[14]

Weak agro-climatic conditions, poor connectivity and infrastructure, physical isolation and low social capabilities among the adivasi or tribal characterise this region into a region of tribal backwardness, hill area backwardness and natural calamities prone to backwardness. During last one decade most of the KBK districts have faced the Naxalite-Maoist movement leading to killing of number of people and the counter-insurgent movements lead by CRPF and BSF have also killed number of cadres. In 2012, the Malkangiri District Collector, Mr Vinil Krishnna was abducted by the Maoist and was released after a talk by the state government with the Maoists through three interlocutors. The Maoists have damaged number of government institutions and installations and thus obstructed the development process. Another significant agitation of farmers and labourers under the banner of 'Chasi Mulia Sangha' took place against the large scale land transfer from the hands of tribal to non-tribal and large farmers. The movement was spear headed by a tribal leader named Nachika Linga. This movement was crushed by the state government and Nachika Linga was forced to surrender before the police. The presence of Maoists or Naxalites is also seen in other area of KBK districts. The Khaprakhol block of Bolangir district and the Sunabeda wildlife sanctuary area of Nuapada district witness frequent activities of this extremist group. The naxal groups predominately operate in the tribal areas of KBK districts. It helps them to get easy access to Andhra Pradesh. They are fighting mainly for three causes (i) Restoring land right of the tribal and thereby oppose entry of companies to the mineral rich tribal land, (ii) Protecting people against police atrocities and (iii) Providing food to the draught hit people. They have also the intention to control administration through arm revolution. Thus, we see a troubled hit under developed KBK region with large scale internal migration. It has questioned the implementation of development programmes in the region. However, the state government with the special central assistance launched several welfare measures to calm the movements in the region. A few selected such programmes are focused below in a brief manner only to project an idea about such plans.

3.9 Migration in Odisha and KBK Region

Although migration of people from under developed areas to developed areas is associated with push and pull factors and is common in a developing country like India, but the KBK districts do face the problem in a larger scale. The official migration data on number of labour contractor and migrant labour for 2009-14 of different districts in the state is presented in Table 3.10. In 2014, Bolangir district top the migrant list and is followed by Khurdha. The Deogarh district exceptionally shows no migration. The migrants from Khurda, Ganjam, Chhatrapur usually move to Surat in Gujarat to work in the different industrial establishments like textiles, gems, ceramic, etc.

The data further reveals that the industrially developed districts like Jharsaguda, Sundargarh, and Sambalpur also have the presence of internal migration. The agriculturally developed district, Bargarh also witness migration in under developed region of Padampur sub-division. The costal districts of Odisha such as Puri, Baleswar, Kendrapada etc also experience the situation of migration but of different nature from KBK region. Thus, migration is present more or less in most the districts of the state. But the migration in the KBK region is distress induced seasonal in character, which needs special attention of the policy-makers. The migration data derived from state figure is presented in Table 3.11.

Table 3.11 shows the official data relating to the number of licensed labour contractors and migrant labour of different districts in the KBK districts for the period from 2009-14. It is revealed from the data that Bolangir district has the largest number of labour contractors and migrant labour followed by Nuapada district during the last six years. Whereas it is least in case of Sonepur, and is followed by Rayagada district. The number of migrant labour in the region is rising constantly from 41,871 in 2009 to 61,632 in 2014 although there was a decline in 2012 and 2013. This is the figure of migrants under licensed contractors but in practice a significantly large number of migrants' labour move

Table 3.10: Odisha Migration Data

Sl. No.	*Name of the District*	*2009 Cont./Lab.*	*2010 Cont./Lab.*	*2011 Cont./Lab.*	*2012 Cont./Lab.*	*2013 Cont./Lab.*	*2014 Cont./Lab.*
1.	Angul	18/704	18/704	28/1,415	34/3,070	35/3,120	36/3,170
2.	Balasore	—	—	01/50	01/50	04/50	04/50
3.	Bargarh	35/520	36/635	36/530	39/850	39/850	43/1,190
4.	Bhadrak	17/402	19/502	09/361	11/401	13/401	13/441
5.	Bolangir	694/32,935	698/33,035	240/25,334	292/28,748	400/39,863	490/44,075
6.	Boudh	01/20	01/20	01/20	01/20	02/20	02/40
7.	Cuttack	31/1,099	38/1,239	44/1,379	47/1,469	46/1,469	62/2,309
8.	Chhatrapur	321/8,582	360/10,542	168/4,651	296/7,190	456/10,635	472/16,002
9.	Deogarh	—	—	—	—	—	NA
10.	Dhenkanal	20/694	45/1,657	46/1,606	51/1,885	57/2,157	68/2,542
11.	Gajapati	09/246	10/266	02/40	02/40	02/40	02/40
12.	Ganjam	152/4,382	158/4,442	164/4,636	169/4,161	175/4,926	176/4,941
13.	Jagatsinghpur	03/150	04/170	03/50	05/93	05/93	05/93
14.	Jajpur	30/906	34/1,091	33/1,421	60/2,583	60/2,866	78/3,477
15.	Jharsuguda	49/3,549	56/3,904	90/6,969	150/8,752	180/10,227	199/11,022
16.	Kalahandi	32/1,805	49/4,074	55/3,346	56/3,466	60/3,636	66/3,809
17.	Kendrapara	14/285	17/335	20/384	21/403	22/403	22/413
18.	Keonjhar	23/285	29/1,217	40/1,267	40/1,267	40/1,267	40/1,267
19.	Khurda	755/18,988	790/19,598	823/20,233	823/20,233	827/20,233	833/20,408
20.	Koraput	25/665	26/680	09/215	11/255	13/295	12/285
21.	Malkangiri	14/445	19/565	23/665	28/765	32/905	33/925

(Cond...)

22.	Mayurbhanj	34/860	35/960	35/960	35/960	35/960	35/960
23.	Nayagarh	40/707	44/827	48/943	58/1,153	58/1,153	58/1,153
24.	Nabarangapur	37/795	41/875	24/588	29/758	35/758	35/888
25.	Nuapada	97/4746	98/4,786	106/5,796	180/5,306	123/5,306	186/10,905
26.	Kandhamal	18/480	18/480	19/510	23/590	25/590	27/670
27.	Puri	94/2335	102/2,472	180/2,647	118/2,864	123/2,964	125/3,057
28.	Rayagada	08/240	09/260	06/149	15/559	19/770	20/745
29.	Sambalpur	48/186	86/3,450	92/3,388	105/5,013	110/5,447	115/6,527
30.	Subarnapur	03/186	03/186	—	—	—	—
31.	Sundargarh	18/750	25/2,705	30/1,279	32/1,313	36/1,489	39/1,549
32.	Talcher	17/450	18/450	30/1,080	34/1,211	50/2,009	58/2,899
	Total	**2,657/88,397**	**2,886/1,06,437**	**2,333/91,205**	**2,772/10,5428**	**3,082/1,24,902**	**3,354/1,45,852**

N.B. Chhatrapur and Talcher is not district but the presence of Labour office in these areas provides data. Figures in bold letters indicate no. of labour contractors and figures in normal letters indicate no. of inter-state migrant labour relating to the corresponding year.

Source: State Labour Commission, Bhubaneshwar.

Table 3.11: Migration in KBK Districts

Sl. No.	*District*	*2009*	*2010*	*2011*	*2012*	*2013*	*2014*
1.	Kalahandi	32/1,805	49/4,074	55/3,346	56/3,466	60/3,636	66/3,809
2.	Nuapada	97/4,746	99/4,786	106/5,796	108/5,306	123/6,345	186/10,905
3.	Bolangir	694/32,935	698/33,035	240/25,334	292/28,748	400/39,863	490/44,075
4.	Sonepur	03/186	03/186	NA	NA	NA	NA
5.	Koraput	25/665	26/680	09/215	11/255	13/295	12/285
6.	Nabarangapur	37/795	41/875	24/588	29/758	35/888	35/888
7.	Rayagada	08/240	09/260	06/149	15/559	19/770	20/745
8.	Malkangiri	14/445	19/565	23/665	28/765	32/905	33/925
	Total	**910/41,871**	**944/44,461**	**463/36,093**	**539/39,857**	**682/52702**	**842/61,632**

N.B. Figures in bold letters indicate no. of labour contractors and figures in normal letters indicate no. of inter-state migrant labour relating to the corresponding year.

Source: Records of State Labour Commission, Bhubaneshwar.

through unlicensed contractors. The entire undivided Koraput district is under TSP area shows a less degree of migration than the other KBK district. A study on the tribal of KBK by Sinha and Behera (2009) shows that the tribal do not consider wage earning as respectable job and labour is done on exchange basis. There is no employer and employee in their community. Seasonal migration is low. It is 8.68 per cent in case of Dongaria Kondha. This exposes that the tribal are less mobile than the non-tribal people of the KBK region.

3.10 State Policy in KBK Region for Reduction of Poverty and Regional Disparity

To overcome regional disparities, number of development strategies has been adopted by Government of India as well as the state government during successive plan periods. In spite of huge flow of fund under different special development programmes, this region (KBK) of Odisha has not yet shared the gains of development in an equitable manner and continues to languish in underdevelopment.

Due to several economic, social, institutional and political obstacles all regions in Odisha have not shared the gains of economic development in an equitable manner. The undivided districts of KBK form one such region where the incidence of poverty is very high. Several other pockets of southern and western Odisha are also socially and economically depressed (Odisha Economic Survey, 2013-14, p. 279).

The State Government constituted a Regional Imbalance Enquiry Commission (RIEC) in 2004, headed by Justice Sri S.K. Mohanty (Retired) to look into various aspects of regional imbalance in the State and to make necessary recommendations. The Commission took four years and submitted its report in 2008. But it has neither been made public nor any action been taken in line with the recommendation.

Removal of regional disparities has been one of the important development strategies of the Central and State Governments. To supplement this strategy several International and Civil Society Organisations including DFID, UNICEF, CARE and Local NGOs have joined hands with the government to assist people in modifying their behaviour and improving their living standard through better access to sanitation and safe drinking water.

3.10.1 KBK Plan

This KBK region could see the visit of three Prime Ministers at quick succession after the infamous incidence, of child sale. As a special drive against poverty, a special KBK plan was started in 1995 to ensure economic and social development. All the present eight districts comprising 14 sub-divisions, 80 C.D. Blocks, 1437 panchayats and 12293 villages were covered. But huge corruption in the implementation of the plan has led to failure in achieving its objectives. During 1998-99 to 2006-07 a sum of Rs 7850.16 crore was released to fight against poverty, hunger, starvation death, child sale, dadan (migration) labour etc. A Special Central Assistance to the tune of 1573.95 cr. has come and 1552.96 cr. has already been spent. But poverty continues to reign in this region.[15] Seasonal migration has been adopted by the people of this region as an escape from unemployment and poverty. Discrimination tactics within KBK were also adopted by the state in release of grants to higher education.

In the underdeveloped region of the state, nine key initiatives have been taken to address the problem of under development and regional disparities. These are (i) Special plan for KBK districts, (ii) Biju KBK plan, (iii) Biju Kandhamal 'O' Gajapati Yojana, (iv) Backward Regions Grant Fund (BRGF), (v) Integrated Action Plan (IAP), (vi) Gopabandhu Gramin Yojana (GGY), (vii) Western Odisha Development Council (WODC) for backward western districts, (viii) Grants-in-aid received under Article 275 (1) of the Constitution of India to bridge critical infrastructure gaps in identified sectors in the Tribal Sub-Plan (TSP) areas and (ix) Implementation of Development Programmes in TSP areas funded out of Special Central Assistance.[16]

3.10.2 Modified Area Development Approach (MADA)

By the end of fifth five year plan MADA was introduced in the identified pockets of ST population with 50 per cent or more ST population with a total population of minimum10,000. The total no. of MADAs identified so far in various TSP state is 259. It is implemented through district authorities in 46 pockets in Odisha.

3.10.3 Integrated Tribal Development Projects/Agencies (ITDPs/ITDAs)

The ITDPs are generally contiguous area of the size of a Tahasil or Block or more where the ST population is 50 per cent or more of the total. In view of the demographic composition, however ITDPs in Assam, Karnataka, Tamil Nadu, and West Bengal may be smaller or not contiguous. Andhra Pradesh and Odisha have opted for an Agency model under the recognition of Societies Act and ITDPs are known as ITDAs. So far 194 ITDPs/ITDAs have been delineated in the country. In 21 pockets, 118 blocks in the state are covered under TSP. The TSP is basically smaller plan for the tribal areas within the state plan.

3.10.4 Tribal Development Blocks (TDB)

In India, the ST population is 104.2 million, which is 8.6 per cent of the total population. (Census 2011). States like Madhya Pradesh, Maharashtra, Odisha, Gujarat, Rajasthan, Jharkhand, Chhattisgarh, Andhra Pradesh, West Bengal and Karnataka have large number of ST population. The diversity and magnitude of the problems of the tribals could not be integrated with the ongoing development programmes and to focus specially on tribal the concept of Tribal Development Blocks was evolved. This resulted in identification of 25 TDB in the state and concerted efforts were put in the sphere of health, education, irrigation and drinking water programme. It continues till the end of fouth plan. The demographic figures reveal that the tribal population is the most disadvantaged, exploited and the neglected lot in India. Despite certain constitutional provisions, they are backward compared to the general population, even their situation is worse than the Schedule Caste (SC) and Other Backward Class (OBC) population [(Xaxa, 2012), as cited by Paltasingh and Paliwal, 2014].[17]

3.10.5 Cluster Programme

The cluster programme is in the identified pockets of tribal concentration having 50 per cent or more ST population within a total population of 5000 or more. As in the case of MADA pockets, there are no separate administrative structures for the Clusters. So far 82 Clusters have been identified in various TSP states. This programme covers under Dispersed Tribal Development Programme (DTDP) implemented through SC and ST Development Finance Cooperative Corporation Ltd.

3.10.6 Long Term Action Plan (LTAP)

The Government of Odisha in consultation with the of Government India, has adopted a Long Term Action Plan (LTAP) for the KBK districts for the period from 1995-96 to 2001-02 with two principal objectives (i) draught proofing and (ii) poverty alleviation and development saturation.

A senior IAS Officer has been posted as the Chief Administrator, Special Area Development (KBK) Project with headquarters at Koraput. Revenue Divisional Commissioner (RDC), Southern and Northern Divisions have been made ex-officio Deputy Chief Administrators to strengthen the Office of the Chief Administrator.

The LTAP and Revised Long Term Action Plan (RLTAP) focused on improving productivity infrastructure, strengthening livelihoods of the marginalised communities, improving literacy levels and accelerating the pace of development in this region. Special Central Assistance to the extent of Rs 2593.95 crore has been received by the State during 1998-99 to 2013-14. This has resulted reduction of poverty to 25.40 percentage point from 73.40 per cent in 2004-05 to 48.00 per cent in 2011-12 as per the Tendulkar Committee methodology.

3.10.7 Odisha Tribal Employment and Livelihood Programme (OTELP)

In India, Odisha, with 62 categories of Scheduled Tribes, has the second highest number of tribal population. There are 75 ‘Particularly Vulnerable Tribal Groups’ (PVTGs) in India, Odisha has 13 such groups, the highest in the country. The PVTGs, considered to be most backward tribal population, are characterised with diminishing population, low level of literacy, with habitations in remote areas. In certain development indicators, a number of pockets of KBK districts lag even behind Sub-Saharan Africa. Ecological degradation, erratic rainfall and high risk of draught in the area has resulted food insecurity, increasing out-migration and periodic deaths from starvation. The concept of PVTG was introduced by Government of India since the fifth five-year plan. Development interventions are being undertaken for these groups through Micro Projects. The PVTGs of Odisha are localised groups found in specific compact areas spread over 541 habitations in 82 Gram Panchayats of 20 blocks in 12 districts namely, Kalahandi, Nuapada, Sundergarh, Deogarh, Angul, Mayurbhanj, Keonjhar, Malkangiri, Raygada, Kandhamal, Gajapati and Ganjam. Population of these PVTGs, as per a survey conducted in 2011, is 82808. For total development of these PVTGs, 17 Micro Projects have been set up in the state, out of which 13 are located within the TSP area and the rest 4 are outside the TSP area. In the KBK districts the following Micro Projects are operating: (i) Banda Development Authority, (ii) Didayi Development Authority, Malkangiri, (iii) Chakutia Bhunjia Development Authority, Nuapada, (iv) Dongaria Kondh Development Authority, Rayagada, (v) Kutia Kondh Development Authority, Kalahandi. These Micro Projects cover a total of 20 Gram Panchayats of these districts. The ST and SC Development Department, Government of Odisha engages leading NGOs/Government promoted Agencies to develop and facilitate implementation of relevant Livelihood Development/Income Generation/Integrated Natural Resource Management/Drinking Water and Sanitation Projects in the areas of Micro Projects for the twelfth five-year plan period, viz. 2012–17.

To overcome these critical situations, a special programme namely, Odisha Tribal Employment and Livelihood Programme (OTELP) was launched from 2nd October 2004. This programme focuses on empowering the tribal and enabling them to enhance their food security, increasing their income, and improving their quality of life by means of efficient management of natural resources through watershed management and sound agricultural practices. This programme will be implemented in three phases in 30 of the most backward blocks in seven districts of Odisha over a period of 10 years. These districts are Koraput (seven blocks), Malkangiri (three blocks), Nabarangapur (three blocks), Rayagada (five blocks), Kalahandi, (two blocks), Kandhamal (five blocks), and Gajapati (five blocks). So under this special tribal development plan the districts under undivided Koraput district are covered. And the Kalahandi district of KBK is partly covered.

3.10.8 Western Odisha Development Council (WODC)

The WODC has been constituted in 1998 by taking ten districts namely, Bargarh, Bolangir, Boudh, Deogarh, Jharsuguda, Kalahandi, Nuapada, Sambalpur, Sonepur and Sundargarh districts and Athamallick sub-division of Angul district, spreading over about 57,384 Sq.Km which is 36.85 per cent of the total state area. It has been formed to accelerate the pace of development and reduce regional disparities with the creation of infrastructure and better livelihood options for the people of this region. But the headquarters of the council still function in the state capital, and there is lack of political will to establish it in Western Odisha. Under this institutional arrangement the undivided Bolangir and Kalahandi districts are covered, whereas the undivided Koraput district is not covered because it comes under the southern part of the state.

3.10.9 Western Odisha Rural Livelihood Project (WORLP)

In 2000, the Government of Odisha in supports of the DFID, under Watershed Development Mission launched the Western Odisha Rural Livelihood Project (WORLP) in four district of western Orissa. These districts are Bolangir, Kalahandi, Nuapada and Bargarh. The WORLP focuses to reduce poverty by promoting livelihoods initiatives for the poorest through building and working with people's existing strengths and resources. The approach of the programme is about creating an enabling environment for empowering people, and allowing them to make informed choices for their long-term well being.

3.10.10 Backward Region Grand Fund (BRGF)

BRGF, a Central funded scheme launched during 2006-07 in 19 districts of Odisha, namely Bolangir, Boudh, Deogarh, Dhenkanal, Gajapati, Ganjam, Jharsuguda, Kalahandi, Kendujhar, Koraput, Malkangiri, Mayurbhanj, Nabarangapur, Nuapada, Phulbani, Rayagada, Sambalpur, Sonepur and Sundargarh and from 2012-13 the Bargarh district has been included in the scheme. Thus, a total of twenty districts have been included during Twelfth Plan (2012-17). All KBK districts are under this scheme since its inception. To bridge the critical infrastructure gaps, strengthening local governance, and delivery mechanism are principal objectives. A total of Rs 1,648.43 crore has been sanctioned till March, 2013.

3.10.11 Integrated Action Plan (IAP)

The IAP has been introduced by the Government of India since 2010-11 in selected tribal and backward districts. Initially, 15 districts, namely Bolangir, Deogarh, Gajapati, Kalahandi, Kandhamal, Keonjhar, Koraput, Malkangiri, Mayurbhanj, Nabarangapur, Nuapada, Rayagada, Sambalpur, Sonepur and Sundargarh. From 2011-12 three more districts, namely Ganjam, Jajpur and Nayagarh have been included in the scheme. So, including all the KBK districts now there are 18 districts under IAP scheme. A total of Rs 1677.57 crore has been received by the State till March, 2014. Under this scheme ST/SC hostels, Anganwadi Centres, Primary Health Centres, roads, culverts, bridges, tube-well, check dams, pipe water supply programmes are undertaken.

3.10.12 National Rural Livelihood Mission (NRLM)

National Rural Livelihood Mission (NRLM) as a poverty alleviation programme has been launched in 2011 by the Ministry of Rural Development, Government of India. Under this programme the women Self Help Group (SHG) are organised for the promotion of self employment among rural poor. This scheme replaces Swarnajayanti Grameen Swarojgar Yojana (SGSY) in 2013. This programme is supported by the World Bank. It includes financial and capital services production and productivity enhancement, services, technology, knowledge, skills, market linkages etc. The SHGs and NGOs would play a key role to strengthen the NRLM operation. Through NRLM programme Rural Self Employment Training Institutions will be established through the public sector banks in all districts of the country. Under NRLM the Aajeevika scheme targets to the poor rural youth in the age group of 18-35 for skill formation. In case of the PVTG the upper age is 45 years. In addition to this the State Rural Livelihood Mission is also in operation.

3.10.13 Mahatma Gandhi National Rural Employment Guarantee Act (MGNREGA)

The National Rural Employment Guarantee Act (NREGA) 2005 was passed in the Lok Sabha on 23 August 2005. It came into force in 200 districts on 2 February 2006 and was extended to the whole of rural India within five years. It is a step towards legal enforcement of the right to work, as a part of the fundamental right to live (with dignity).

This formed a flagship programme of the UPA Government is also under operation to enhance livelihood security of the rural poor by providing at least 100 days of guaranteed wage employment per household per year. The work guarantee applies in rural areas only. This programme has also other objectives like generating productive assets, protecting the environment, empowering rural women, social equity and reducing rural-urban migration. Now NREGA has been renamed as Mahatma Gandhi National Rural Employment Guarantee Act (MGNREGA).

One hundred days of guaranteed employment at the minimum wage is not a great privilege, but for those who live on the margin of subsistence, it can make a big difference. Secondly, the Act is likely to lead to a substantial reduction of rural-urban migration: if work is available in the village, many families will stay in their native places instead of heading for cities.[18]

This flagship programme of employment generation has also the objective to check distress seasonal migration in the KBK region. But due to corrupt practices in its implementation level the programme has failed to deliver the desired result and migration continues unabated. The nexus between officials, contractors and politicians has questioned the validity of the programme.

3.10.14 Working of MGNREGA in KBK

In spite of thousands crores of grant allotment from the central government in the MGNREGA programme, the state administration has failed to provide the targeted 100 man-days of employment to the registered labour in this much sensitive KBK districts. This has come as a reply by the Panchayat Raj Minister Mr Arun Sahu to the question put by Mr Nabakishor Das, MLA. This has become clear with the information presented by the minister in the floor of the Assembly. The data presented in Table 3.12 shows that during the last seven years i.e. 2007-08 to 2013-14 a family has been provided 37 to 53 days of work in a year. In these years a total of 30,24,451 families have worked under MGNREGA. The administration has failed to provide the required 100 days of work at least to one member of a family which has registered. But no reason has been assigned for such dismal performance of the programme. The allotted funds have remained unutilised during these years. This pushes the people to adopt migration as the only livelihood strategy. For corrupt practices in MGNREGA, Odisha is well known and there is no doubt to this dismal performance in the KBK districts. In this context a case is pending with the Supreme Court of India. Under this condition of state employment provision the poor people have no alternative except to adopt migration of short and long distance within the state or outside the state for their livelihood and survival.

Table 3.12: MGNREGA in KBK

Financial Year	*No. of Registered Labourer*	*Work Demanded*	*Work Provided*	*No. of Days of Work Provided*
2007-08	1369672	423262	408994	37
2008-09	1438850	366754	360635	37
2009-10	1480816	382129	376637	40
2010-11	1562343	553691	549228	53
2011-12	1591212	417325	414603	33
2012-13	1613939	488378	436167	36
2013-14	1642817	532692	478187	41

Source: The Samaj, Odia Daily 11th February, 2015, p.11.

3.10.15 Non-Government Organisation (NGO)

In the democratic set up of a welfare state like India, the Non-Government Organisations (NGOs) play a crucial role in the development initiatives of the state. There are number of NGOs working in the KBK districts. More than 30 NGOs are engaged in the field of migration/dadan, livelihood, watershed, education, health, and rehabilitation of displaced people etc and to promote better living of the people of this area. These organisations are funded by different national and foreign donors to work for the people of this backward region. NGOs' role in the area for the betterment of the people is undeniable. But sometime back the role of a few NGOs has been questioned by the Intelligence Bureau and has been coined as obstructionists of development and promoting peoples' movement against development projects. Fighting for peoples' right can never be termed as obstructionists or anti-development. Serving the goals of the corporate sector is not the only measurement of development. Where the government functionaries are not able to reach the NGOs have the capacity to reach and perform, provided they, have the will and determination to serve the people. The prominent NGOs operating in the KBK districts are, Lokadrusti, Agragamee, Gram Vikas, Antadoya, Gaon Mukti Sangathan, Action Aid, Aide et Action, Udayam, Adhar, Youth Service Centre, Aajivika Bureau, Spread, Rites Forume, Harsha Trust, FARR, OVA, Pradan, Pragati, RARE, YCDA, Sai, Karmi, Jindabad, Sramik Adhikar Sangathan, Seva Jagat etc.

3.10.16 Conclusion

The KBK is an abbreviation of the erstwhile undivided districts of Kalahandi, Bolangir and Koraput. KBK became a popular term during 1980s in the circle of economic and political discussion not only in Odisha but also in the national and international sphere for its hunger and poverty. Although development measures in term of industries and agriculture have been taken still the region is known for its underdevelopment. In this underdevelopment scenario, push factor has become strong enough to push the labour force to adopt internal migration in the form of seasonal/circular nature within the region or between states to search for their livelihood or better/regular employment. The KBK region experiences Naxalite activities frequently, which has affected the development process and employment of people in different projects.

In addition to above noted special schemes there are other general state programmes which also operate in the KBK districts. These programme are like supply of 25 kg rice at one rupee to the BPL families, old age pension, widow allowance, handicap allowance, Indira Awas Yojana, Mo Kudia, Biju Pucca Ghar Yojan, food security yojana etc are in operation. In course of time some old schemes have been renamed or replaced by new schemes.

The underdeveloped KBK region has received state support in terms of number of development programmes, for infrastructure development and livelihood of the people of these districts. In spite of these host of programmes, inter-state migration in KBK districts has become a common phenomenon which raises the basic question towards the implementation and trickledown of such development programmes to the targeted people group. It needs a special study over the outcome of such special development programmes in the KBK region. The level disparity between developed and underdeveloped still continues.

References

1. Bal, C, A. Das and S.C. Kumar (2015). *Silver Lining in Odisha's Organised Manufacturing Sector,* Economic and Political Weekly, Vol. No. 15 April 11, pp. 69-79.
2. Sainath, P. (1996). *Everybody Loves a Good Draught, Stories from India's Poorest Districts.* Penguin Books, New Delhi.
3. *Samaj The Odia Daily* 14th January, 2015.
4. Government of Odisha (2014) *Odisha Economic Survey 2013-14,* Planning and Coordination Department, Government of Odisha, Bhubaneswar, p. 332.
5. Mehta, A.K. and Amrita Shah (2003). *Chronic Poverty in India Incidence, Causes and Policies*, World Development 31(3), p. 492.
6. Haan, A. and A. Dubey (2005). *Extreme deprivation in remote areas in India: social exclusion as an explanatory concept,* Draft paper for Manchester Conference on Chronic Poverty, April, 2003.
7. ORD CRD Report, *Impact Assessment of Externally Aided Project Interventions on Livelihood of the poor and Marginalised in KBK Districts of Orissa, Sponsored by Planning Commission of India*, Centre for Rural Development, Bhubaneswar.
8. Mishra, D. and R.S. Rao (1992). *Hunger in Kalahandi, Blinkered Understanding*, Economic and Political Weekly, Jan. 13-20, pp. 1245.
9. Pradhan, Jagadish (1993). *Drought in Kalahandi: The Real Story,* Economic and Political Weekly, May 29, pp. 1084-1088.
10. Senapati, N. and N.K. Sahu (1968). *Odisha District Gazetteers – Bolangir,* Govt. Press, Cuttack.
11. Vasundhara (2005). *Development Policies and Rural Poverty in Orissa: Macro Analysis and Case Studies: A Study by Vasundhara,* Bhubaneswar, Supported by Planning Commission of India, New Delhi.
12. Mahalik, N (2014). Cultural Heritage of Undivided Koraput District of Odisha (Origin and Growth of Janajati Culture), Odisha Review, April-May, pp. 105-105.
13. Gupta, S.K. (1965). *Dandakaranya: A Survey of Rehabilitation, I-The State of Agriculture,* The Economic Weekly, January 2, p. 15.
14. Behera, N.K., (2011). *Displacement, Resettlement and Rehabilitation* Abhijeet Publications, New Delhi, p. 27.
15. The Dharitri Odiya Daily, 4th April, 2014.
16. Government of Odisha (2014). Odisha Economic Survey 2013-14 Planning and co-ordination Department, Bhubaneswer, p. 279.
17. Paltasingh, T. and G. Paliwal (2014). *Tribal Population in India: Regional Dimensions and Imperatives,* Journal of Regional Development and Planning, Vol. 3, No. 2, pp. 27-36.
18. Dey, N., J. Dreze and R. Khera (2006) Employment Guarantee Act: A Premier, National Book Trust, India, p. 5.

Chapter - 4

Legal Framework for Labour and Migrants

4.1 Introduction

The 2001 census figure shows, migrant population constitutes around 30 per cent of the total population in India. The tendency of migration has shown an increasing trend over the decade. This indicates the important role of migration in the economy. A larger section of the people at the lower strata of the society participates in the process. Migration is governed by push factors at source, such as lack of employment, low wage, failure of agriculture due to natural calamities, debt bondage etc. Todaro (1976) explains migration in terms of expected rather than real income difference between rural and urban sector.[1] Whatever may be the factor responsible for migration within the country, undoubtedly migrants do contribute substantially to the productivity and national income of the country. In a large country like India, uneven course of development has opened the gates of opportunities in an uneven manner. It has become an opportunity for the people in distress and otherwise who have been migrating in large number within the state or between states in search of employment and livelihood. This internal migration for livelihood was present before independence and is continuing even after six decades of planning and post liberalisation period. The mega development projects such as dams and large scale industries, which were considered as infrastructures for development, launched after independence attracted migrant workers from different parts of the country. These mega projects not only attracted migrant workers, but also became the origin of migrant workers due to population displacement, without proper arrangement for their resettlement and livelihood.

4.2 Legal Provision for Migration

The Constitution of India allows such movements as a fundamental right under Article 19(1) (d) and (e). Under the provision of the article the citizen of a country has the freedom of movement and freedom to settle in any part within the territory of India. (Except in certain States, which enjoy some special status in the Constitution). In addition to this freedom of movement as a fundamental right, the state also performs as a guardian of citizen's right through Directive Principles of State Policy. Under these directive principles the State ensures protection of workers from exploitation and prevalence of equal rights to all the workers. In order to pursue better conditions for the working citizens the Parliament of India has enacted many laws from time to time to deal with the issues of external and internal migration.

International laws govern legal relations between states. Historically, migration was regulated at the national level. In this context, The Emigration Act, 1983 plays a significant role in the field of external migration. With the increase in global mobility, states have begun to realise that migration is no longer something they can manage in autarchy. The main elements of International Migration Law deals with the issues of human rights, the duty of the states to accept the returning migrants, the obligation to provide consular as access to non-residents human trafficking and migrant smuggling, specific areas that are the subject of specific internal agreements e.g. labour migration. The International Migration is governed by a set of rules of immigrating and emigrant country.

On the other hand, the internal migration which takes place within the country is also assuming a significant role in the demographic study of the country. The Inter-State Migrant Workmen Act, 1979 tries to address the problem of internal migrant workers of the country. In addition to this Act there are several other Central Acts and State Rules to deal with the issues of labour working in different formal and informal sectors and its related problems. The workers of informal sector need more state support and protection because of their unorganised nature. The migrants are largely engaged in informal jobs without security of wage and livelihood. Here is a list of different Acts and Rules dealing with labour issues.

1. The Workmen's Compensation Act, 1923 and Rules 1924.

2. The Trade Unions Act 1926 and Regulation, 1941.
3. The Payment of Wages Act, 1936 and Rules 1936.
4. The Industrial Employment (Standing Orders) Act, 1946 and Rules 1946.
5. The Industrial Disputes Act, 1947 and Amendment, 2010.
6. The Minimum Wages Act, 1948 and Rules 1954.
7. The Working Journalists (Condition of Service) and Miscellaneous Provision Act, 1955.
8. The Odisha Shops and Commercial Establishments Act, 1956 and Rules 1958.
9. The Maternity Benefit Act, 1961 and Rules 1966.
10. The Motor Transport Workers Act, 1961 and Rules 1966.
11. The Payment of Bonus Act, 1965 and Rules 1975 and Amendment Ordinance 1977.
12. The Beedi Cigar Workers (Condition of Employment) Act, 1966 and Rules 1969.
13. The Odisha Industrial Establishment (National Festival) Holiday Act, 1969 and Rules 1972.
14. The Contract Labour (Regulation and Abolition) Act, 1970, and Rules 1975.
15. The Payment of Gratuity Act, 1972 and Rules 1974.
16. The Equal Remuneration Act, 1976.
17. The Sales Promotion Employees (Condition of Service) Act 1976 and Rules 1976.
18. The Inter-State Migration Workmen (Regulation of Employment and Condition of Services) Act, 1979 and Rules 1980.
19. The Cine Workers and Cinema Theatre Workers (Regulation of Employment) Act, 1981.
20. The Child Labour (Prohibition and Regulation) Act, 1986 and Rules 1994.
21. The Labour Laws (Exemption from Furnishing Returns and Maintenance of Registers by certain Establishment) Act, 1988.
22. The Employees Provident Fund and Miscellaneous Provisions Act, 1952.

23. The Bonded Labour System (Abolition) Act, 1976.
24. The Building and other Construction Workers (Regulation of Employment and Conditions of Services) Act, 1996 and Rules 2002.
25. The Building and other Construction workers Welfare and Cess Act 1996 and Rules 2002.
26. The Unorganised Workers Social Security Act, 2007 and Rules 2010.
27. Mahatma Gandhi National Rural Employment Guarantee Act, 2005 (NREGA, 2005).
28. Rastriya Swasthya Bima Yojana Scheme.

4.3 Inter-State Migration Workmen Act, 1979 (ISMW)

These Acts/laws show that in India there is no dearth of legal provision to deal with problems of labour. In the matter of inter-state migration, the Inter-State Migration Workmen (Regulation of Employment and Condition of Services) Act, 1979 plays a vital role in ameliorating the condition of such migrants. The purpose of the act is to protect workers whose services are requisitioned outside their native states in India. Whenever an employer faces shortage of unskilled/skilled labour among the locally available workers, the act creates provision to employ better skilled workers available outside the state.

The employment of inter-state migrant labour prevailing in different states is more or less exploitative in nature. This practice was rampantly institutionalised in Odisha and some other states. The migrant labour called *dadan* labour were sent through agents called sardars/ khatedars to work outside the states in tea plantation of Assam, West Bengal and large construction projects. This system lends to various types of abuses. To minimise the problems of dadan labour, Odisha is the first state to enact a law called Odisha Dadan Labour (Abolition) Act, 1975, to recognise and define the role of agents/dalals in the recruitment procedure and sending the labour to work outside the state.

Once the workers come under the clutches of the contractors who take them to a far off place on payment of railways fare only it become difficult on their part to come out of the tentacles of owner-agent nexus.

For them no working hour is fixed and they are forced to work on all days in a week under extremely awful working conditions. The condition of employment of inter-state migrant labour is exploitative in nature which prevails in many states of the Indian Union. This system lends itself to various abuses. The provisions of available labour laws are not observed and wages are not paid under the Minimum Wage Act, 1948. As per 2001 census, 314.54 million persons moved for various reasons within the country. Out of these nearly 29.90 million migrated for employment reason alone.

The conditions of inter-state migrant workers were acknowledged by the political representatives of the country. In cognizance of the serious problem of inter-state migrant workers, the 28th State Labour Ministers Conference held on 21st October, 1976 recommended for setting up a small compact committee to examine all issues and recommend measures for elimination of the abuses prevalent in the inter-state workers deployment. The committee was formed in February, 1977 and recommended for the enactment of a separate central legislation to regulate the employment of inter-state migrant workers as it was observed that the provisions under Contract Labour (Regulation and Abolition) Act, 1970 could not adequately take care of the variety of malpractices adopted by the employers and agents.

The recommendations of the compact committee had been examined in consultation with the State Governments and the relevant Central Ministries. The Inter-State Migrant Workmen (Regulation of Employment and Conditions of Services) Act, 1979 was passed by the Parliament and received the Presidential assent on 11.06.1979 and came into force from 1st June, 1987.

The Act applies –

(a) To every establishment and contractor in which five or more Inter-State migrant workmen (whether or not in addition to other workmen) are employed or who were employed on any day of the preceding twelve months;

Labour contractor used to supply workmen to the establishment either directly by him or through a sub-contractor, khatadar, sardar, dalal, agent or any person, by whatever name called who recruits or employs workmen.

The Inter-State migrant workmen are those workers who are recruited by or through a contractor in one state under an agreement (usually unrecorded) or other arrangement for employment in an establishment in another state, whether with or without the knowledge of the principal employer in relation to such establishment. This does not cover such recruitment arrangement or carried out for the establishment within the state itself.

The purpose of the Act is to discourage inter-state migration of workers against the interest of local workers as the principal employers would have to incur more cost in deploying inter-state workers. The Act provides some rights to the inter-state migrant workers in terms of:

- Equal or better wages for the similar nature and duration of work applicable for the local workers or as stipulated under the Minimum Wage Act, 1948.
- The inter-state migrants are to be provided with non-refundable Displacement Allowance Equal to 50 per cent of monthly wage at the time of recruitment, home journey allowance, including payment of wages during journey period.
- The employers are to provide suitable residential accommodation and medical facilities free of cost on mandatory basis.
- The employment is subject to termination after the contract period without any liability.
- Wages shall be paid in cash. Regular payment wages to inter-state migrant workers (ISMWs) and shall be equal for equal work to both sexes.
- The worker is given the right to file complaints with the authorities within three months of any incident or accident.
- If the contractor fails in his duties to ISMW, it is the duty of the principal employers to make the payments and recover the amount paid to the contractor.

Thus, the Act intended to extend certain minimal protection measures against exploitation under labour laws to the inter-state migrant workmen. The Act provides avoidance of bonded labour by both the principal employer and contractor that no loan is given to workmen or remain outstanding after the completion of the period of employment. If anything remains outstanding, it is supposed to be extinguished and no suit shall lie to recover the debt from such immigrant workers.

The law allows (a) licensing contractors who employ or supply workmen to different establishments which includes government departments/offices or a local authority under the activities of industry, trade, business or manufacturing carried on. (b) Registering the concern establishment employing inter-state migrant workmen.(c) Any establishment providing employment to five or more inter-state migrant workmen or any day of the preceding 12 months will bring contractors and establishment under the purview of the Act.

"Workmen" means any person employed in or in connection with the work of any establishment to do any skilled, semi-skilled or unskilled, manual, supervisory, technical or clerical work for hire or reward, whether the terms of employment by express or implied, but does not include any such person –

(i) Person employed in a managerial or administrative capacity; or

(ii) Person employed in a supervisory capacity, draws wages exceeding five hundred rupees per month, or exercises, either by the nature of the duties attached to the office or by reason of the powers vested in him, functions mainly of a managerial nature. In other words, the Act, don't take into account the white colour workers engaged in States other than their native states.

4.3.1 Major Provisions of ISMW Act, 1979

(1) Registration of all principal employers/contractors employing migrant labour.

(2) Licensing of contractors.

(3) Issue of passbook affixed with a passport sized photograph of the workman indicating the name and place of the establishment where the workman is employed, the period of employment, rates of wages etc. to every inter-state migrant workman. Payment of minimum wages under Minimum Wages Act, 1948, payment of equal wages for inter-state migrant workman performing similar nature of work along with local labour,

payment of journey allowance including payment of wages during the period of journey.

(4) Payment of displacement allowance. Providing suitable accommodation, providing medical facilities free of charge.

(5) Punishment with imprisonment up to one year or with a fine up to Rs 1,000 or both for contravening the provision of the Act.

4.3.2 Enforcement Machinery

The responsibility for enforcement of the provisions of the Act in establishments where the Central Government is the appropriate authority lies with the office of the Chief Labour Commissioner (Central) and the responsibility for enforcement of the provisions of the Act in the establishments located under the state sphere lies with respective State Government in which they are working and from where they have been recruited.

4.3.3 Recruitment Process of Inter-State Migrant Workers

The ISMW Act, 1979 prescribes certain rules for the recruitment of skilled, semi-skilled and unskilled labourer to work in states other than their natives. These recruitment processes are to be carried on by a license agent/contractor as per the act. The licensed labour contractor is to register at the District Labour Office. After obtaining the permission letter, the contractor is allowed to recruit more than five persons; no upper limit has been fixed on the recruitment of such workers. The contractor is issued with one license for one year i.e. Jan-Dec. and is subject to submit half yearly return. There is also provision that one contractor can obtain more than one licence and no limit has been set. The licence contractors are supposed to supply inter-state migrant workers to the registered establishments of other States. Under the provision of the Act the contractor has to pay displacement allowance of 15 days of wages before leaving their house, which is not to be deducted from the wages of the workers. The licenced contractor bears the transportation cost, with food and wage during journey period. He is also to ensure minimum standard of living conditions and wages not less than the minimum wage presented for different categories of workers. In addition to these the workers are to be provided medical facilities during their stay at the destination.

Thus, the legal part of the labour recruitment processes for the inter-state migrant workers presents a rosy picture. But, in practice through extra legal provision, a sizable section of inter-state migrant workers move to other states for work. In this process neither formal licence nor other official formalities are maintained to recruit such workers.

The process of *dadan*/migrant labour recruitment begins from the time of the local festival called 'Nuakhai', a mass agricultural festival observed in the month of September by the people of western Odisha or even before Nuakhai. Nuakhai symbolises beginning of new season with the consumption of rice from new or fresh rice. Both licenced and non-licenced labour agents on behalf of the owners of brick kiln mostly from the south Indian states adopt same path and pay cash advance to each family to the tune of Rs 60,000-80,000 (per head @ 15,000-20,000) depending on the number of members in a family. (The brick kiln owners of the state do not pay this type lump sum advance/ dadan) This becomes the most important source of attraction and saving or for creation of certain durable assets like of houses construction, and repair, purchase of jewellery or consumer durables like TV, mobile phone etc. As the labour migration involves family members for the brick kilns in general, the children are supposed to accompany and assist as out of pay roll workers in brick making, because brick making involves piece work. After receiving cash advance *(baina)* their movements start from *Dushara* i.e. October to December. The agents collect such migrant labour and keep them at a place for two-four days and arrange to send them by trains or trucks. The common station for their departure is Kantabanji railway station. These migrant labourers have to move in general compartments. The train tickets for the workers are arranged through agents/dalals on commission basis. In this process there is the direct or indirect involvement of local political people, police and administration right from the bottom level to the higher level. Agents have revealed that in this process they have to bribe at different stages for the easy passage of dadans and escape from the legal procedures well. The dadan challan or labour trafficking goes on in mass scale in the KBK districts. The Kantabanj railway station of Bolangir district is known as *'Dadan Corridor'* from where thousands of *dadan* labourers are dispatched every day to work in other

Table 4.1: Documented Information on Internal Migration in the KBK Districts, 2005-2014

Sl. No.	*District*	*No. of licensed issued/ Renewed*	*No. of Labour migrated the contractor*	*No. of migrant labour returned*	*No. of cases of torture/ harassment*	*No. of migrant rescued*	*No. of child labour*	*Common destination of migrant labour*	*Common nature of work at destination*	*Remarks*
1	*2*	*3*	*4*	*5*	*6*	*7*	*8*	*9*	*10*	*11*
1.	Kalahandi	14	435	435	05	148	NA	Andhra Pradesh	Brick Making	
2.	Nuapada	554	28,185	28,185	34	1026	NA	Andhra Pradesh, Tamil Nadu, Karnataka, Uttar Pradesh	-do-	
3.	Bolangir	963	71620	NA	NA	12	NA	Andhra Pradesh, Karnataka, Tamil Nadu.	-do-	Data for 2011-14 have been provided
4.	Sonepur	05	1649	1649	NA	NA	NA	Maharashtra, Karnataka, Andhra Pradesh, Tamil Nadu, Ganjam (Odisha)	-do-	27 migrants have been rescued in the 1st quarter of 2015.
5.	Koraput	87	2371	735	52	88	NA	Gujarat, Maharashtra, Karnataka, Chhattisgarh, Andhra Pradesh, Tamil Nadu	Construction work, Buildings and roads	The migrants of 2014 have not yet returned.

(Cond...)

6.	Nabarangpur	147	4301	3991	NA	NIL	NA	Tamil Nadu, Karnataka, Andhra Pradesh, Gujarat, Maharashtra.	Construction work, Buildings, roads, brick making and Plantation	-do-
7.	Rayagada	17	378	194	NA	376	NA	Karnataka, Maharashtra, Gujarat, Himachal Pradesh, Tamil Nadu, Rajasthan.	Construction work, building and roads	-do-
8.	Malkangiri	104	3025	2915	NA	NA	NA	Maharashtra, Karnataka, Tamil Nadu, Andhra Pradesh, Punjab, Pondicherry, Assam, Madhya Pradesh.	Construction work, Buildings roads and plantation.	
	Total	**1891**	**1,11,964**	**38,104**	**91**	**1650**	**NA**			

Source:- Information collected through RTI and the District Labour Offices.

states. The labour contractors earn a good amount as commission for the supply of labour.

The workers are selected on the basis of the intimation received from the registered brick kilns owners through the DLOs of the destination to the DLO at source. Agent's commission on recruitment of labour is neither determined by the DLO at source nor at destination nor by the labour department. The principal employers provide it to the agent depending upon the demand for labour and supply of labour. The data on number of inter-state migrant labour is determined on the basis of report made by the licensed agents only. And the non-licensed labour movement remains outside the orbit of such data. It is also noted that a few former *dadans* who could establish some rapport with the owners also become agent to collect dadans from their native areas. Inter-state migration through non-licensed agents/sardars has become more prominent than the registered agents.

To avoid official procedures and complexity, the agents do not register themselves and manage the *dadan* network through other process. The inter-state migrant workers from Bargarh, Bolangir, Nuapada, Kalahandi and Sonepur mainly specialise in brick making. The Bihari migrant labour also work in brick kilns and they specialise in managing the kilns, firing and maintaining adequate temperature for proper baking of bricks. On the other hand, the migrants from Koraput, Nabarangpur, Rayagada and Malkangiri districts are engaged in construction sector, road, building, wood work etc. Recently, the Government of Odisha has signed a MOU with the Governments of Andhra Pradesh, Telengana and Tamil Nadu to deal with the problems of ISMW and to provision different social security schemes. The condition of inter-state migrant labour will not improve without the cooperation of the administration of destination states, since these migrants have to work in adverse condition and face oppression at different levels. These migrants move to other states under distress and have little option to comeback from their place of work. In addition to this, migration awareness programme through NGOs have been undertaken from 2014, in order to pursue them to stay in their locality and to work in various public work programme particularly under MGNREGA, SHGs etc. so as to prevent themselves from exploitation in other states. Another motive of the awareness campaign is to enlighten the migrants about different legal provision for the protection and safeguard of inter-state migrant workers.

Table 4.1 shows the secondary data relating to the situation of migration in the KBK districts during the last one decade i.e. 2005-2014. The information has been collected through personal contact and through RTI provision. The official data in the table reveals that highest number of inter-state migrants is seen in two districts, namely Bolangir and Nuapada with 71,620 and 28,185 respectively. Bolangir and Nuapada have 963 and 554 numbers of labour contractors respectively, which is considered to be highest in the region. A total of 1,891 licenced labour contractors are engaged in the labour migration of 1,11,964 during the period stated. The figure of migrants fluctuates over the year depending upon the demand and supply of labour. The total number of migrant return is 38,104. Strangely enough there is no data relating to number of return migration in case of Bolangir district. There is also no data relating to harassment or torture cases of migrant labour at the destination. On the other hand very often, we come across several cases of torture and harassment from print and electronic media. A total of 91 harassment/torture cases have been recorded in all in the KBK districts out of which Nuapada district has the highest of 34 such cases.

Kalahandi, which was known for its hunger and poverty in the 1980s, does not show a high rate of migration. After the reorganisation of districts, the migration of labour is largely seen in the newly carved out district of Nuapada from Kalahandi. Bolangir continues to show a high rate of migration. In case of undivided Koraput district, the present Nabarangpur and Malkangiri districts record higher migration than the districts of Koraput and Rayagada. In case of Nabarangpur 4309 persons have migrated through 147 labour contractors and in case of Malkangiri 3025 persons have migrated through 104 labour contractors. The data does not show any child labour from any of the district of KBK region is a doubtful one. We come across a number of cases of child labour and their torture in different places. In bricks kilns children work to supplement the family income, which has been confirmed during our visit to different brick kilns. It is also confirmed through media report and NGOs working in this field about the prevalence of child labour and their exploitation. These child labourers are working in different mills, hotels and houses. The migrant workers from

Kalahandi, Nuapada, Bolangir and Sonepur are generally employed in brick kilns of Andhra Pradesh, Telengana, Tamil Nadu, Karnataka, and Maharashtra. A few of them from Sonepur have also adopted intra-district migration to Ganjam district for brick making. So also a few migrants of Nuapada district have gone too far off states like Uttar Pradesh and others.

In contrast to the migrants of these districts, the migrants from undivided Koraput district are employed in the construction sector of roads and buildings. Migrants from the districts of Nabarangpur and Malkangiri are engaged in brick making and plantation as well. The common destinations of migrants of these districts are Gujarat, Maharashtra, Karnataka, Andhra Pradesh, Telengana, Rajasthan, Tamil Nadu, and Kerala. A few migrants from Malkangiri have moved far off states like Punjab, Pondicherry, Assam, Madhya Pradesh, and Himachal Pradesh.

To sum up the scenario of migration from KBK region, on the basis of above secondary data we can say that a significant number of migrants adopt inter-state migration of distressed induced seasonal nature with a common destination to the southern and western states of India. They are generally engaged in the brick kilns and construction sectors. The main reason responsible for this large scale inter-state migration from KBK region unemployment, higher wage at destination, regular employment and the vicious cycle of debt bondage.

4.4 Minimum Wage Act

The initiative for minimum wage was started in 1920 with the placing of a resolution by Sir K G R Choudhry for setting up Boards for the determination of minimum wage in each industry. In 1928, the International Labour Conference adopted the Convention No. 26 and Recommendation No. 30 for wage fixation. A draft bill was considered by Indian Labour Conference in 1945. A Minimum Wage Bill was introduced in the Central Legislative Assembly on 11.04.1946 to provide for fixation of minimum wage on certain employment. It was passed in 1946 and came into force with effect from 15.03.1948. A tripartite committee, namely "The Committee on Fair Wages" was set up in 1948 to provide guidelines for wage structure in the country. It recommended certain key concepts of the 'living wages', 'minimum wage', and 'fair wage' besides setting out guidelines for wage fixation.

The central and state governments are appropriate authorities to notify scheduled employment and fixed/revise minimum wage. There are two parts of the schedule, part I deals with non-agricultural employment and part II deals with agricultural employment.

Article 39 directs its policy towards securing (a) that the citizens, men and women equally shall have the right to an adequate livelihood and (b) there is equal wage for equal work for both men and women.

Article 43 further states that the state shall endeavour through legislation/organisation or other way to provide all workers agricultural, industrial or otherwise work a living wage, condition of work ensuring a decent standard of life and full enjoyment of leisure and social and cultural opportunities. It is enforced through (i) Central Chief Labour Commissioner and (ii) State Labour Commissioner. At present there are five Regional Minimum Wages Advisory Committees in the country. The State of Odisha comes under Eastern Region.

On May 1, 2015, the government of Odisha revised the minimum wages for different broad category of workers (a) Unskilled Rs 200, (b) Semiskilled Rs 220, (c) Skilled Rs 240 and (d) Highly Skilled Rs 260. Previously these wage rates were Rs 150, 170, 200, and 220 respectively. The employers are to pay to the workers accordingly. Any violation of the Act is liable to punishment of six months imprisonment along with penalty. But it is observed that violators escape from punishment. The Odisha government's report revealed that action was taken in only one of the 426 cases filed for nonpayment of minimum wages last year. The government further admitted that only six cases were solved during the period. The state CPI (M) secretary Mr Janardan Pati added that surprisingly the Labour Inspectors are neither making field visits to check ground reality nor registering cases against employers violating the provision. However, laxity on the part of the concerned authority has made the policy impractical as the benefit is not fully reaching the toiling class.[2]

In this context it may be added that the tea plantation industry is one of the oldest sector in the country to employ migrant workers. Currently a little over 10 lakh permanent workers, the largest employer in the private sector and second largest employer after the railway. Tea plantation of Assam and West Bengal employ around 8,00,000 workers while the two southern states employ around 2,00,000 workers.

A little more than half are women. (Bhowmik, 2015, p. 19). In spite of this large employment and organisation, plantations owners in the northern states don't implement the statutory provision of Plantation Labour Act of 1951. The record of implementation of provisions of the Act is dismal; the findings showed that not a single tea plantation on the three tea districts had implemented the Act. The record of plantation in Tamil Nadu and Kerala is much better in term of wage rate and provision of basic amenities than the northern plantation states. Apart from paying ridiculously low wages they do not fulfill any conditions that could be regarded as Decent Work as prescribed by the ILO.[3] If condition of workers in one of the oldest organised sector, tea plantation remain like this, it can be visualised the condition of temporary/seasonal migrant workers who are not organised and working in different sectors in other states. Violation of minimum wage also takes place in an extensive manner in the name of contractual labour working in different public, private and semi-public organisations.

4.5 Child Labour and Migration

Indian brick kilns industry is the second largest brick producer next to China only. Annually, over 14 billion bricks are produced from more than 1,00,000 units. Generally brick kiln requires manual labour for earth molding, stacking, head loading, baking, firing, transportation etc. A large number of migrant families including women and children are recruited by labour contractors through advance payment. Child labour is an integral part of these brick kilns. The study made by Aide et Action International South Asia, in the brick kilns of Andhra Pradesh and Tamil Nadu shows the harsh condition of children who live with their parents for 6-8 months and struggle to access the bare minimum facilities for human survival.

The children are forced to work in the brick kilns as part of family labour, without any payment and are subjected to abuses and exploitation. The children are deprived up nutrious food, drinking water, sanitation, social security measures and schooling. Migration leads to loss of education for generations.

India recognised the Right to Education (RTE) as a fundamental Right in 2009. The country is also striving to achieve the Millennium Development Goals (MDGs), of which the second goal is to achieve universal primary education by 2015. However, through the more ambitious Sarva Shiksha Abhiyan (SSA) programme, the Indian Government is working to achieve universalisation of elementary education (UEE) by 2010. India is also a signatory of the UN Convention on the Rights to the Child (1989). Amidst this positive scenario, there is little attention to the plight of the children of a migrant labourer, although year after year their ranks are swelling. In India, the Ministry of Human Resource (MHRD) and the State Education Departments do not even have the record with respect to this category of children, let alone a strategic plan in place to address related concerns. Urgent steps are thus needed for their education and development if the UEE targets and the MDGs are to be achieved.[4] The goals set these programme are far away from its achievements.

The Child Labour (Prohibition and Regulation) Act, 1986 prohibits employment of children in number of occupation set forth in part of 'A' of the schedule or in any workshop wherein any process set forth in part 'B' of the schedule to this Act. The ISMW of KBK districts are largely engaged in brick kilns and their children are also engaged with them in these brick kilns also come under the list of workshop prohibited for engaging children, but little care has been taken to the provisions of this Act and the owners of brick kilns have employed children of ISMW families in an indiscriminate manner. A number of child abuse cases have come to the light through media.

It is also a known fact that ISMW involves family labour, it is obvious that children accompany the families are also subject to exploitation in many ways. There are cases of child exploitation and abuses. An example of such exploitation can be cited here. The hand of Sushanta Kumbhar son of Bhanumati and Santosh Kumbhar of Village Kadalimunda of Patnagarh Block in the district of Bolangir was broken by the owner of a brick kiln in Gulbarga district of Karnataka. His hand was broken by the owner of kiln by beating with an iron rod. A few social activists and lawyers could bring the matter to light and rescued the family. Sushanta was treated at SCB Medical College and Hospital, Cuttack. It received the government attention after much hue and cry by the opposition and civil society. He was paid compensation of Rs 50,000 on 21st October, 2014.

On the issue of child labour we can conclude with the observation of the editorial of Economic and Political Weekly that, "there is no pat solution to end child labour. That is evident after years of effort by many non-governmental organisations, as well as by government. Giving children the right to be educated is a very small step. It has to be followed up with specific enabling tools such as accessible and affordable schools, subsidised books and uniforms, transport and other specific assistance. Where governments have done this, as in Bihar for instances, there has been a marked increase in enrollment, especially girls".[5]

In the recent (2015) past the Union Cabinet has decided to allow child labour below the age of 14 to work in family enterprises and in audio-visual entertainment sector, including advertisement, films, and television serial etc. This move has diluted provisions under the Child Labour (Prohibition and Regulation) Act, 1986. It will be difficult for labour departments in the states to supervise and distinguish between children merely helping their parents or working to supplement their parents' income.

4.6 Seasonal Hostels for the Children of Dadan Families

In view of reports from the different quarters of the state, the Government of Odisha has taken step to look after the education of the children of dadan/migrant labour families in the districts of Bolangir, Balasore, Bargarh, Cuttack, Kalahandi, Mayurbhanj, Nuapada and Khurda. The Government has proposed to open seasonal hostels for such children to provide education during the migration period of their parents. For each child a sum of Rs 20,000 has been estimated for schooling, fooding and boarding. In this plan a total of 9960 children in the age group of 6-14 will be covered.

The above data (Table 4.2) clearly indicate the high rate of internal migration in the two districts of KBK i.e. Bolangir and Nuapada on the basis of which the number of children in the seasonal boarding schools have been determined. The expenditure on fooding and education will be borne by the school management committee. The scheme involves health check up and provision of medicine, blanket, mosquito net, bed sheet, soap, oil, talcum powder etc. It will function for a period of 6-9 months in the absence of the children's parents. It will prove to be worthy if the scheme operates fairly.

Table 4.2: Proposed Seasonal Hostels for Children of Migrant Families

Sl. No.	*Districts*	*Nos. of Children*
1.	Bolangir	5,000
2.	Balasore	50
3.	Bargarh	983
4.	Cuttack	250
5.	Kalahandi	500
6.	Khurdha	235
7.	Nuapada	2642
		Total = 9,660

Source: The Samaj, Odiya Daily, 7th October, 2014.

4.7 Bonded Labour and Internal Migration

Earlier bonded labour system was in the form of customary obligation, forced labour, beggar or debt-bondage under which a debtor agrees to render service and in different parts of the country it was name differently. In Odisha it was known as *gothi, kuthia, baramashia* etc. who were working in a traditional agricultural economy where the payments were made largely in kinds. These labourers were given a relationship tie with the members of the owners' families. Some sort of familial relation was maintained between the master and the worker to ease any type of bitter relation between them. A *Jajmani* system was also prevailing in the village economy. The serving castes like barber, washer-man, Brahmins ware serving their masters against the payment of annual wage in kinds. But with monetisation of the economy, spread of education and market economy the *Jajmani* system has vanished even in the remote rural life.

The Voice of Odisha, a NGO reports that about 40 to 60 thousand bonded labour from the districts of Bargarh, Bolangir, and Nuapada in western Odisha are working outside the state. It further states that about two lakhs of male and female along with their children are moving the southern states such as Andhra Pradesh, Tamil Nadu, Karnataka etc. about 46 per cent of bonded labour are below 14 years of age and 96 per cent of them do not get proper food and 22.5 per cent suffer from malnutrition. These children do not get education neither at their place of origin nor at their destinations. Around 85 per cent of these children work in brick factory. Girls of 14-18 years of age suffer from sexual harassment. This is a grim picture of migrant families working in other states.

The ISMW Act, 1979 can be supplemented by other Acts such as Minimum Wages Act, 1948, Bonded Labour System (Abolition) Act, 1976, Child Labour (Prohibition and Regulation) Act, 1986 and Equal Remuneration Act, 1976, for the betterment of the inter-state migrant workers. The prevailing dadan labour, in inter-state migration is a kind of debt bondage called *Lakti* give rise to a new form of bonded labour system in the country.

India ratified ILO Convention No. 29, Forced Labour Convention, 1930 on 30.11.1954; accordingly, the Bonded Labour System stand abolished throughout the country with effect from 25th October, 1975 with the enactment of Bonded Labour System (Abolition) Act 1976. It freed all the bonded labour from the bondage by simultaneously liquidating all the debts. Although, unilaterally the government declare the abolition of Bonded Labour System, still it prevails in other forms especially in the case of inter-state migrant workers who are going under dadan.

4.7.1 Who is a Bonded Labour?

A bonded labour arises out of loan/debt/advance or dadan. It represents a relationship between creditor and debtor, wherein the debtor undertakes to mortgage his services/s of his family members to the creditor for a specified or unspecified period with or without wages accompanied by a bar on the choice of any alternative avenues of employment or to deny him the freedom of movements. Under this definition of bonded labour the 'dadan' system of labour recruitment prevails in KBK districts for the inter-state migration of labour can easily be covered up.

4.7.2 Release and Rehabilitation of Bonded Labour

The numbers of ISMWs who have been rescued from time to time by the government officials forms the category of bonded labour with the certification from the appropriate authority in the working destinations.

Table 4.3: Bonded Labour Released and Rehabilitated in the KBK Districts

Sl. No.	*Districts*	*Year*	*No. of Bonded Labour Released*	*No. of Bonded Labour Rehabilitated*	*No. of labour yet to be released*	*Provision made for the rehabilitation*	*States/Area from which the bonded labour are released*
1	*2*	*3*	*4*	*5*	*6*	*7*	*8*
1.	Kalahandi	Up to 2014	57	03	54	Certificate of bonded labour and financial Assistance of Rs 20,000	NA
2.	Nuapada	2011, 2013, 2014	238	92	146	Work under MGNEGA, IAY/Mo Kudia	NA
3.	Bolangir	2011-12 to 2013-14	525	215	310	Financial Assistance Rs 20,000	Nellor, Tiruvallur, Bangalore, Ozil, Bhupalhipu, Tirupati, Pelakur
4.	Sonepur	2013-14	50	38	12	Financial Assistance Rs 20,000	Bangalore, Tiruvallur
5.	Koraput	2004-2012 2013-2014	Nil 107	60	47	47 labourers have not yet been identified	Andhra Pradesh, Uttar Pradesh
6.	Nabarangpur	2013-14	47	24	23	Financial Assistance Rs 20,000	Andhra Pradesh, Kerala, Tamil Nadu
7.	Rayagada	2008-09 to 2013-14	23	16	07	Financial Assistance Rs 20,000	Andhra Pradesh and Tamil Nadu, Chittor, Karimnagar
8.	Malkangiri	2004-05 to 2013-14	61	61	44	Rs 20,000 F.A.. A house under IYA or Mokudia, Job card, 2 bullocks and Agriculture inputs	Krishan District, Andhra Pradesh

Source:- Data from the DRDAs of KBK Districts through RTI and personal contact.

Table 4.3 shows the number of bonded labour of KBK districts released by the concerned departmental authorities from different places mainly from Andhra Pradesh, Karnataka, and Tamil Nadu and confirms the frequency of bonded labour in the country. Although there is complete prohibition to the practice of bonded labour in the country under the Abolition and Prevention of Bonded Labour Act, 1976, it is seen that large number of labourers from KBK districts are moving to other states to work as bonded labour. The bonded labour are working there under dadan or monetary advances paid to them. It is a debt bondage process through which they work through labour contractors.

The law is not being enforced in its true spirit to prevent bonded labour system. After receiving complaints, the appropriate authority at the destination takes action to release such bonded labour in cooperation with the officials of source districts. A released certificate of bonded labour is issued by the authority at the destination. After getting the certificate the Project Director, DRDA of concerned district tries to rehabilitate such labour as per the provision of the Act. Such labours are provided Rehabilitation Assistance to the tune of Rs 20,000 in general. In case of Malkangiri district, a house under Indira Aabas Yojana (IAY) or Mo Kudia Yojana has been provided, along with a job card to work under MGNREGA. In some cases a pair of bullock and agricultural inputs have been provided. The children of such bonded labourers are provided free schooling and boarding at ST/SC schools.

In the matter of bonded labour and their release, the Bolangir district tops the list with 525 bonded labour out of which 215 have already been provided rehabilitation assistance and the rest 310 will be provided shortly. Thus, the Bolangir district in the KBK region is prone not only to distress induced seasonal internal migration but also the system of bonded labour. It is a picture of two sides of the same coin. Where there is the prevalence of distress migration it is bound to be followed by the instances of bonded labour. In case of Nuapada district, data for 2011-14 shows that 238 bonded labour have been released and out of them 92 have so far been rehabilitated.

The data on release and rehabilitation of bonded labour in KBK districts clearly shows that the practice of bonded labour continues to exist in the form of debt cycle bondage which may be termed as neo-bonded labour system, in the expanded world of capitalism. This system is likely to perpetuate due to indirect promotion of the practice and least punishment to the violators. Capitalism begets inequality and in this process exploitation is supposed to exist. Bonded labour is one such form of exploitation which is seen in the twenty-first century India. The traditional way of workers engaged in agricultural sector by the farmers was somehow less exploitative than the so called modern working system of dadan. It exemplifies the system of exploitation of neo-capitalism under the guess of liberalisation. The redress mechanism has a tendency to provide protection to the employers of such bonded labour. As we are heading towards a more unequal society in the name of liberalisation and capitalistic model of development, the interest of labour is supposed to be trampling upon. The labourers of this category are not yet united to press for their right in right forum.

The process of release of such bonded labour starts on the approach of the bonded labour to the District Magistrate, who is the Chairman of Vigilance Committee, or Sub-Divisional Magistrate or any other person who is a member of the Vigilance Committee. Once they are rescued from such bond the bonded labour is provided with a certificate from the appropriate authority of the destination. After meeting all the official formalities a rehabilitation grant of Rs 20, 000 is provided to each of the bonded labour. This grant is shared by Centre and concerned State Government on 50:50 basis.

Recently, 75 children including 333 dadan labour have been rescued from Tiruvalla district, of Tamil Nadu, who were working in JDM Brick, an unregistered brick kiln. These labourers were from Paikmal, Gaisilate, Jharbandh areas of Bargarh district in Western Odisha. The district administration of Tiruvalla had issued 258 Bonded Labour released certificates.[7]

The Supreme Court of India, in its judgment of 15th October, 2012, relating to writ petition (Civil) No. 3922 of 1985, peoples union for Civil Liberty PUCL Vs. State of Tamil Nadu and Odisha observed that bonded labour is rampant in brick kilns, stone quarries, bidi manufacturing, carpet weaving, construction industries, agriculture in rural areas and urban unorganised and informal sectors, power looms, fish processing etc. Taking note of the previous orders passed by the Supreme Court, the Judges gave new instructions that fresh surveys of bonded labour should be conducted once in three years in all the States/ UTs and that the findings of these surveys should be made a part of a computerised data base and should be submitted to NHRC. District and Sub-Divisional Vigilance Committees were directed to give more attention to the sectors listed above and to take prompt action in case violation is noticed. The above observation made by the apex court proves the presence of bonded labourers who are working in the brick kilns. A joint study made by MiRC, Aide et Act and ILO, shows the out-migration from Bolangir, Nuapada and Kalahandi has increased from 12 per cent to eighty per cent between 2011-12. Further a study done by SOVA a NGO, in Koraput and Harmony (NGO) in Malkangiri reflects the trend of 82 per cent of increment during 2010 to 2012. 80 per cent of these people are migrating in distress situation.[8]

The rehabilitation of such released bonded labour is done by the Collector or the Project Director, District Rural Development Authority which comes under the state Panchayati Raj Department. During field visit, several respondents have shown their release certificates and expressed their dissatisfaction over the delay in the release of rehabilitation assistance.

The DLO at the destination issue a certificate to that effect and pays Rs 1,000 and rest Rs 19,000 is paid by the PD, DRDA of the source area. As per the recent guidelines all the migrants moving through the licenced agents will be treated as construction workers and the benefit of Odisha Construction Workers Rules, 2002 will be extended to them. With this extension, three purposes can be served.

(i) More inter-state migrant workers will move through the licenced contractors.

(ii) Registration of workers and a data base will be possible.

(iii) Financial benefits, insurance coverage and other benefits provided to construction workers can also be extended to them in an easier way. The state provides various assistances to the workers engaged in different construction and building works under the Building and Other Construction Workers (Regulation of Employment and Conditions of Services) Act, 1996 and Rules 2002. The detail of such provisions is presented in appendix II.

4.8 Conclusion

In a welfare state like India, provision for the protection of workers is an obligation of the state for adequate legal safeguards. Accordingly, the governments in pre-independent as well as post-independent periods have enacted several laws for the causes of labour in general and migrant labour in particular. As listed in the previous discussion, there are as many as 28 such laws to deal with labour issues. The ISWM Act, 1979 is a landmark in this regard. To supplement this Act, Minimum Wages Act 1948, the Bonded Labour (Abolition) Act 1976 and Child Labour (Prohibition & Regulation) Act, 1986 strengthen the rights of labour class in the country. In spite of large number of legal provisions, the conditions of inter-state migrant labour/dadan or child labour engaged in various hazardous and exploitative works do not seem to impressive. There are several cases of such exploitations which come to the notice of the civil society at regular intervals. The bonded labour system has been abolished but it is prevailing in another form or we may call neo-bonded labour system. So enactment of laws is not the solution of the problem rather a greater part of solution lies in its implementations.

References

1. Tadaro, M.P. (1976) *Internal Migration in Developing Countries: A Survey,* I.L.O,Geneva.
2. The OTV, News, 5th May. 2015.
3. Bhowmik, Shartak (2015). *Wages of Tea Plantation Workers,* Gap between North and South, Economic and Political Weekly, Vol. L. No. 19, May 9, p. 19-20.
4. MiRC (2011). *Children in Brick Kilns*. Aid et. Action p. 9.
5. Editorial (2015). *Let the Children Play,* Economic and Political Weekly April 18, Vol. L. No. 16, p. 8.
6. The Samaj Odiya Daily 13th April, 2015.
7. The Samaj Odiya Daily 13th Feb. 2015.
8. MiRC. *Debt Migrant Labour, Bondage and Rehabilitation.* Aid et. Action, p. 607.

Chapter - 5

Data Analysis and Testing of Hypotheses

5.1 Introduction

The present study of Internal Migration: from KBK Districts of Odisha is based on the primary data collected directly from the sample households of these districts. The field data have been collected on a multi-stage random sample technique. In the first stage, all the eight districts of KBK region are taken into account. In the second stage, blocks from each district has been selected by the method of random sampling. In the third stage, villages/hamlets from each block have been selected depending upon the number of migrants available by the method of simple random sampling. In the fourth stage, the numbers of households were selected from each village by the method simple random sampling that represents the sample, (as presented in Table 2). The respondents were interviewed through a scheduled questionnaire (Appendix-I) and the responses were recorded and presented in tabular forms in this chapter. The data so collected were analysised by SPSS16.0 and MS Excel software under window Xp environment.

On the macro studies of rural urban migration Samal, Meher and Mishra (2012) find that the work participation rate (WPR) in the urban areas of Odisha has declined from 37.52 per cent in 1961 to 29.67 per cent in 1991. It has declined at a higher percentage during 1961-71 but slackened thereafter. This shows that the slowdown in urbanisation is closely related to the decline in the work participation rate in urban Orissa. This decline in WPR may be due to either the "weak pull" or "weak push" or both.[1]

No doubt these observations hold good during the above stated decade of slow economic growth and certain level of uncertain political and economic conditions in the country. But with adoption of New Economic Policy, 1991 and consequent changes in the economic scenario of the country, migration both external and internal has assumed a significant role in the development of the country. The pace in the growth of urbanisation has been continuously rising and the participation of migrant workers particularly in construction sector has increased. It is an accepted fact that major construction projects, roads, buildings and agricultural activities cannot be undertaken properly without the participation of the migrant workers. The role of migrant workers cutting across different sectors and the overall development of economy cannot be ruled out.

Another observation made by Samal *et al* (2012) shows a decline share of the migrant workers in the total urbanisation force of Odisha may be due to implementation of various rural development programmes since early 1970s which might have improved the living condition in rural areas thereby reducing rural-urban migration. Due to these programmes including employment generation schemes, skill development, credit at a subsidised rate for self-employment and other income-generating programmes, in spite of its various leakages, there was dramatic decline in the incidence of rural poverty during 1972-1988 in India (Planning Commission: 1993). Rural migrants in Orissa, instead of coming to towns of Orissa, might be going to towns and cities outside Odisha such as Ahmedabad, Surat and Calcutta. (pp. 45-46).

The above study has relevance in relation to the rural-urban migration context pertaining to that period. But with the changing condition and the socio-economic characteristics of KBK region we find a different trend of internal migration of seasonal in nature arising out of distress, which may not be exactly rural-urban migration, rather a mix of rural urban migration of inter-state and intra-state in nature.

In spite of growing number of poor people oriented programme like, rice @Re 1, cooked food @ Rs 5, distribution of umbrella, blanket, and many other things the intensity of internal migration from KBK region has increased over the period of time. The *dole economic* policy adopted by the state has failed to check distressed migration from this region. With the changing socio-economic characteristics of KBK region we find a different trend of internal migration of seasonal in nature arising out of distress in search of livelihood in the neighbouring states or even to far distance states of India, which is migration of inter-state and intra-state in nature.

5.2 MGNREGA and Migration

In spite of a mammoth employment generation programme like MGNREGA, the seasonal internal-migration perpetuates in this region. There is a consistent increase in the state expenditure on MGNERGA since its inception in 2005-06. It is noticed that the number of internal migrants have also increased continuously over this period. To provide job to poor and agricultural labour the central government has started this programme and till September 2015 more than Rs 7,501 crore have been provided to the state as central assistance and the state government has provided Rs1,043 crore as state share to this programme. But it is a paradoxical situation that with the increase in the amount of expenditure the numbers of migrants from the state have increased. In the statistics of migrant labours only the registered labours and contractors have been taken into account. Whereas the unaccounted dadans who migrate through unregistered labour contractors are not accounted and if their number is added the actual figure will be much more. Thus, the operation of push and pull factors at source and destination respectively or in combination of both have worked together to create more of internal migrants in the KBK region.

Table 5.1 shows the data pertaining to state expenditure over a period of one decade and the number of migration shows that there is increasing tendency of migration in the region along with number of Man days Created (in Lakh) created through MGNREGA Programme.

From the figures (Figures 5.1 and 5. 2) it is quite clear that there is an increasing trend in migration from the state to other states continuously from 2005-06 to 2013-14. Figure 5.3 reveals an increasing expenditure under MGNREGA from Rs 347.17 crore in 2005-05 to Rs 1289.13 crore in 2013-14, a continuous increase in state expenditure under this programme. Therefore, it is felt worth to study the rate of

Table 5.1: State Expenditure on MGNREGA and Trend of Migration in the State

Sl. No.	*Year*	*Expenditure under MGNREGA (Rs in Crore)*	*No. of Man days Created (in Lakh)*	*No. of Migrants out of the state*
1.	2005-06	347.17	355.29	39,261
2.	2006-07	733.47	799.34	44,940
3.	2007-08	690.59	430.90	40,391
4.	2008-09	678.29	432.58	87,983
5.	2009-10	932.58	551.59	88,397
6.	2010-11	1530.35	975.59	1,02,127
7.	2011-12	1032.56	453.74	91,872
8.	2012-13	1177.68	546.01	1,08,132
9.	2013-14	1289.13	711.83	1,27,038
10.	2014-15 (Up to Sept. 2015)	707.56	307.19	1,35,713

Source:- The Samaj (Odiya Daily) 23 December, 2014, p. 4.

migration and the rate to total expenditure per year for the period 2005-06 to 2013-14. Figure 5.2 presents a linear trend fitted to the data for the migrants out of the state which shows a steep increasing trend with a slope of 10963, (R^2 =0.877) (R^2=Coefficient of multiple determination) with the regression equation Y=10963X+26313 (Y=year, X= No. of migrants). Thus, it can be inferred that there is an increase of 10,963 migrants out of state for each year. Figure 5.3

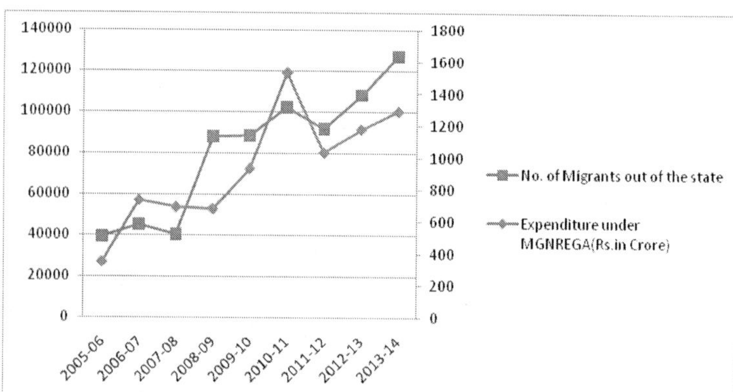

Figure 5.1: Trends of Migration and Expenditure (in Crores) under MGNREGA.

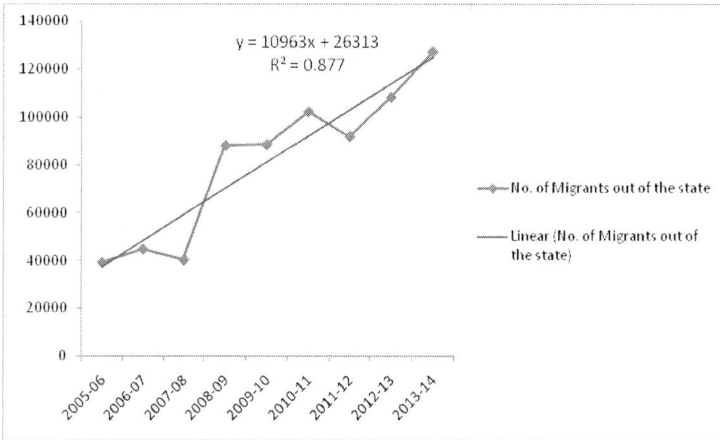

Figure 5.2: No. of Migrants out of the State.

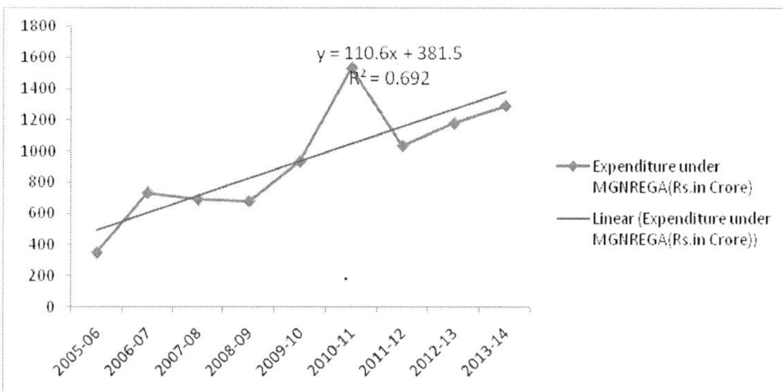

Figure 5.3: Trend of Expenditure under MGNREGA (Rs. in Crore) for the Period 2005-06 to 2013-14.

presents the trend line for the expenditure under MGNREGA for the period 2005-06 to 2013-14. The regression equation Y=110.6X+381.5 (R^2=0.692, Y=Year, X=Expenditure) shows that there is an increase in 110.6 crore per year for the above mentioned period. Figure 5.4 presents the trend of man days created in lakh for the above period i.e. 2005-06 to 2013-14. The regression equation Y=20.91X+479.5 (R^2=0.078) reflects that there has been an increase in the number of man days (X) created in lakh (20.91) per year for the period.

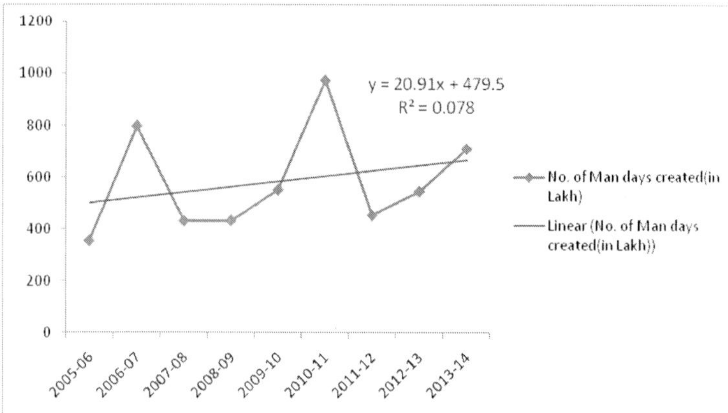

Figure 5.4: No. of Man Days Created (in Lakh)

5.3 Sample Design for the Study

Table 5.2: Sample Design for Internal Migration in KBK Districts

Districts							
1	*2*	*3*	*4*	*5*	*6*	*7*	*8*
Kalahandi	Nuapada	Bolangir	Sonepur	Koraput	Nabaran-gapur	Rayagada	Malkan-giri
Blocks							
Golamunda	Khariar	Belpada	Sonepur and Binka	Kundra and Bai-pariguda	Jharigaon	Muriguda and Bisamkatak	Mithali
No. of Sample Villages							
04	04	02	04	09	06	12	02
No. of Sample Households							
104	100	100	106	107	74	120	62

Total No. of Sample Households – 773.

Table 5.2 indicates sample design of the field study. A total of 773 sample households were selected for the collection of primary data from eight districts of KBK region. Depending on the availability of migrant households and size of village or hamlet and its location the number of villages/hamlets varies from district to district. A maximum of 12 hamlets/villages have been taken in case of Rayagada district and minimum of 02 villages have been covered in Bolangir and Malkangiri districts. These villages/hamlets come under different blocks of their respective districts as indicated in the table. All the blocks of undivided Koraput district come under TSP category, whereas blocks of other districts come under general category.

The official data do not fully capture the magnitude of migration particularly seasonal in nature, let alone its determinants, consequent results and policy implementation of the state. To assess the ground reality of internal migration of seasonal in nature, field study was conducted to collect data from different villages prone to the adoption of internal migration, with regard to their socio-economic conditions, income level and problem faced at sources and destinations. In view of their migrating time period and their scatterings habitation data have been collected by different groups of investigators during June-November, 2014.

5.4 Demographic Features of Sample Households

Table 5.3 and Figure 5.5 show the total number of sample households taken from the eight districts of KBK regions. It represents a total population of 3162, with 53.23 per cent of male and 46.77 per cent of female population. The total working population of all the sample households stands at 2333 persons, both male and female of 15 to 65 years of age and a total (829) 26.21 per cent constitute the children of 0-14 age group. The mean household size of all the districts is 4.09, and the household generally includes husband, wife and their 2-3 unmarried children. The percentage of female is highest (65.66 per cent) in case of Rayagada district and lowest in case of Malkangiri (30.22 per cent). The number of children participation is

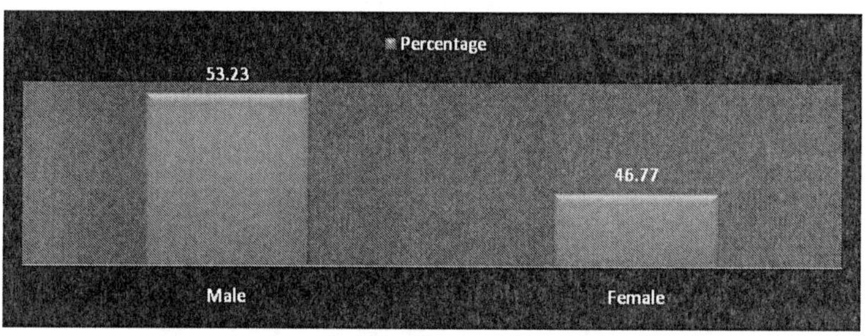

Figure: 5.5: Per cent Distribution of Male and Female (Total No. of Househods=773)

Table 5.3: Demographic Features of Sample Households

Sl. No.	Districts	Total No. of HH	No. of			Percentage		Working population (15 to 65 Yrs)	No. of Children (0 to 14 Yrs)	Mean Household Size
			Male	Female	Total	Male	Female			
1	Kalahandi	104	196	168	364	53.85	46.15	254(69.78)	110	3.50
2	Nuapada	100	200	222	422	54.95	60.99	290(68.72)	132	4.22
3	Bolangir	100	217	229	446	59.62	62.91	277(62.11)	169	4.46
4	Sonepur	106	243	202	445	66.76	55.49	362(81.35)	83	4.20
5	Koraput	107	225	178	403	61.81	48.90	305(75.68)	98	3.77
6	Nabarangpur	74	161	131	292	44.23	35.99	224(76.71)	68	3.95
7	Raygada	120	299	239	538	55.58	44.42	427(79.37)	111	4.48
8	Malkangiri	62	142	110	252	39.01	30.22	194(76.98)	58	4.06
	Total	**773**	**1683**	**1479**	**3162**	**53.23**	**46.77**	**2333(73.78)**	**829(26.21)**	**4.09**

highest (169) in case of Bolangir followed by Nuapada (132) district. The male-female composition of all sample households of all the districts represents more or less a balanced one.

5.5 Social (Caste) and Religious Affiliation of Sample Households

Table 5.4 and Figures 5. 6.1 and 5.6.2 indicate the social caste break up and religious affiliation of the sample households of all the eight districts. All the castes in the society have been broadly put into four categories namely, schedule caste (SC), schedule tribe (ST), other backward caste (OBC) and general caste (Gen). The people of general caste are at the top of the social structure followed by OBC,

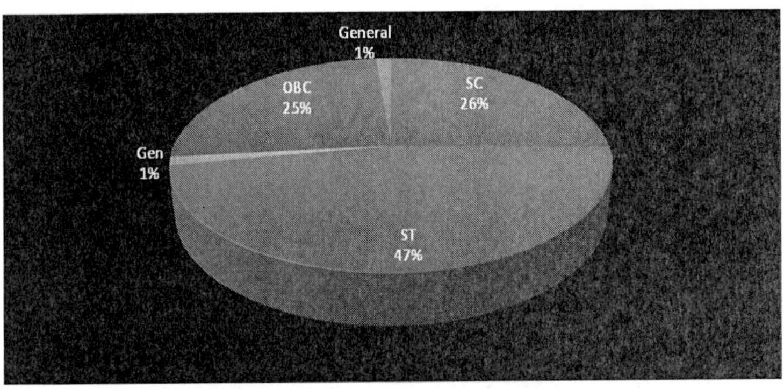

Figure 5.6.1: Social Caste of Sample Household.

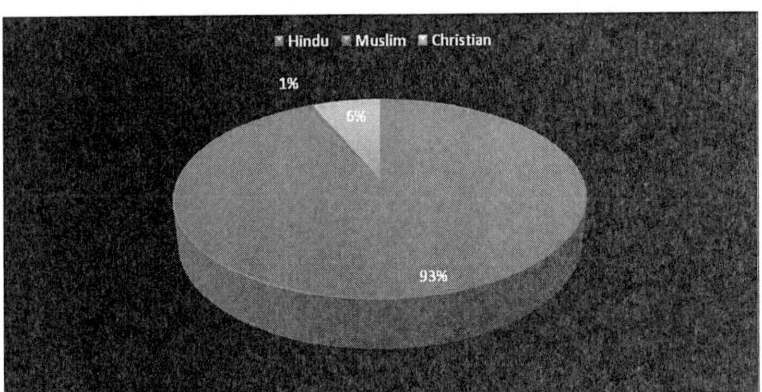

Figure 5.6.2: Religious Affiliation of Sample HH.

Table 5.4: Social (Caste) and Religious Affiliation of Sample Households

Sl. No.	*Districts*	*Total No. of Households*	*No. of HH and Percentage*				*Religious Affiliation*		
			SC	*ST*	*OBC*	*Gen*	*Per cent of Hindu*	*Per cent of Muslim*	*Per cent of Christian*
1	Kalahandi	104	43 (41.35)	15 (14.42)	44 (42.31)	2 (1.92)	103 (99.04)	0	1 (0.96)
2	Nuapada	100	16 (16.00)	69 (69.00)	15 (15.00)	0 (0.00)	100 (100.00)	0	0
3	Bolangir	100	36 (36.00)	26 (26.00)	38 (38.00)	0 (0.00)	100 (100.00)	0	0
4	Sonepur	106	58 (54.72)	8 (7.55)	40 (37.74)	0 (0.00)	106 (100.00)	0	0
5	Koraput	107	11 (10.28)	78 (72.90)	13 (12.15)	5 (4.67)	90 (84.11)	0	17 (15.89)
6	Nabarangpur	74	10 (13.51)	45 (60.81)	19 (25.68)	0 (0.00)	60 (81.08)	5 (6.76)	9 (12.16)
7	Raygada	120	14 (11.67)	102 (85.00)	4 (3.33)	0 (0.00)	110 (91.67)	0	10 (8.33)
8	Malkangiri	62	11 (17.74)	24 (38.71)	24 (38.71)	3 (4.84)	50 (80.65)	0	12 (19.35)
	Total	**773**	**199 (25.74)**	**367 (47.48)**	**197 (25.49)**	**10 (1.29)**	**719 (93.01)**	**5 (0.65)**	**49 (6.34)**

Source: Field Survey, 2014.

ST and SC. Taking all the districts; SC population represents 25.74 per cent. It is highest in case of Sonepur district (54.72 per cent) and lowest in case of Koraput district (10.28 per cent). The ST population constitutes 47.48 per cent in the KBK region as a whole. It is highest in case of Rayagada district (85 per cent) followed by Koraput with (72.90 per cent) and it is lowest in case of Sonepur district with 7.55 per cent only and Kalahandi with 14.42 per cent. The OBC as a whole constitute 25.49 per cent among the sample households. It is highest in case of Kalahandi with 42.31 per cent and lowest in Rayagada district with only 3.33 per cent. On the other hand the participation of general caste in the process of seasonal migration of is only 1.29 per cent. The table indicates that the participation of SC and ST population in internal migration is significantly higher and is followed by OBC class.

So far as religious affiliations are concerned, a majority of 93.01 per cent then are Hindu. Christians constitute 6.34 per cent and Muslims constitute only 0.65 per cent of the migrant population. There is the presence of Christian population in the undivided Koraput district of KBK. Except Nabarangpur district, the sample does not indicate the presence of Muslim migrants.

5.6 Educational Status of Migrants

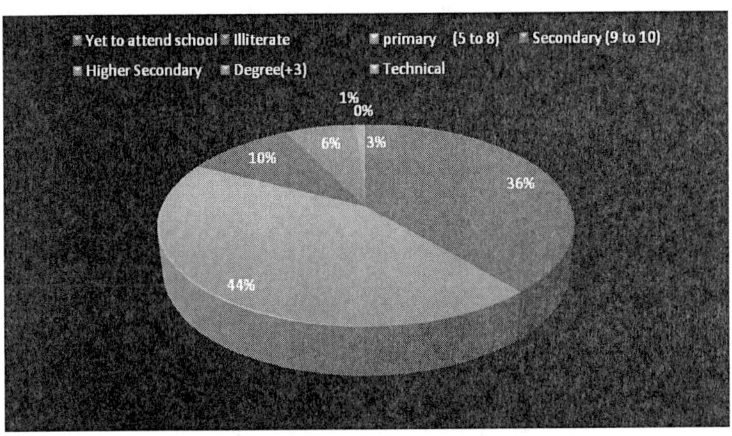

Figure 5.5.2: Educational Status of Female Migrants (in per cent).

Table 5.5.1: Educational Status of Male Migrants

Sl. No.	*Districts*	*Total No. of HH*	*Total Male*	*Yet to attend school*	*Illiterate*	*Primary (5 to 8)*	*Secondary (9 to 10)*	*Higher Secondary*	*Degree (+3)*	*Technical*
1.	Kalahandi	104	196	6(3.06)	68(34.69)	85(43.37)	6(3.06)	27(13.78)	4(2.04)	0
2.	Nuapada	100	200	16(8.00)	79(39.50)	74(37.00)	15(7.50)	16(8.00)	0	0
3.	Bolangir	100	217	5(2.30)	80(36.87)	127(58.53)	3(1.38)	2(0.92)	0	0
4.	Sonepur	106	243	6(2.47)	38(15.64)	105(43.21)	57(23.46)	33(13.58)	2(0.82)	2(0.82)
5.	Koraput	107	225	4(1.78)	91(40.44)	110(48.89)	16(7.11)	4(1.78)	0	0
6.	Nabarangpur	74	161	4(2.48)	62(38.51)	59(36.65)	26(16.15)	10(6.21)	0	0
7.	Raygada	120	299	5(1.67)	121(40.47)	122(40.80)	34(11.37)	12(4.01)	5(1.67)	0
8.	Malkangiri	62	142	5(3.52)	63(44.37)	55(38.73)	11(7.75)	6(4.23)	2(1.41)	0
	Total	**773**	**1683**	**51(3.03)**	**602(35.77)**	**737(43.79)**	**168(9.98)**	**110(6.54)**	**13(0.77)**	**2(0.12)**

Table 5.5.2: Educational Status of Female Migrants

Sl. No.	*Districts*	*Total No. of HH*	*Total Female*	*Yet to attend school*	*Illiterate*	*Primary (5 to 8)*	*Secondary (9 to 10)*	*Higher Secondary*	*Degree*	*Technical*
1.	Kalahandi	104	168	5(2.98)	78(46.43)	73(43.45)	6(3.57)	6(3.57)	0	0
2.	Nuapada	100	222	16(7.21)	116(52.25)	74(33.33)	9(4.05)	6(2.70)	0	1(0.45)
3.	Bolangir	100	229	5(2.18)	115(50.22)	106(46.29)	2(0.87)	1(0.44)	0	0
4.	Sonepur	106	202	8(3.96)	61(30.20)	92(45.54)	21(10.40)	19(9.41)	1(0.50)	0
5.	Koraput	107	178	5(2.81)	117(65.73)	46(25.84)	10(5.62)	0	0	0
6.	Nabarangpur	74	131	8(6.11)	80(61.07)	30(22.90)	9(6.87)	4(3.05)	0	0
7.	Raygada	120	239	2(0.84)	157(65.69)	59(24.69)	12(5.02)	4(1.67)	4(1.67)	1(0.42)
8.	Malkangiri	62	110	4(3.64)	77(70.00)	25(22.73)	2(1.82)	2(1.82)	0	0
	Total	**773**	**1479**	**53(3.58)**	**801(54.16)**	**505(34.14)**	**71(4.80)**	**42(2.84)**	**5(0.34)**	**2(0.14)**

Source: Field Survey, 2014.

Table 5.5.1 and Figure 5.7 show the educational status of male migrants of sample households. The migrants as a whole of the region show illiteracy of 35.77 per cent and primary education up to class VIII of 43.79 per cent. There is also presence of migrants with education of higher secondary (6.54 per cent), degree (0.77 per cent) and technical education of (0.12) per cent. The highest percentage of illiteracy among the migrants is seen in case of Malkangiri (44.37) followed by Koraput 40.44 per cent. The migrants from Bolangir districts have highest percentage (58.53) of primary education. The educational status of these migrants from KBK region shows that majority of them are either illiterate or only having primary education. The migrants with higher education and some sorts of technical education are of insignificant proportion among the male migrant population. Thus, the overall education of male migrants from KBK region constitutes a very low level of education.

The Table 5.5.2 and Figure 5.8 show the educational status of female migrants of sample households taking the female migrants as a whole the level of illiteracy is higher (54.16 per cent) than their male counterparts. The level of illiteracy among female is highest in Malkangiri with 70 per cent and lowest in Sonepur district with 30.20 per cent. The female population as a whole has received primary education to the extent of 34.14 per cent. The level of female education relating to higher secondary, degree or technical education

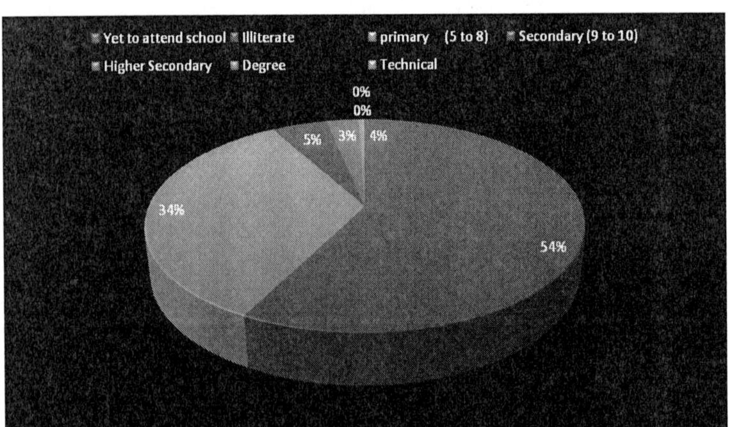

Figure 5.8: Educational Status of Female Migrants (in Per cent).

is very insignificant and it is less than the male migrants. Taking together both the male and female sample population on education count, it can be stated that the level of education is low among the migrants adopting internal seasonal migration. In view of their low level of education they are generally employed in such jobs which need physical strength. Their jobs generally do not need any specific institutional training and educational degree or standard.

5.7 Landholding of Migrants Households

Table 5.6 and Figure 5.9 show the land holding status of the migrant workers in the KBK region. For land holding position the migrants have been divided into landless agricultural labour, marginal farmers (0-1.99 Ac) small farmers (02-4.99 Ac) medium farmers (05-9.99 Ac) and large farmers (10 Ac and above). Some of them lease out their land to other farmers, some others cultivate land of other farmers on lease basis. The other categories reflect cultivation of forest/ government land without any title over such land. In western Odisha, the landless category is called *Sukh Basi* meaning happy resident, because they do not possess any obligation of land or cows and buffalos and they have nothing to lose in the event of damage in the agricultural production process. Whatever they earn, they are happy with that. With the changing socio-economic and political situation, the concept of *Sukh Basi* has lost its ground reality. The data shows that in the KBK region 94 per cent of migrants belong to landless, marginal and small farmer category. Among the migrants, the landless constitute 38 per cent, marginal farmers 35 per cent, and small farmer 21 per cent. These people cannot take agriculture as the sole source of livelihood for the entire year. The percentage of landlessness is as high as 68.87 per cent in Sonepur district and lowest in Nabarangpur district (15.57 per cent). In view of landlessness or small quantity of land in their possession and having no alternative employment opportunity, they have been forced to adopt migration, during lean agricultural season. The irregular nature of job accompanied by low wage in the local area they are unable to meet their needs properly. The participation of medium farmer and large farmer in inter-state migration is of insignificant proportion (less than two per cent). They might have adopted casually due to failure of crop or some extraordinary social or family situation.

Table 5.6: Status of Landholding of Migrant Households

Sl. No.	Districts	Total	No. of Households								Area in Acre		
		No. of HH	Landless	0 to 1.99 Marginal farmer	02 to 4.99 Small farmer	05 to 9.99 Medium farmer	10 & Above Large farmer	Leased Out	Leased in	Other-wise possessed	Average Irrigated	Average Non-Irrigated holding	Average land holding
1.	Kalahandi												
	SC	43	30(69.77)	12(27.90)	1(2.33)	0	0	0	1	0	0	0.27	0.27
	ST	15	4(26.67)	10(66.67)	0	1(6.66)	0	0	1	14	0	1.05	1.05
	OBC	44	16(36.36)	25(56.82)	3(6.82)	0	0	0	2	0	0	0.69	0.69
	GEN	2	1(50.00)	1(50.00)	0	0	0	0	2	2	0	0.5	0.50
	TOTAL	104	51(49.04)	48(46.15)	4(3.85)	1(0.96)	0	0	6	16	0	0.56	0.56
2.	Nuapada												
	SC	16	12(75.00)	2(12.50)	2(12.50)	0	0	0	0	0	0	0.41	0.41
	ST	69	22(31.88)	38(55.08)	9(13.04)	0	0	0	0	1	0.01	0.77	0.78
	OBC	15	12(80.00)	3(20.00)	0	0	0	0	0	0	0	0.23	0.23
	GEN							0					
	TOTAL	100	46(46.00)	43(43.00)	11(11.00)	0	0	0	0	1	0.01	0.63	0.64
3.	Bolangir												
	SC	36	11(30.56)	23(63.89)	2(5.55)	0	0	0	1	1	0.00	23.50	0.65
	ST	26	3(11.54)	17(65.39)	6(23.07)	0	0	0	2	0	0.19	1.01	1.21
	OBC	38	20(52.64)	14(36.84)	3(7.89)	1(2.63)	0	0	1	0	0.00	0.68	0.68
	GEN	0						0					
	TOTAL	100	34(34.00)	54(54.00)	11(11.00)	1(1.00)	0	0	4	1	0.05	0.76	0.81
4.	Sonepur												
	SC	58	50(86.21)	6(10.34)	2(3.45)	0	0	0	0	0	0.05	0.10	0.16
	ST	8	6(75.00)	2(25.00)	0	0	0	0	0	0	0.00	0.13	0.13
	OBC	40	17(42.50)	22(55.00)	1(2.50)	0	0	0	0	0	0.00	0.48	0.48
	GEN							0					
	TOTAL	106	73(68.87)	30(28.30)	3(2.83)	0	0	0	0	0	0.03	0.25	0.28

(Contd...)

5.	Koraput												
	SC	11	3(27.27)	3(27.27)	3(27.27)	2(18.19)	0	0	1	0	0.00	2.09	2.09
	ST	78	18(23.07)	31(39.75)	26(33.33)	3(3.85)	0	0	1	0	0.13	1.60	1.73
	OBC	13	7(53.85)	4(30.77)	1(7.69)	1(7.69)	0	0	12	0	0.00	1.50	1.50
	GEN	5	1(20.00)	0	4(80.00)	0	0	0	2	0	1.00	1.40	2.40
	TOTAL	107	29(27.10)	38(35.51)	34(31.78)	6(5.61)	0	0	16	0	0.14	1.63	1.77
6.	Nabarangpur												
	SC	10	2(20.00)	2(20.00)	5(50.00)	1(10.00)	0	0	0	0	0.41	2.09	2.50
	ST	45	9(20.00)	6(13.34)	18(40.00)	11(24.44)	1(2.22)	0	10	7	0.46	3.30	3.76
	OBC	19	2(10.53)	3(15.79)	9(47.37)	3(15.78)	2(10.53)	0	4	4	0.08	5.08	5.16
	GEN	0						0					
	TOTAL	74	13(17.57)	11(14.86)	32(43.24)	15(20.28)	3(4.05)	0	14	11	0.35	3.59	3.95
7.	Raygada												
	SC	14	5(35.72)	2(14.29)	5(35.71)	2(14.28)	0	0	4	5	1.50	1.50	3.00
	ST	102	24(23.53)	11(10.78)	49(48.04)	15(14.71)	3(2.94)	0	31	46	1.82	2.54	4.36
	OBC	4	1(25.00)	1(25.00)	2(50.00)	0	0	0	2	4	4.63	5.63	10.25
	GEN	0						0					
	TOTAL	120	30(25.00)	14(11.66)	56(46.67)	17(14.17)	3(2.5)	0	37	55	1.87	2.52	4.40
8.	Malkangiri	62											
	SC	11	4(36.36)	5(45.45)	2(18.19)	0	0	0	1	0	0.00	0.72	0.72
	ST	24	9(37.50)	8(33.34)	6(25.00)	1(4.16)	0	0	0	0	0.00	1.30	1.30
	OBC	24	3(12.50)	17(70.84)	4(16.66)	0	0	0	2	1	0.00	1.13	1.13
	GEN	3	0	0	3(100.00)	0	0	0	0	0	0.67	2.33	3.00
	TOTAL	62	16(25.81)	30(48.39)	15(24.19)	1(1.61)	0	0	3	1	0.03	1.18	1.21

Source: Field Survey, 2014.

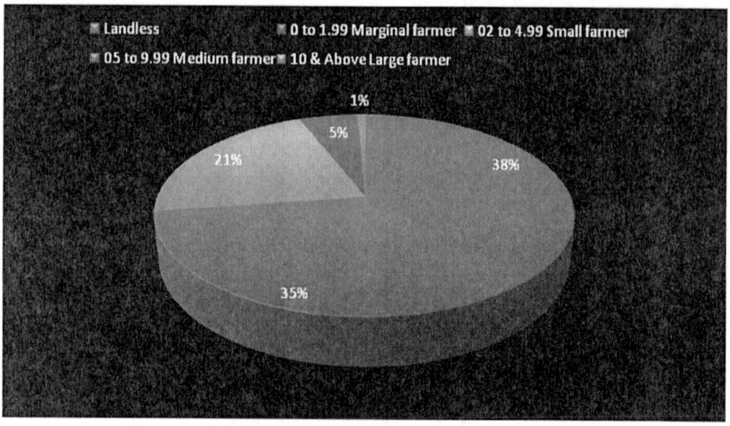

Figure 5.9: Land Holding Status of Migrants.

Further it is noticed from the table that SC and ST people are more of landless in nature than the OBC and general caste categories in the entire KBK region. The average land holding among the sample household ranges from 0.28 Ac in Sonepur to 4.40 Ac in Rayagada district. The average irrigated land area is less than half acre in all districts except Rayagada where it is only 1.87 acre. The non-irrigated area dominates the land holding characteristics of the migrants. None of the sample migrant household lease out their land to others, which shows that they continue to cultivate their land whatever they possess. It is also seen that a few migrants household in all the districts have leased in land from other farmers for cultivation. Thus, the land ownership structure of the migrants clearly demonstrates a picture of landlessness or insignificant amount of land holding, which fails to provide a livelihood support to their family. As a result they have to adopt a distress induced seasonal migration as a means of livelihood strategy. Increased landlessness, decline profitability, repulsive attitude towards agricultural activities and easy availability of lump sum cash advance lure people of this region to migrate. The young migrants usually adopt migration to different industrial and construction sectors to fulfill their modern needs like mobile phone, television, clothing, visiting different places etc. which may not be available to them in their locality. The migrant labours also find it easy to work in inferior category of jobs in an unknown place than in their own locality.

This is also a reason which promote people to migrate to a distance destination.

5.8 Living Conditions of Migrants at Source

Table 5.7 and Figure 5.10 indicate the housing condition of migrants at their place of origin. The migrants as a whole in the region have a very high percentage (74.64) of kacha houses which are made of mud/brick with a roof of straw or country tile or tin or asbestos. These houses usually have only 1-2 rooms for their living, kitchen and other purposes. Migrants from Koraput have highest number of kacha houses (95.33 per cent) followed by Sonepur with 93.40 per cent. It is found that 13.46 per cent of migrants in Kalahandi district do not have their own house. The percentage of semi-pucca and pucca houses, which are considered to be better than kucha houses are 18.24 and 5.30 per cent respectively for the region as a whole. A semi-pucca house is one which has cement flooring or a partially cement and brick constructed. On the other hand a pucca house is made of baked bricks with cement flooring either with country tile or asbestos sheet roof or cement concrete roof. The highest percentage of semi-pucca houses are seen in case of migrants from Kalahandi (55.77 per cent) whereas it is lowest in case of Koraput (2.80). In case of migrants from Bolangir have highest percentage (10.00 per cent) pucca houses, whereas in case of Koraput it is lowest 1.87 per cent. The housing condition of migrants do not represent a good dwelling condition in general. These houses are of simple living rooms without any gadget. As far as access to electricity is concerned, 60 per cent of the migrants as a whole have electricity. Migrants from Bolangir have 70 per cent access to electricity. The percentage of access to electricity is due to rural electrification programme like Rajiv Jyoti Yojana. So far as the provision of latrine/toilet is concerned only 3.10 per cent of sample households have such provision, which clearly indicates that almost all the migrants adopt open defecation, a source of environmental pollution. Regarding drinking water the migrants usually have access to three water sources namely, open well/pond, tube well and other sources such as stream, pipe water supply etc. They have the access to pond and nearby rivers/streams for other uses and drinking water as well. For drinking water, taking the region as a whole 27 per cent use the traditional sources like open well, pond, river/stream, 60 per cent

Table 5.7: Housing Condition and Other Basic Amenities of the Migrant Households at Source

Sl. No.	*Districts*	*Total No. of HH*	*Type of Dwelling House*						*Sources of Drinking water*		
			Kacha	*Semi-Pucca*	*Pucca*	*No. own House*	*Electricity*	*Latrine/ Toilet*	*Open well/pond*	*Tube well*	*Other Sources*
1.	Kalahandi	104	27(25.96)	58(55.77)	5(4.81)	14(13.46)	70(67.31)	3(2.88)	25(24.04)	70()67.31)	9(8.65)
2.	Nuapada	100	77(77.00)	17(17.00)	6(6.00)	0	55(55.00)	3(3.00)	24(24.00)	66(66.00)	10(10.00)
3.	Bolangir	100	71(71.00)	19(19.00)	10(10.00)	0	70(70.00)	3(3.00)	20(20.00)	30(30.00)	50(50.00)
4.	Sonepur	106	99(93.40)	3(2.83)	4(3.77)	0	68(64.15)	4(3.77)	15(14.15)	81(76.42)	10(9.43)
5.	Koraput	107	102(95.33)	3(2.80)	2(1.87)	0	56(52.34)	3(2.8)	40(37.38)	67(62.62)	0
6.	Nabarangpur	74	59(79.73)	11(14.86)	4(5.41)	0	36(48.65)	2(2.70)	30(40.54)	39(52.70)	5(6.76)
7.	Raygada	120	99(82.50)	13(10.83)	8(6.67)	0	72(60.00)	4(3.33)	35(29.17)	73(60.83)	12(10)
8.	Malkangiri	62	43(69.35)	17(27.42)	2(3.23)	0	35(56.45)	2(3.23)	20(32.26)	42(67.74)	0
	Total	**773**	**577(74.64)**	**141(18.24)**	**41(5.30)**	**14(1.81)**	**462(59.77)**	**24(3.10)**	**209(27.04)**	**468(60.54)**	**96(12.42)**

Source: Field Survey, 2014.

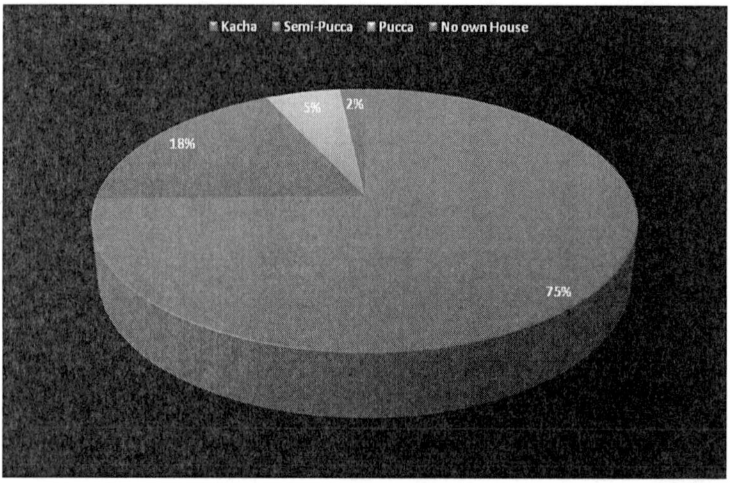

Figure 5.10: Housing Condition of Migrants at Source (in Per cent).

use tube well water and only 12 per cent of them use other sources. During field study, it has come to the notice that a few villages of Kalahandi and Nuapada districts are suffering from a disease like fluorosis due to intake of tube well water which contains high rate of fluorite (more than 3-5 p.p.m). In this disease the affected person suffer from mottling of teeth. This problem should be addressed with the provision of alternative sources of drinking water having least fluorite contain or provision for the treated water. No individual household has his personal water supply provision. The left behind family members of the migrants face difficulties of water during summer. The water table goes down; tube well fails to provide water, ponds and wells also dried up. There is no provision of irrigation facilities in these areas. The living condition of the migrants in the villages is simple and lacks proper sanitary conditions. The unhygienic living condition give birth to number of diseases for which there is an urgent need to implement the programme of Swachha Bharat Abhijan in a more vigorous manner in the rural areas to stop open defecation and environmental pollution and provision of clean drinking water.

5.9 Reasons for Migration

Table 5.8 and Figure 5.11 show different reasons behind migration of people in the KBK region. The general reasons attributed for migration are unemployment, higher wage at destination, in search of regular employment, to overcome debt bondage; lump sum cash advance (dadan), natural calamities and social obligation. Among all these reasons, unemployment and higher wage constitute major reasons for their migration. The respondents of Nuapada and Sonepur have attributed unemployment (33 per cent and 36.79 per cent respectively) as the major reason. Lump sum cash advance constitute as a prominent reason for migrants from Kalahandi, Nuapada, Bolangir and Sonepur

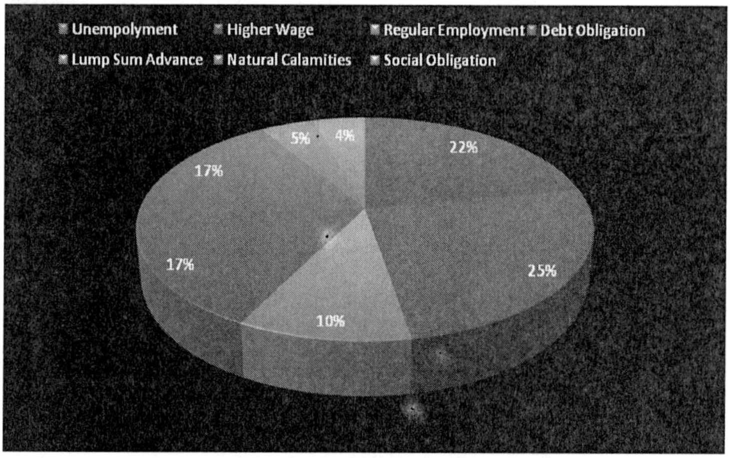

Figure 5.11: Reason for Migration (in Per cent).

districts. The owners of southern states put huge amount advance through agents to capture the migrant labour in comparison to the owners of the locality or other parts of the state. But it has less significance in the undivided districts of Koraput. The reasons for this may be attributed to the fact that migrants of these districts are largely going to work in brick kilns, whereas the workers from undivided Koraput are generally engaged in construction sector. This is an important difference in the reason of migration within the KBK region. The migrant of the region as a whole attribute 22 per cent to unemployment, 25 per cent to higher wage and 17 per cent to lump sum cash advance as major factors for migration. So also the debt cycle occupies nearly 17 per cent as a reason for migration. On the other hand the migrant have attributed least importance to the

Table 5.8: Reasons for Migration

Sl. No.	*District*	*No. of HH*	*Unemploy-ment*	*Higher Wage at Destination*	*Regular Employment*	*Debt Bondage/Cycle*	*Lump sum Advance*	*Natural Calamities*	*Social Obligation*
1.	Kalahandi	104	31(29.81)	7(6.73)	14(13.46)	20(19.23)	27(25.96)	0	5(4.81)
2.	Nuapada	100	33(33.00)	6(6.00)	4(4.00)	18(18.00)	20(20.00)	15(15.00)	4(4.00)
3.	Bolangir	100	18(18.00)	11(11.00)	29(29.00)	21(21.00)	10(10.00)	5(5.00)	6(6.00)
4.	Sonepur	106	39(36.79)	19(17.92)	0	17(16.04)	20(18.87)	8(7.55)	3(2.83)
5.	Koraput	107	29(27.10)	40(37.38)	7(6.54)	12(11.21)	14(13.08)	3(2.80)	2(1.87)
6.	Nabarangpur	74	5(6.76)	24(32.43)	20(27.03)	15(20.27)	8(10.81)	0	2(2.70)
7.	Raygada	120	11(9.17)	46(38.33)	5(4.17)	20(16.67)	28(23.33)	0	10(8.33)
8.	Malkangiri	62	4(6.45)	42(67.74)	1(1.61)	5(8.06)	4(6.45)	4(6.45)	2(3.23)
	Total	**773**	**170(21.99)**	**195(25.23)**	**80(10.35)**	**128(16.56)**	**131(16.95)**	**35(4.53)**	**34(4.40)**

Source: Field Survey, 2014.

factor like natural calamities (4.53 per cent) and social obligation (4.40 per cent) as reason for migration. They are forced to adopt migration for unemployment and livelihood, which may be stated as distress induced factors contributing towards internal migration.

5.10 Motivation for Migration

Table 5.9: Means of Motivation for Migration

Sl. No.	*District*	*No. of HH*	*Sources of Information*			
			Friends	*Relatives*	*Neighbour*	*Agents*
1	Kalahandi	104	19(18.27)	21(20.19)	12(11.54)	52(50.00)
2	Nuapada	100	0	23(23.00)	5(5.00)	72(72.00)
3	Bolangir	100	0	2(2.00)	0	98 (98.00)
4	Sonepur	106	20(18.87)	22(20.75)	10(9.43)	54(50.94)
5	Koraput	107	49(45.79)	12(11.21)	2(1.87)	44(41.12)
6	Nabarangpur	74	17(22.97)	13(17.57)	6(8.11)	38(51.35)
7	Raygada	120	35(29.17)	24(20.00)	27(22.50)	34(28.33)
8	Malkangiri	62	19(30.65)	9(14.52)	4(6.45)	30(48.39)
	Total	**773**	**159(20.57)**	**126(16.30)**	**66(8.54)**	**22(54.59)**

Source: Field Survey, 2014.

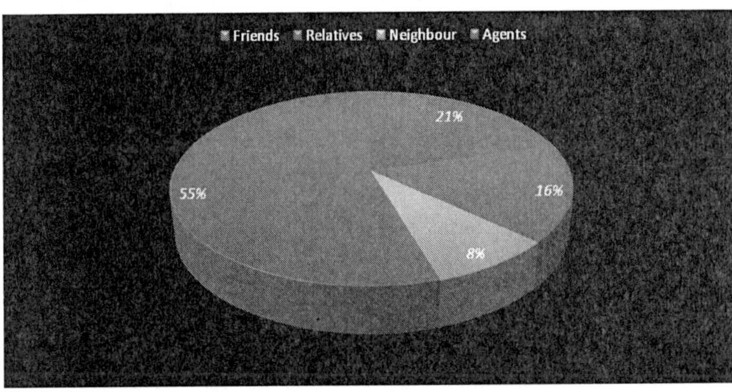

Figure 5.12: Means of Motivation for Migration (in Per cent).

Table 5.9 and Figure 5.12 show the driving forces behind the motivation for migration. The motivation for migration takes place by friends, relatives and neighbours who have migrated earlier. Their role may either be persuasive or in connivance with the agents. The region as a whole, friends, relatives and neighbour has an influence on migration to the extent of 20.57, 16.30 and 8.54 per cent respectively whereas 54.59 per cent of migration takes place through labour contractors/agents/dalal/sardar. The role of such labour agent/sardar is highly prominent in two districts namely, Bolangir (98 per cent) and Nuapada (72 per cent). These two districts are prone to high degree of distress seasonal migration, and the migrants usually move to work in brick kilns, through agents/sardars. These agents play a vital link between the brick kiln owners and the migrant labours.

These agents/sardars system has been recognised in the inter-state migration play dominant role to recruit labour for the brick kilns located mainly in the southern states of India. The agents may either be registered or unregistered one. It has come to the notice that the migrants have a little knowledge about the registration of the dalal and their own. That is why the unregistered dalals come to the picture in a big way for recruitment of migrant labour. The function of registered or unregistered dalal is more or less the same. The difference is that the registered labour agents/contractors use to follow a few rules of ISMW Act, 1979 like registration of migrants and record of the working place and destination. The recognition of dalals in the labour recruitment system has somehow recognised the exploitation of labour right from the payment of cash advance till their return to the place of origin. The dalals or agents adopt various means to capture the labour pool for their dispatch to different brick kilns, particularly located in the states of Andhra Pradesh, Telengana, Tamil Nadu, Maharashtra, Karnataka, Gujarat etc. The migrant labourers of Nuapada, Bolangir, Kalahandi, Sonepur generally specialise in the making of bricks. A family of three to four members generally forms a group called "pathuria" and work on piece wage basis, i.e. per 1000 of bricks, they are paid a fixed amount of Rs 800-1000. Although the piece wage for per 1000 brick making within the state varies between Rs 600 to 800, it is the lump sum cash advance which pulls these migrant labours to work in other states. The demand for these migrant labours is high in these states because they work at a lower wage than the local labour. They do not have the bargaining strength due to absence of labour organisation. In the recent past it has come to the notice that a few student volunteers and NGO have come forward to organise these migrant workers in a platform to show their solidarity in Andhra Pradesh. But the result of such organisation is yet to come. The problem of language pushes them to a disadvantageous position, which becomes advantage for the employers and agents. While recruiting the labour, the labour agent/ dalal pays a lump sum of Rs 60, 000 to Rs 80,000 as advance or dadan to a pathuria family. The amount may vary from family to family and agent to agent, depending upon the number of adult working members and dealing of the agent. The children of such pathuria family assist during the process of brick making but they remain out of the pay rolls of the employers. The more bricks, they make the more will be their earning. These migrant workers move to different states through these agents on the payment of railway fare of general compartment and fooding only. No wage compensation is made for their journey period. The agents may visit once or twice to the place of work to know about the state of migrant workers and to receive commission from the owners. If any difficulty arises in between owner and workers, the agents usually do not come to the picture. There are incidences of exploitation and tortures by the brick kiln owners at different points of time. To overcome such problems, the administration, labour department, come to rescue them and bring back to their place of origin. During our visit to different brick kilns it is noticed that the migrant workers were ignorant of their exact rate of making bricks. They told that at the end of the work they are paid the rest amount after deduction of advance and weekly maintenance amount. Some family get surplus some may become *lakti* that is they become debtor. Of course the owners do not insist to repay it immediately and it becomes a gone case for repayment. This is also a reason for which the migrants move to these states for work. Those who fail to obey the order of the owners and agents are bound to face torture and harassment. Several cases of harassment and torture have come to the light through media. In 2014, the agents chopped of the palms of two migrant labour from Kalahandi is the burning example of torture of migrant labour in the hands of agent and owner. It is also reported that the agent or owner resort to such act of atrocity against the migrants, when they fail to work or run away with advance amount. The cases of sexual harassment have also been reported by a few migrant. Of course such cases do not become public due to fear from society and owner.

5.11 Destination of Migrants

Table 5.10 shows the destination of migrant households to different states and different district/towns within the state. The data shows that 22 per cent of sample households adopt migration within the state, whereas 78 per cent adopt inter-state migration. Eighty-one per cent of migrant from Koraput adopt intra-state migration, whereas migrant household from Nuapada and Sonepur district adopt inter-state migration. Majority of migrants from Nuapada (89 per cent), Bolangir (85 per cent), and Malkangiri (71 per cent) adopt inter-state migration mainly to Andhra Pradesh, Telengana, whereas migrants from Kalahandi prefer Chhattisgarh as their destination. In case of migrants from Rayagada, Kerala has become their work destination. The inter-state migrants from Sonepur have moved to Tamil Nadu (90 per cent) in significant number. The other state where the migrants from KBK region are working are Madhya Pradesh, Karnataka, Pudducherry, Gujarat, West Bengal, Delhi, Punjab, J&K and Himachal Pradesh. Thus the destination of migrants from KBK shows their movement mainly directed towards the southern states of India whereas movement towards northern states is of limited. It is clear that states like Andhra Pradesh, Tamil Nadu, Karnataka, Chhattisgarh, and Kerala have become common destination for the inter-state seasonal migrants of KBK region.

5.12 Nature of Work of the Migrants at Destination

The migrant workers are provided different types of work through the agents/dalals depending upon the contracts between the employers and the agents. The common work which the seasonal migrants from the KBK region are assigned at the destination is presented in the table. Table 5.11 and Figures 5.13.1 and 5.13.2 show the nature of work of the migrants at their respective destination. The migrants of the region as a whole are mainly engaged in brick making (48 per cent), construction sector (31 per cent), plumber, mason etc. (8 per cent), plantation and textile (5 per cent each), rickshaw pulling and other (3 per cent). It is noticed that migrants from Nuapada, Bolangir, Kalahandi and Sonepur are mainly engaged in brick making (90-72 per cent) (Figure 5.13). On the other hand majority of migrants from undivided Koraput district works in the construction sector.

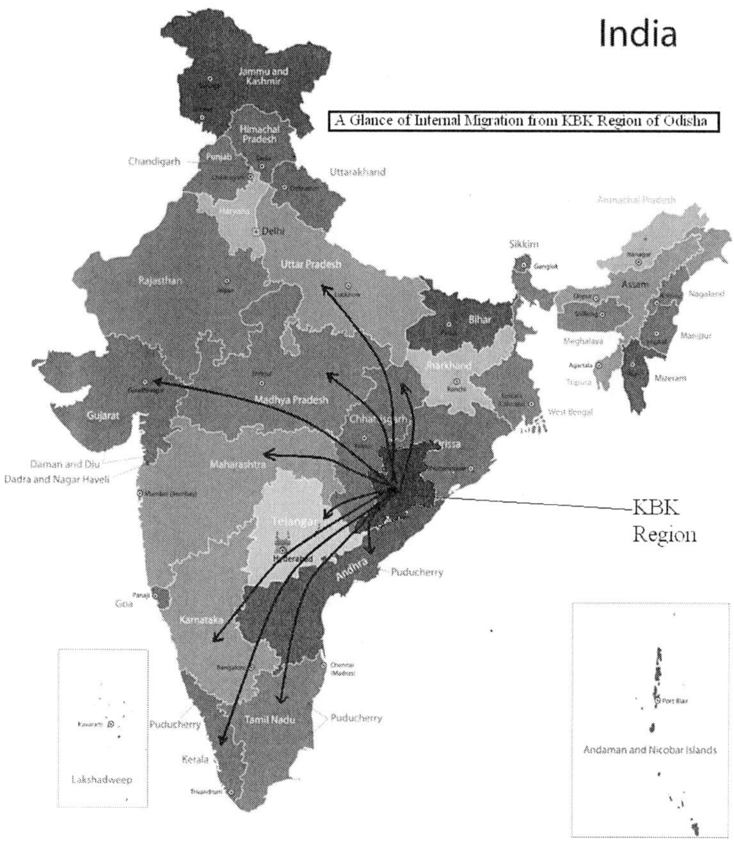
India
A Glance of Internal Migration from KBK Region of Odisha
KBK Region
Jammu and Kashmir
Himachal Pradesh
Chandigarh
Punjab
Uttarakhand
Haryana
Delhi
Uttar Pradesh
Rajasthan
Sikkim
Assam
Nagaland
Bihar
Manipur
Meghalaya
Mizoram
Jharkhand
Madhya Pradesh
West Bengal
Gujarat
Maharashtra
Orissa
Daman and Diu
Dadra and Nagar Haveli
Telangana
Hyderabad
Andhra
Puducherry
Goa
Karnataka
Tamil Nadu
Kerala
Lakshadweep
Andaman and Nicobar Islands

Table 5.10: Common Destination of Migrant Households

		Common Destination	*Inter-State Migration*													
District	*No. of HH*	*Within District/ state*	*Andhra Pradesh/ Telengana*	*Chhattis-garh*	*Madhya Pradesh*	*Maha-rashtra*	*Karnataka*	*Tamil Nadu*	*Pondic herry*	*Kerala*	*Gujarat*	*West Bengal*	*Delhi*	*Pun-jab*	*J&K/ Himachal Pradesh*	*Total (Inter-State)*
Kalahandi	104	5 (4.81)	5 (5.05)	62 (62.63)	2 (2.02)	17 (17.17)	1 (1.01)	4 (4.04)	0	0	0	0	5 (5.05)	1 (1.01)	2 (1.01)	99 (95.19)
Nuapada	100	0 (0.00)	89 (89.00)	5 (5.00)	0	0	2 (2.00)	4 (4.00)	0	0	0	0	0	0	0	100 (100.00)
Bolangir	100	40 (40.00)	51 (85.00)	0	0	0	6 (10.00)	3 (5.00)	0	0	0	0	0	0	0	60 (60.00)
Sonepur	106	0 (0.00)	10 (9.43)	0	0	0	0	96 (90.57)	0	0	0	0	0	0	0	106 (100.00)
Koraput	107	87 (81.31)	10 (50.00)	1 (5.00)	3 (15.00)	0	1 (5.00)		0	4 (20.00)	1 (5.00)		0	0	0	20 (18.69)
Nabarangpur	74	35 (47.30)	19 (48.72)	0	3 (7.69)	0	2 (5.13)	13 (33.33)	0	0	0	1 (2.56)	0	1 (2.56)	0	39 (52.70)
Raygada	120	1 (0.83)	2 (1.68)	0	0	0	2 (1.68)	8 (6.72)	0	107 (89.92)	0	0	0	0	0	119 (99.17)
Malkangiri	62	3 (4.84)	42 (71.19)	0	0	0	2 (3.39)	1 (1.69)	4 (6.78)	10 (16.95)	0	0	0	0	0	59 (95.16)
Total	**773**	**171 (22.12)**	**228 (37.87)**	**68 (11.30)**	**8 (1.33)**	**17 (2.82)**	**16 (2.66)**	**129 (21.43)**	**4 (0.66)**	**121 (20.10)**	**1 (0.17)**	**1 (0.17)**	**5 (0.83)**	**2 (0.33)**	**1 (0.17)**	**602 (77.88)**
NB	Within Districts/state i.e. Berhampur, Ganjam, Cuttack, Bhubaneswar.															

Source: Field Survey, 2014.

Table 5.11: Nature of Work at Destination

Sl. No.	*District*	*No. of HH*	*Brick Making*	*Construction of Roads and Buildings*	*Plumber/ Mason/ Carpenter*	*Plantation/ Agriculture*	*Textile/ Spinning Mills*	*Rickshaw Pulling*	*Others*
1.	Kalahandi	104	80	12	05	03	04	—	—
2.	Nuapada	100	89	05	03	—	—	03	—
3.	Bolangir	100	85	08	—	—	02	05	—
4.	Sonepur	106	76	09	03	—	10	—	08
5.	Koraput	107	18	67	12	08	02	—	—
6.	Nabarangpur	74	08	21	22	08	09	02	04
7.	Raygada	120	12	70	15	11	08	—	04
8.	Malkangiri	62	—	49	02	10	—	—	01
	Total	**773**	**368**	**241**	**62**	**40**	**35**	**10**	**17**

Source: Field Survey, 2014.

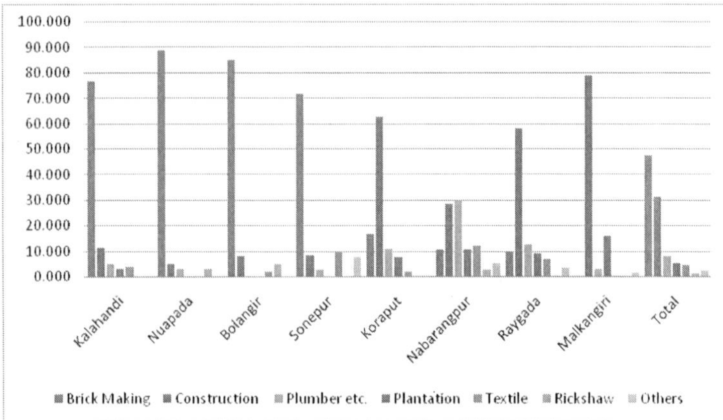

Figure 5.13.1: Nature of Work at Destination (District-wise).

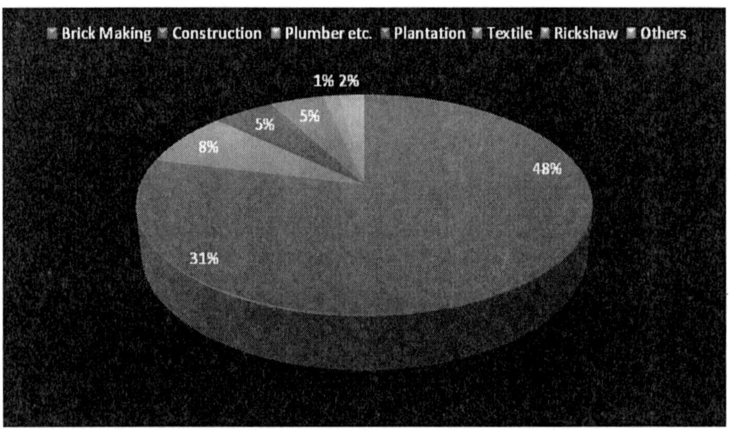

Figure 5.13.2: Nature of Work at Destination.

5.13 Migrants Living Condition at Destination

Table 5.12 and Figure 5.14 show the views of migrants about their living condition at their destination. To assess the ground reality of their living conditions we visited number of brick kilns located in Anandapuram village, which is around 35 km away from Visakhapatnam in Andhra Pradesh. We found that the living condition of migrants at their destination is very poor in general. To substantiate the fact a few photographs taken at the work site are places here.

Table 5.12: Living Condition of Migrants at Destination

Sl. No.	District	No. of HH	Poor	Very Poor	Manageable
1.	Kalahandi	104	10(9.62)	68(65.38)	26(25.00)
2.	Nuapada	100	12(12.00)	62(62.00)	26(26.00)
3.	Bolangir	100	11(11.00)	77(77.00)	12(12.00)
4.	Sonepur	106	33(31.13)	48(45.28)	25(23.58)
5.	Koraput	107	53(49.53)	37(34.58)	17(15.89)
6.	Nabarangpur	74	4(5.41)	58(78.38)	12(16.22)
7.	Raygada	120	28(23.33)	79(65.83)	13(10.83)
8.	Malkangiri	62	5(8.06)	49(79.03)	8(12.90)
	Total	**773**	**156(20.18)**	**478(61.84)**	**139(17.98)**

Source: Field Survey, 2014.

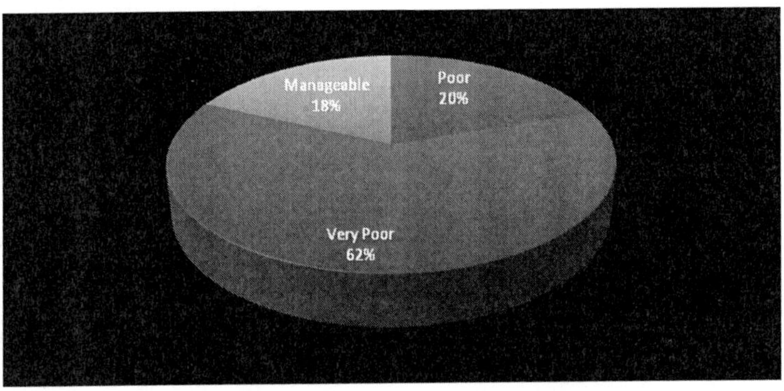

Figure 5.14: Living Condition of Migrants at Destination (in per cent).

Data on the response of the migrants also shows that majority of them (62 per cent) have expressed it as very poor. The migrants working in brick kilns in particular are provided temporary polythene sheeted hut of one room made out of raw bricks which is locally known as 'Gudushiali'. Water arrangement is made as a part of its requirement in brick making. No special provision for drinking water is made for then. During our visit it is observed that their living condition is sub-human and extremely poor. They usually live close to the brick kilns which are located in villages or periphery of urban areas. In some areas it was found that they were living in close proximity to grave-yard. Very often poisonous snake enter their sheds. In the entire scorching summer they have to live in such low height polythene cover sheds in extremely difficult situation. They are not allowed to interact with the local people. Of course language is a barrier for exchanging ideas. As they live close to the brick kilns and work on piece wage basis, there is no fixed working hour. Most of them work for 12-14 hours to make more bricks for the owner as well as for their earning. Any labour who fails to carry out instruction of the owner is subjected to physical assault. The cases of physical assault and torture are coming to the light at regular interval. Sometime the migrant labours are also killed.

The migrants are provided weekly maintenance charges ranging Rs 500-600 per family to purchase grocery and vegetables from the local market. In some places it is provided by the owner himself. These migrant workers are deprived of foodgrain supplied through public distribution system. By this their real income is reduced. The food what they take is mainly 'pakhal' i.e. wet rice with little quantity of curry or dal which lacks a balance diet. As a result they suffer from anemic tendency. The maintenance charges and cash advance are calculated at the end of the work and remaining amount is paid to the migrants. In some cases the migrant workers are cheated in the process of accounting. Eighteen per cent of migrants have reported a manageable living condition whereas 62 per cent have expressed very poor and 20 per cent have expressed poor the living condition at their respective destinations. The rate of dissatisfaction is high among the migrants in general. Thus, it is clear that living condition of the migrants at the destination is sub-human, particularly in case of migrants engaged in brick kilns. It is also noticed that the migrants were unable to answer about the payment of wage per 1000 bricks. They have joined the migration stream only after receiving the lump sum cash advance along with a promise of good rate of wage from the employers. The local labourers expressed that the migrants are paid less wage than them. But the migrant workers engaged in industrial sector like spinning and textile mills have stated that they are provided somehow good/ manageable living condition with minimum basic amenities by the factory owners. Whereas the migrant workers engaged in construction sectors are of no different living condition than the brick kiln workers. Thus, the living condition of migrant workers at the destination is abject and sub-human. This aspect needs a proper surveillance by the administration and Department of Labour.

5.14 Treatment of Owner towards Migrants

Table 5.13: Treatment of Owner to the Migrants at Destination

Sl. No.	*District*	*No. of HH*	*Normal Treatment*	*Inferior*	*Physical Torture*	*Sexual Harassment*
1	Kalahandi	104	60(57.69)	36(34.62)	6(5.77)	2(1.92)
2	Nuapada	100	52(52.00)	35(35.00)	9(9.00)	4(4.00)
3	Bolangir	100	53(53.00)	36(36.00)	5(5.00)	6(6.00)
4	Sonepur	106	62(58.49)	35(33.02)	8(7.55)	1(0.94)
5	Koraput	107	65(60.75)	32(29.91)	10(9.35)	0
6	Nabarangpur	74	38(51.35)	31(41.89)	5(6.76)	0
7	Raygada	120	68(56.67)	40(33.33)	12(10.00)	0
8	Malkangiri	62	28(45.16)	30(48.39)	4(6.45)	0
	Total	**773**	**426(55.11)**	**275(35.58)**	**59(7.63)**	**13(1.68)**

Source: Field Survey, 2014.

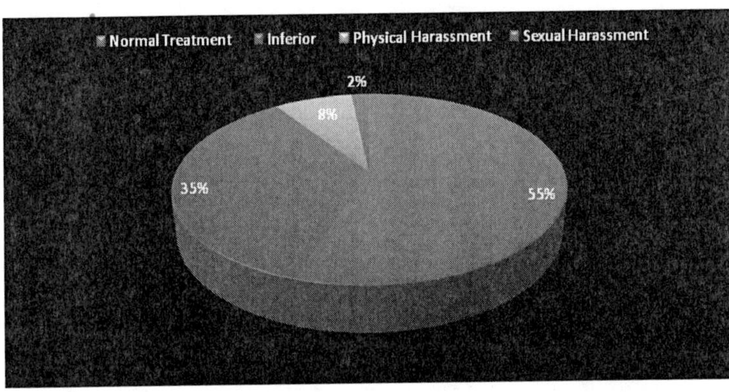

Figure 5.15: Treatment of Owner to the Migrants at Destination (in per cent)

Table 5.13 and Figure 5.15 show the treatment of the owners towards the migrant workers. The treatment of owners to the migrants at work place depends on their character and the labour themselves. Once the migrants come to the clutches of the owners either through labour contractor or through other means, it becomes difficult on their part to come out. By taking the advantage of distance, lack of union, illiteracy and their distress conditions the migrant labour fall easy prey to the exploitation of owner in the form of long working hour, denial of wage, physical torture, sexual harassment etc. But it is not the general scenario. Had it been so, the migrants would not have been going every year to the same destination. The migrant workers of other states working in Odisha are treated normally by the employers. The data reveals that 55 per cent migrants have reported normal treatment by the employers, whereas 35.60 per cent of migrants have reported inferior treatment by the employers and 7.60 per cent of migrants have reported physical torture. Regarding sexual harassment only 13 cases (1.68 per cent) have been reported by the respondents. It is not possible to get the exact number of such cases due to social taboos and fcar of further exploitation. They usually do not report to the police also.

5.15 Role of State Labour Department

Table 5.14: Role of Labour Department towards Migrants

Sl. No.	*District*	*No. of HH*	*Positive*	*Negative*	*Neutral*
1.	Kalahandi	104	10(9.62)	4(3.85)	90(86.54)
2.	Nuapada	100	22(22.00)	7(7.00)	71(71.00)
3.	Bolangir	100	12(12.00)	8(8.00)	80(80.00)
4.	Sonepur	106	25(23.58)	9(8.49)	72(67.92)
5.	Koraput	107	42(39.25)	7(6.54)	58(54.21)
6.	Nabarangpur	74	8(10.81)	41(55.41)	25(33.78)
7.	Raygada	120	33(27.50)	11(9.17)	76(63.33)
8.	Malkangiri	62	28(45.16)	14(22.58)	20(32.26)
	Total	**773**	**180(23.29)**	**101(13.07)**	**492(63.65)**

Source: Field Survey, 2014.

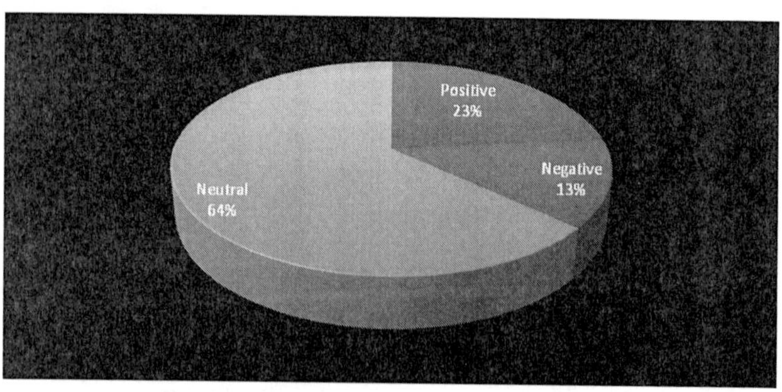

Figure 5.16: Role of Labour Department towards Migrants (in per cent).

Table 5.14 and Figure 5.16 show the views of migrant labour towards the role of Department of Labour of the state. In view of the large scale illiteracy among the inter-state migrants, they do not feel the role of the department and are not aware of the laws and provisions governing the inter-state migration. The role of this department towards the migrants has been limited in the ISMW Act. The department issues licence to the labour contractors only but is not involved in the process of the labour recruitment. That is why the migrants do not feel the role of the Department and majority (64 per cent) of them have expressed neutrality,13 per cent of migrants expressed negative role whereas 23 per cent find positive role of the department. In general the role of this department towards the inter-state migrants has not shown any impressive job as a result, migration under unregistered labour contractors far out weights the labour movement than under registered contractors. In the event of any torture or harassment the department cooperates the administration. The ISMW Act does not empower this department to do something for the migrants at the destination. In case of release of bonded labour, the department does not rehabilitate, therefore its role is limited. The rehabilitation is done by the DRDA. In case of construction workers, the department has a role to play in the matter of their registration, and extension of other state benefits to the workers. Now, the provisions under Odisha Building and Other Construction Workers' Welfare Board have been extended to the cases of inter-state migrant workers. The details of such benefits have been listed in appendix IV. It is a welcome initiative of the state for the betterment of the migrant workers. To receive such benefit the migrants have to register themselves. This will enable for the creation of authentic migration data for further course of action. To expand the role of labour department for the causes of migrant workers, the Government of Odisha has signed memorandum of understanding (MoU) with the Governments of Andhra Pradesh, Telengana and Tamil Nadu. It is expected that these MoUs will help for the betterment of migrants from KBK region working in these states. One common problem faced by the labour department is the lack of man power to implement various provisions as enunciated in the Acts and Rules.

5.16 Migrants' Future Plan

Table 5.15: Plan for Future Migration

Sl. No.	*District*	*No. of HH*	*To Migrate*	*Not to Migrate*
1.	Kalahandi	104	67(64.42)	37(35.58)
2.	Nuapada	100	85(85.00)	15(15.00)
3.	Bolangir	100	70(70.00)	30(30.00)
4.	Sonepur	106	72(67.92)	34(32.08)
5.	Koraput	107	93(86.92)	14(13.08)
6.	Nabarangpur	74	56(75.68)	18(24.32)
7.	Raygada	120	108(90.00)	12(10.00)
8.	Malkangiri	62	45(72.58)	17(27.42)
	Total	**773**	**596(77.10)**	**177(22.90)**

Source: Field Survey, 2014.

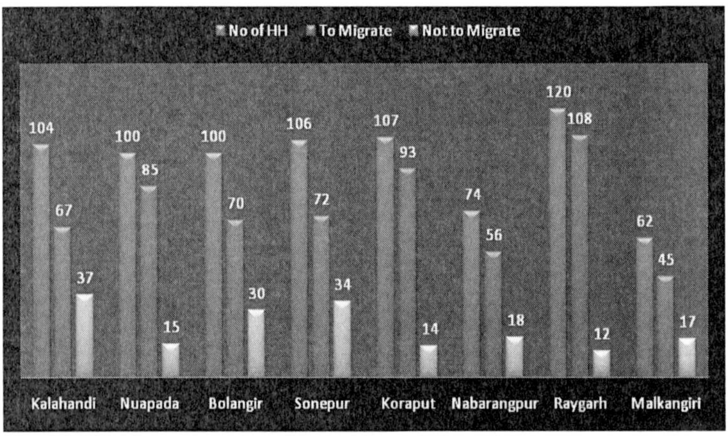

Figure 5.17: Plan for Future Migration (District-wise).

Table 5.17 Figures 5.17 and 5.18 indicate the desire of the migrants to migrate next year or not or their future plan for migration. Taking all the migrants in the KBK region 77 per cent of them have the plan to adopt migration next year whereas only 23 per cent of all the sample migrant households have expressed unwillingness towards migration in future (tentatively). Figure 5.17 shows the district-wise household

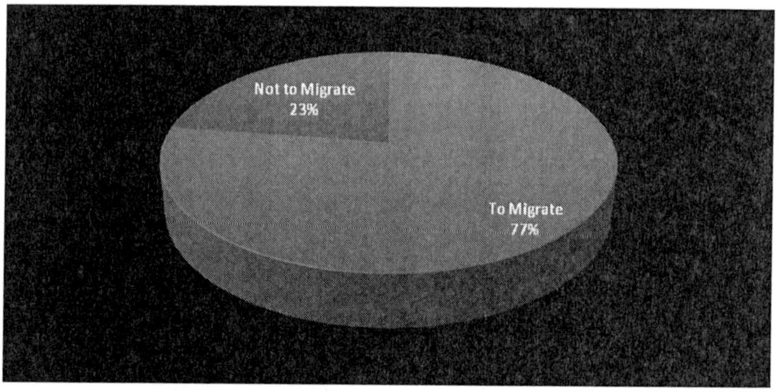

Figure 5.18: Plan for Future Migration [KBK Region] (in per cent).

migrants' willingness for migration in the next season. This shows that in spite of difficulties/tortures at the destinations the migrants have to adopt migration in future for their livelihood because they face distress situation at source. From this analysis it is clear that migration from KBK region will continue to exist so long as they are not provided employment and livelihood at their respective sources.

5.17 Testing of Hypothesis

To test if there is significant improvement in income level due to migration, a testing of hypothesis was carried out. The test applied was a paired 't' test which is given by $t = \frac{\overline{d}}{S/\sqrt{n}} \sim t_{n-1}$, where $\overline{d}$ is the mean of the difference of the income levels before and after the migration

S is the standard deviation of d's.

n is the number of pairs of observations.

t follows a student t distribution with (n-1) degrees of freedom.

The following Null and Alternative hypothesis were formulated for the testing of hypothesis.

Null Hypothesis (H_0): There is no significant change in the income level of the migrants.

Table 5.16: Testing of Hypothesis (District-wise and KBK Region as a Whole)

Sl. No.	*Districts*	*Mean Income Difference*	*Std. Deviation*	*t*	*df*	*Significant*	*Remark (á=0.05)*
1.	Kalahandi	-4969.71	16626.60375	-3.048	103	.003(<0.05)	significant
2.	Nuapada	-1493.00	18046.45663	-.827	99	.410(>0.05)	insignificant
3.	Bolangir	-5070.00	11957.20906	-4.240	99	.000(<0.05)	significant
4.	Sonepur	-17148.1	14337.66423	-12.314	105	.000(<0.05)	significant
5.	Koraput	-10341.1	14854.26026	-7.201	106	.000(<0.05)	significant
6.	Nabarangpur	-12094.6	28452.87809	-3.657	73	.000(<0.05)	significant
7.	Rayagada	-12074.2	22719.65608	-5.822	119	.000(<0.05)	significant
8.	Malkangiri	685.484	9021.02911	.598	61	.552(>0.05)	insignificant
9.	KBK Region	-8277.81	18655.82366	-12.336	772	.000(<0.05)	significant

Alternative Hypothesis (H_1):There is a significant change in income level of the migrants.

Test Criterion: If the value of *t* is significant at 5 per cent level of significance i.e. (if $p<0.05$) the null hypothesis is rejected otherwise, it may be accepted.

Table 5.16 shows the '*t*' test value along with the mean income difference and standard deviation of the eight districts of the KBK region and KBK region as a whole. From the table it is quite evident that pair '*t*' values of all the districts except Malkangiri and Nuapada are significant as the corresponding significant values of these districts are less than 0.05. So the null hypothesis is for the districts namely, Kalahandi, Bolangir, Sonepur, Koraput, Nabarangpur, Rayagada are rejected. It implies that there exist significant differences in the mean income level of these districts before and after migration. The negative sign in the mean difference in income level as indicated in Table 5.16 reveals that the mean income levels of migrants of these districts have increased and not worse off at the post-migration period. On the other hand two districts namely, Malkangiri and Nuapada depicts insignificant difference in the '*t*' value. So the null hypothesis may be accepted. Which means that there exists no significant difference between the mean income level of the migrants before and after the migration. We may also treat the income level of the people before and after migration as equal.

If we look at the variations of the difference of income it is found that, Nabarangpur has maximum variability in the income level and Malkangiri has the least variability in income level. Thus, it is found worthy to measure the degree of relationship in the income level before and after the migration through a correlation analysis.

Table 5.17, shows the paired sample correlation of the annual income before and after migration of the eight KBK districts. From the correlation table it is observed that there exists a significant correlation between the annual income level before and after migration of migrants from the districts viz. Bolangir (0.516), nepur (0.564), Koraput (0.342), Rayagada (0.303), Malkangiri (0.569). It is also found that income of Kalahandi district (-0.028), Nuapada (0.051) Nabarangpur (0.188) shows an insignificant association in the mean income level before and after migration. The income level before and after migration may be treated as independent.

Table 5.17: Paired Sample Correlation for Individual Districts

		N	*Correlation*	*Sig.*
Pair 1	Annual Income Before Migration_ Kalahandi & Annual Income After Migration_Kalahandi	104	-.028	.774
Pair 2	Annual Income Before Migration_ Nuapada & Annual Income After Migration_Nuadada	100	.051	.613
Pair 3	Annual Income Before Migration_ Bolangir & Annual Income After Migration_Bolangir	100	.516	.000
Pair 4	Annual Income Before Migration_ Sonepur & Annual Income After Migration_Sonepur	106	.564	.000
Pair 5	Annual Income Before Migration_ Koraput & Annual Income After Migration_Koraput	107	.342	.000
Pair 6	Annual Income Before Migration_ Nabarangpur & Annual Income After Migration_Nabarangpur	74	.188	.109
Pair 7	Annual Income Before Migration_ Rayagada & Annual Income After Migration_Rayagada	120	.303	.001
Pair 8	Annual Income Before Migration_ Malkangiri & Annual Income After Migration_Malkangiri	62	.569	.000

However, if the whole scenario of KBK region is taken into consideration it is found that there exists a significant difference in income levels of the migrants at the post-migration period. (as t value is significant at five per cent level of significance in Table 5.18). A negative difference in the mean income level (-8277.81) indicates a rise in the income level of migrants as a whole at the post-migration period.

Table 5.18: Paired Samples Test (KBK as a Whole)

		Paired Differences					*t*	*df*	*Sig. (2-tailed)*
		Mean	*Std. Deviation*	*Std. Error* Mean	95 per cent Confidence Interval of the Difference				
					Lower	*Upper*			
Pair -1	Annual Income Before Migration – Annual Income After Migration	-8277.81	18655.82366	671.00334	-9595.02119	-6960.60623	-12.336	772	.00 0

5.18 Conclusion

The field data collected from 773 households from the eight KBK districts pertaining to migrants of this area have been analysed on number of aspects. Majority of migrants of this region usually adopt internal migration which is seasonal and temporary in nature. It is not only seasonal but also a distress induced migration mainly going for their livelihood. The reason behind migration shows that they are migrating due to lack of regular employment opportunity in their place of origin, to get higher wage, and attraction of lump sum cash advance (Dadan). The debt cycle (Lakti) of migrant household also acts as a prominent factor of migration. The demographic feature of the migrant households show that 53 per cent of male and 47 per cent of female population are in the age group of 15-65 years constitutes the working population. The mean size of migrant household is 4.09, which indicates that size of the migrant families is not large one. Majority of migrants belong to SC and ST categories they are followed by OBC category whereas the participation of general caste people in this type of migration is almost negligible. It is further noticed that majority of migrants (93 per cent) belongs to Hindu religion.

On the analysis of educational status of the migrants, it is found that 36 per cent are illiterate and 44 per cent are literate and the level secondary and higher education is insignificant among the migrants. The overall educational status of both male and female shows a poor condition which leads to ignorance of laws and government schemes. The housing condition of the migrants in the origin is poor one and there is lack of access to basic sanitation. Sixty per cent of such households have access to electricity so also 60 per cent have access to the drinking water from the tube wells. Use of latrine/toilet by the migrants is almost non-existent. Hence, they are largely environmental polluters. The migrants are usually motivated to adopt migration by agents, friends and relatives. The labour contractors or dadan sardar is the prime motivator to migrate them only on payment of cash advance, which form the main attraction for migration. For them it is a business to supply labour to the owners of brick kilns and construction sector. The general destinations of these distress induced migrants are Andhra Pradesh, Telengana, Tamil Nadu, Karnataka, Kerala and Gujarat. A few migrants have also moved to the north Indian states.

So far as their land holding position is concerned, majority of them belong to landless, marginal and small farmer categories. The support of land as a means of livelihood is not strong enough to retain them in their place of origin during lean agricultural season. Due to poor land holding and lack of local employment, they are forced to adopt temporary migration for their survival.This process continues like a *vicious cycle of migration.* In the entire process of distress induced seasonal migration from KBK districts, the labour department has a very limited role to play. The department has nothing to do neither with their condition at the destinations nor with their betterment at origin. The migrants live in a very poor condition at their destinations or places of work and remain at the mercy of the owner. They are subjected to various types of exploitation by the owners and labour contractors. Media has played as important role to rescue such tortured migrants.

In spite of hardship and exploitation, the migrants of KBK districts, who are generally adopting distress induced migration have planned to migrate in future mainly due to lack of employment opportunities. The state programme of MGNREGA for rural employment which ensures 100 days of employment at least to one member of a family suffers from many shortcomings and fails to keep the migrants at their native places. Migration cannot be checked completely but measures should be taken to keep them in the locality through different labour intensive work programmes.

References

Samal, K.C, S. Meher and S. Mishra (2012). *Migration of Workers to Urban Informal Sector*, Avon Publications, New Delhi, p. 45.

Chapter – 6

Summary, Conclusion and Policy Implications

6.1 Brief Note on the Study of Internal Migration

6.1.1 Migration of population is a complex phenomenon. It is taking place since the beginning of the civilisation; there has always been an uneven and imbalance nature of development in terms of its economic, political and social dimension in different parts of a country and regions within the state. In this context, the study of migration has become one of the important aspects in a changing world of globalisation and liberalisation. Migration involves movement of people within and across national boundaries. The former is termed as internal migration and the later external or international migration. The study of migration has been undertaken by the scholars of different branches such as, economics, sociology, demography, political science and geography from different angles but their analysis tend to be interdisciplinary one. Hence, the study of population migration is a multi-dimensional and multi-disciplinary. Mobility is an integral part of human existence. But all types of human mobility are not migration. It involves movements which result in the change of usual place of residence during the period of enumeration (at least for a period of six months) migration may be temporary or permanent. It is a study of such migration which has received least attention of the scholars, but has serious economic, social and political implications. The present study basically deals with the temporary nature of distress seasonal migration of the region.

6.1.2 This study has been organised into six chapters. The first chapter deals with the introduction to the concept of labour migration internal/external nature and its associated issues, such as definition, typology, determinants, and history of migration in India. It also deals with estimates, effects of migration, along with importance of the study, objective of study, hypothesis and scope of the study. This chapter provides the scheme and brief outlines of the study.

6.1.3 The second chapter is devoted to the analysis of review of literature to the issues of migration. The migration is of several dimensions that is why the review of literature has been carried out from different angles such as external and internal aspects of migration, basis of migration, displacement and migration, circular and seasonal migration, data on internal migration, migration and informal sector, condition of migrants and state action, migration and child labour, effects of migration and prevention of migration. As labour migration is not specific to any particular country or region, it is quite obvious to take notes of literature relating to the studies of international, national and regional levels. In the above sections views of economists, geographers, psychologists, sociologists and other social scientists have been placed with a reference to the present study.

6.1.4 The third chapter covers the regional profile of the study area such as topography, administrative set up, demographic profile and separate sections relating to a brief profile of each district of the region. It also covers the migration data of the state and region as well. The region under study is considered as underdeveloped, and the state has launched several economic measures to uplift the people, a brief analysis has been made about such state plan and programme for this region.

6.1.5 The fourth chapter deals with the legal provision associated with the issues of internal migration in the country/state. It covers briefly, different Acts in general and the Inter State Migration Workman (Regulation of Employment and Condition of Services) Act, 1979 in particular. The other related Acts such as Bond Labour System (Abolition) Act, 1976 and Child Labour (Prohibition and Regulation) Act, 1986, Minimum Wage Act 1948 etc have been focused in relation to the study of internal migration.

6.1.6 The fifth chapter covers the analysis of primary data collected from the region for study of internal migration. It covers the assessment of socio-economic condition of migratory labour of KBK region. In this context, data have been presented in tabular and graphical form to discuss their caste, education, demographic character, reason for migration, future plan for migration, plight of migrants at destination etc. The land holding status of different categories of migrants has also been analysed to know their asset position. A student '*t*' test has been carried out to test the hypotheses of the study and to determine the level of significance in their change in income before and after migration. Apart from push and pull factors, the social network and other factors associated with migration have been analysed.

6.1.7 The last chapter presents summary and conclusion of the study. It highlights the contents of the chapters in the study and general conclusions derived from the analysis of primary data of internal migration and policy implication in relation to the study have been provided for the betterment of the migrants.

6.1.8 The common determinants of migration in rural areas are abject poverty, persistent unemployment, low and irregular wage conditions, landlessness, poor facilities of education and health which push these people to those areas like urban centres where they identify the possibilities to overcome the above problems. Natural calamities like flood, draught and famine can also become a push factor for migration. Migrants may settle permanently in such areas where there is the presence of pull factors. Whereas there are migrants who move different places for regular employment and higher wage but do not settle there and again come back to the place of origin. This type of migration can be termed as circular or seasonal migration and it generally occurs during the lean agricultural season. It can be termed as distress induced seasonal migration.

In some regions (States like Bihar, Jharkhand, Odisha, Rajasthan, UP and Andhra Pradesh) where the literacy level of STs is low; are not fully aware of the schemes available for them. Such information is not clearly disseminated to them. The main reason for lesser beneficiaries is the complicated procedure of the sanctioning of the schemes and poor implementation. Awareness generation to avail the existing schemes and programmes targeted for tribal community is very much required. In the states with low rate of literacy; special camps can be organised to make them aware of the schemes meant for educational development. The strategic planning with a special focus to the problems and issues of the tribes residing in different regions should be implemented; where a particular segment of the (Paltasing and Paliwal, 2014).

6.1.9 External or international migration relates to population movement from one country to another across the international boundary. It may be voluntary or involuntary. Voluntary migration arises in the form of 'brain-drain' from developing countries to developed countries. The case of Indian Diaspora in the USA and UK is an example of external migration of voluntary in nature. On the other hand involuntary international migration arises due to political factors like partition of British India into two nations namely, India and Pakistan. Millions of people were forced to migrate from one nation to other and vice versa. Migration may also take place to one nation where the refugees of a nation get legal protection in another nation. As it is the case with Tibetan and Bangladeshi refugees in India. India has experienced large scale immigration from its neighbouring countries particularly from Tibet, Bangladesh and Nepal. Although India's population is considered as one of the least mobile population of the world, still it has experienced both types of migration. Internal migration is said to exist when people move within the territorial jurisdiction of the country. Internal migration may take place within the State (Intra-state) and outside the state (Inter-state). It may also take place on an inter-regional basis within a state. Amin (1974) has classified internal migration of labour into rural to urban, rural to rural, urban to urban and urban to rural. Among all these form of migration rural to urban migration find a prominent place in the demographic study of migration. Urban to rural migration has not assumed any significant dimension in the country. Various factors acting towards migration from rural to urban areas may be put into two main factors namely 'push' and 'pull' and push-pull combine.

6.1.10 The basis of distance migration may be short or long. In the long distance, the migrants used to stay a longer period than the case of short distance. On the other hand, the time division of migration may take place, daily, periodic, seasonal, temporary or permanent. That depends on the nature of employment, and distance. For example, brick kilns employ migrant labour during November-June of a year, and the migrants have to come back to their respective places of origin. This type of migration may be termed as seasonal or circular migration.

6.1.11 The motive behind migration may be economic, social and political but usually economic motive predominates other. The decision to migrate may be taken by an individual or by the family members as a unit by a class or caste or a group as a whole. A common interest or common suffering may lead to a decision as a whole of the group to migrate. It is also stimulated by agents/dalal/khatedar, friends, relatives or neighbour. Development of transport and communication facilitates have helped the movement of migrants to accessible places easily than inaccessible places. In general push factor operates prominently in the area of out-migration and pull factors pull them into the in-migration area. The decision to migrate is governed by a set of prevailing factors both in the migrant's place of origin and destination. Lee (1969) has identified, these factors as positive (+), negative (-) or neutral (o). The negative factors or push factors at the place of origin influence the migrant's decision to migrate. On the other hand the positive factors at the destination pull the migrant. The push, pull, or push-pull factors results the volume of migration. Migration is also accompanied by certain intervening factors, as a result it may not be a smooth migration in all cases.

6.1.12 The history of migration shows, in the British India, people migrated as indenture labour to Asian, African, European and American countries to seek their fate in other nation. The adoption of tea plantation in Assam led to large scale internal migration particularly from Bihar, West Bengal and Odisha. These migrants have more or less settled permanently and a unique mixed society has developed in Assam. Labour migration from the study area in western Odisha has also moved to the tea plantation of Assam. During the British rule in India, migration, both internal and external was encouraged by various means in pursuit of the goal of capitalism and colonisation of British Domain.

6.1.13 So far as data on migration is concerned, NSSO is an important source of migration data. To assess the volume and structure of migration in India, NSSO starting with the 9th round (May-August, 1955) conducted a number of surveys and collected data on migration as a part of its employment and unemployment enquiries.

The 64th round of NSSO survey provides an exhaustive data on migration. But so far as inter-state seasonal migration is concerned there is no direct data either in the census or the NSS or with the state. Therefore, one has to relay on surrogate information to arrive at the magnitude of seasonal migration. In recent years the state department of labour has initiated a task to provide data on seasonal migration. The NSS counted 15 million short-term migrants but other estimates have placed the number at 100 million (Abbas and Verma, 2014). The 2001 census figures 307 million as internal migrants. The National Commission of Rural Labour (NCRL) put the number of seasonal/ circular migrant into 10 million (including roughly 4.5 million inter-state migrants and 6 million intra-state migrants). Thus, there is the presence and growth of the phenomenon of internal migrants in the country.

6.1.14 Migration as a demographic phenomenon has a far reaching effect in term of economic and social consequences. Migrants have a positive role in the economic development of a country. After all migration helps in providing employment and remittance by such migrants to the sources helps the left behind members of the family to get livelihood without difficulties. In the case of external migration remittance is considered as a boon to the economy. Migration, particularly for poor people has become a source of livelihood.

6.1.15 The present study area is known for its poverty, frequent drought like situation, under-development and backwardness. Distress/ seasonal/circular migration has become a common phenomenon. In spite of special development measures, it still persists in the region. The study has enabled to know the condition of migrants during pre- and post migration periods, the process of labour recruitment and their problem at different stages of migration.

6.1.16 The review of literature on the issue of migration has been taken up on different related fields of migration. Internal migration in India shows that it takes place mainly due to lack of employment opportunities in the place of origin. The poor and economically disadvantaged groups of people resort to seasonal/circular migration as a means of livelihood during the lean agricultural season. The presence of push, pull and push-pull factors are acting in such a way that internal migration takes place on regular basis. Studies show a mixed result of migrants' improvement in terms of their economic condition.

6.1.17 The study area for internal migration covers the erstwhile undivided districts of Kalahaṇdi, Bolangir and Koraput popularly it is abbreviated as KBK district since 1980s. These districts came to the lime light not for their prosperity but for hunger and poverty. During 1992-93, these three districts have been divided into eight districts namely, Kalahandi, Nuapada, Bolangir, Subarnapur, Koraput, Nabarangpur, Rayagada and Malkangiri. These high, land districts were clubbed together to launch a special development programme in the name of KBK plan and thereafter it is popularly known as KBK districts. Broadly, these districts have more or less a similarity in linguistic and cultural affiliation. In view of under-developed characteristics, these districts are at a lower level in term of HDI rank in relation to other districts of the state, which shows the presence of underdevelopment and regional disparities within the state. According to 1997 BPL census 72 per cent of families was under BPL category. It is highest in Nuapada district (85-70 per cent) where the incidence of sale of a girl child took place in the eighties. A recent study conducted by Meheta and Shah (2003) reported that KBK region of Odisha is one of the poorest region including 10 other regions in India where the incidence of poverty is very severe and 34.08 per cent of people in rural areas of this region were very poor, 69.02 per cent were poor, and the square poverty gap was 6.83 per cent in 1993-94, furthermore, severity of poverty can be expressed in terms of hunger and lack of availability of two full meals a day. The KBK region as a whole has high percentage of ST (33.12 per cent) and SC (17.9 per cent) population corresponding to the state average of 22 per cent and 17.1 per cent respectively.

6.1.18 The entire undivided Koraput district has been covered under the special tribal development programme known as Tribal Sub-Plan Blocks (TSPB). It is a homeland to many primitive tribes such as Bondas, Kayas, Soars, Gadabas, Roans, Pongania Kondha and Kutia Kondh. The Dongria Kondhas live in the hill range of Niyamgiri bordering Kalahandi and Rayagada. There is the presence of huge bauxite deposits in the hills of Panchpatmala, Baplamali, Niyamgiri of Koraput region where these tribal abode. Koraput is famous for its coffee plantation. Numbers of large scale industries have been established under public sector and private sector initiative. For the rehabilitation of a large number of refugees from East Pakistan a special programme was undertaken during 1963-64 in Dandakaranya area of Malkangiri.

6.1.19 In spite of number of large scale industries and various special developmental measures, these districts of KBK have remained by and large under-developed. During the last one decade most of the KBK districts have faced the Naxalite-Mao movement leading to the killing of number of people and the counter-insurgent movement lead by CRPF and BSF have also killed number of extremists' cadres. Thus, we see a troubled KBK region with underdevelopment and large scale internal migration. In spite of the implementation of MGNREGA, these areas experience high rate of distress seasonal migration. Bolangir, Nuapada show the highest rate of internal migration to the southern states of India

6.1.20 The Constitution of India allows movement of people as a fundamental right under Article 19(1) (d) and (e). Under the provision of this Article, the citizen of the country has the freedom of movement and to settle in any part within the territory of India, except in certain states which enjoy some special status under the Constitution of India. The constitutional provision of Directive Principles of State Policy ensures protection of workers from exploitation and prevalence of equal rights to all the workers. In order to pursue better conditions for the working citizens and migrants the Parliament of India has enacted laws from time to time to deal with the issues of internal migration. These acts have been adopted by states in the forms of rules for the state concerned. To deal with the problem of external migration the Emigrant Act 1983 plays a significant role. The international migration is governed by a set of laws of immigrating and emigrant country as well.

6.1.21 The issues of internal migration are addressed mainly by the Inter-State Migrant Workmen Act, 1979 (ISMA). In addition to this Act, there are several other Central Acts and State Rules to supplement the ISMW Act. The purpose of the Act is to protect workers whose services are requisitioned outside their native states in the country. The employment of inter-state migrant labour in different states is more or less exploitative in nature. The migrant labourers/*dadan* were sent through agents known as Sardar or Khatedars to work outside the states in tea plantation of Assam, West Bengal and large construction projects, now they are going to southern states.

6.1.22 During the last three decades this practice of *dadan* labour has been followed to a very large extent in the KBK districts of west Odisha. To minimise the problem of *dadan* labour, Odisha was the first state to enact a law called 'Odisha Dadan Labour (Abolition) Act, 1975' which recognises, defines and regulates the role of agents/dalals in the recruitment procedure and sending the labour to work outside the state. Subsequently, following the recommendation of the Compact Committee and consultation with State Governments and relevant central ministries, the Inter-State Migrant Workmen (Regulation of Employment and Conditions of Services) Act, 1979 was passed by the Parliament and received the Presidential assent on 11.06.1979.

6.1.23 The Act incorporates provisions of Minimum Wages Act, 1936, to ensure payment of minimum wages to the workers working in other states. It also provides cognizance to the Factories Act, 1948, Mines Act, 1952, Industrial Disputes Act, 1947 for the protection and betterment of inter-state migrant workers. Under the ISMW Act, the movements of migrant workers are to be regulated through licensing contractors and registration of employers and migrant workers. The Act provides for the provision of minimum wage, displacement allowance, journey allowance, suitable residential accommodation and medical facilities, regular payment of wages to both sexes. It provides right to the migrant workers to register complaints with the authorities within three months for any incident at their place of work. Violators of the Act are subject to imprisonment up to one year or with a fine up to Rs 1,000 or both. The responsibility for enforcement of the provisions of the Act rests upon the Central Chief Labour Commissioner and State Labour Commissioner of respective State.

6.1.24 In addition to above Acts, the provisions of Bonded Labour System (Abolition) Act, 1976, Equal Remuneration Act, 1976, Child Labour (Prohibition and Regulation) Act, 1986, the Odisha Building and other Construction Workers (Regulation of Employment and Conditions of Services) Act, 2002 can also be add-on for the betterment of inter-state migrant workers. The MGNREGA, 2005 provides a guarantee of job of at least 100 days to one member of a family during a year and if it fails to provide then unemployment allowance will be paid during the period of unemployment, to the worker to whom job cards have been issued. Thus, there are many legal provisions to protect the interest of the inter-state migrant workers. But it all depends on its implementation and practices adopted for such workers, along with the awareness amongst the migrants about their claims and different provisions for their betterment.

6.1.25 The present book on internal migration has been carried out as a case study of KBK district by collecting primary data from the migrant households. The primary data have been collected on a multi-stage random sample technique, through a scheduled questionnaire. A total of 773 sample households have been selected for this purpose. The study has also been supplemented by secondary data. A paradoxical situation is observed in the area that in spite of huge public expenditure on the largest rural employment generation programme, MGNREGA since 2005-06, the number of migrants from the state as a whole has increased considerably and consistently. The state expenditure has increased from Rs 347.17 crore in 2005-06 to 1289.13 crore in 2013-14; simultaneously the numbers of migrants from the state have increased from 39,261 to 1,27,038. This is the figure of registered labour migrated to other states, and if we add the unregistered migrant labour then figure will be much greater. The rising trend of migration has questioned the effective implementation of the scheme for which it is intended. The pattern of migration that occurs in the KBK region is squarely distress induced migration from rural areas to other neighbouring states. It has turned into a more regular livelihood option for the lower strata of population.

6.2 Socio-economic Background of the Migrants

The socio-economic background of migrant labour from KBK region shows that they are generally from economically backward class of the society. The obvious reason for migration may be poverty and lack of employment opportunities in their locality. The migration of labourers does have an impact on the labour supply at destination as well as at their place of origin.

6.2.1 The demographic trend of the migrant population shows that, the seasonal migration to other states involves family migrations which represent 53 per cent of male and 47 per cent of female population. The children also accompany them to participate in the process of working for the family. The working population in the age group of 15-65 years is about 74 per cent of the migrants, which represents a high work participation ratio. The mean household size of the migrants of the region is 4.09, generally includes husband, wife and their two to three unmarried children. The social and religious affiliation of the migrant household in the region shows that 47 per cent of ST, 26 per cent of SC, 26 per cent of OBC and one per cent of general caste people participate in the process of migration combining the ST and SC, migrant population it represents (73 per cent) a significant percentage, these people are at the lower strata of the society. It shows that the internal migration which is taking place in the KBK region largely involves SC and ST population. The number involving the general caste people is very insignificant. Majority of migrants (93 per cent) belong to Hindu religion followed by six per cent of Christian, and less than one per cent of Muslims are in the process of migration.

6.2.2 The educational status of the migrants is very poor. Among them 36 per cent of male and 54 per cent of female are illiterate. Whereas 44 per cent of male and 34 per cent of female have the primary education up to class VIII. The percentage of secondary, higher and technical education among the migrants is of highly insignificant in nature. The total educational scenario of the migrants is poor and not an encouraging one.

6.2.3 The basic amenities and housing condition of the migrant at the place of their origin show that 75 per cent of them have katcha houses, 18 per cent semi-pucca and five per cent pucca houses. Nearly two per cent (1.81 per cent) of the migrants have no house of their own. The number of rooms in their houses ranges between 1-3 and 60 per cent of them have access to electricity. But highly significant number of households of them do not have latrine and bathroom facility, which indicates poor sanitary condition. So far as drinking water sources are concerned, majority of them use (61 per cent) tube well water, on the other hand 27 per cent use open well and rest 12 per cent use other sources. No individual household has their personal water supply provision. The living condition of the migrants at their native places is simple and lacks proper sanitary condition.

6.2.4 When asked about the reason for their migration, they have pointed out different reasons. The main reasons for migration are unemployment (22 per cent), higher wage (25 per cent), regular employment (10 per cent), debt bondage cycle (17 per cent), lump sum advance (17 per cent), natural calamities (4.5 per cent) and social obligation (4 per cent). Employment opportunity and higher wage at destination dominate their decision for migration. It is accompanied by *Baina*/ lump sum advances provided by the employers through agents/dalal and debt bondage cycle. They are attracted by lump sum advance and regular employment at destination during the lean season of the year.

6.2.5 The motivating forces behind migration are agents (55 per cent), friends (21 per cent), relatives (16 per cent) and neighbour (9 per cent). Looking at the opinion of the migrants it can be clearly concluded that the agents/dalals play a vital role in the process of migrant labour recruitment. But one thing that has come to the picture, they fail to distinguish between a registered and unregistered agent/ dalal. The agents take the advantage of their local affiliation. Some of the agents are former migrants, with a little knowledge and intelligence and rapport with the employers are doing the job of agents and earning a handsome amount. The role of labour agent is highly prominent in Bolangir (98 per cent) and Nuapada (72 per cent). There is chain of big players, agents, local politicians, tout, and ticket brokers in the process of migrant labour movement. The migrants from these two districts are prone to distress seasonal migration and they usually work in brick kilns of southern states. The demand for migrant labour is high in these states due to their skill of making bricks, lower wage than the local labour, and absence of bargaining power. The practice of piece wage in making of bricks engages family labour where the children are also engaged but those children do not come under the pay roll. The family of brick-makers are called *pathuria* and they put more effort to maximise bricks production, so as to earn more and to achieve this they have to work more than 12 hours a day.

6.2.6 The agents may visit once or twice to the work site of the migrant labours but often do not comes to the picture when difficulties arise, or in the case of torture or exploitation. It is also noticed that the migrant workers are not told about the rate of brick making and only the weekly maintenance charge per family is paid to them. At the end of the working period, the advance amount and weekly maintenance charges are deducted and if surplus remains they are paid. If there is no surplus, the pathuria group has to return with debt bondage of *lakti or debt.* Of course, the owners do not insist to repay it immediately and becomes a gone case of repayment. This is also a reason for which the migrants become obliged to work for the owner in the next season. Cases of torture and harassment arise when the labour fails to work or do not obey the order of the owner. Sometimes in the process of recruitment of migrant labour, the agents and owners also suffer loss in the event of betrayal by the labour or bad weather which may cripple bricks production. It is also found that some of the brick kiln owners have to stop their business due to heavy losses. The common destinations for the migrants of KBK districts are Andhra Pradesh, Telengana, Chhattisgarh, Maharashtra, Karnataka, Tamil Nadu, and Gujarat. Few migrants have also moved to work in other states like West Bengal, Delhi, Punjab, Kerala, J&K and Himachal Pradesh. Majority of migrants from Nuapada, Bolangir, Malkangiri adopt inter-state migration mainly to Andhra Pradesh and Telengana. The inter-state migrants from Bolangir, Kalahandi, Nuapada, Sonepur generally work in brick kilns whereas the migrant workers of undivided Koraput district work in construction sector. Here we find the different occupation of migrants from the KBK region.

6.2.7 The migrants basically belong to landless, and small marginal farmer category. In this region 98 per cent of migrants form this category which show a class of asset poor. In view of landlessness or small amount of land on their possession and lack of adequate employment opportunity at their native places they have been compelled to adopt migration as an easy and attractive alternative during the lean agricultural phase. The participation of medium farmers and large farmers in the inter-state migration is insignificant and if at all they have migrated, it may be under certain extra-ordinary circumstances, and they use to work in factories or industrial establishment. Increased landlessness, decline profitability in agriculture and repulsive attitude towards agricultural activities coupled with easy availability of lump sum advances lure the people to migrate. The young migrants usually work in factories to meet their growing demand of modern needs like mobile phone, television, clothing etc.

6.2.8 The living condition of the migrants who are working in the brick kilns is very poor in general. More than 60 per cent of respondents have expressed very poor condition about their living condition. They face the problem of drinking water, proper food, decent living condition, medical facilities and schooling facilities for their children. As a result they suffer from different ailments. They live in close proximity to brick kilns in unhygienic condition. In the entire scorching summer they have to live in very low height polythene cover sheets in extremely difficult situation. Most of those migrant workers have to work for 12-14 hours to make bricks for their owners. Numbers of cases relating to physical torture, death/killing at the place of work or during transit have come to the lime light. Hundreds of dadan labours have been rescued by the authorities from different places of Andhra Pradesh, Telengana, and Tamil Nadu. But little action has been taken against the culprits and violators of the ISWM Act. By taking the advantages of distance, unorganised nature, poverty and cash advance the owners in some cases exploit the migrants in the form of physical torture, sexual harassment, and monetary exploitation. But it is not the general scenario in all cases where migrant workers work. But these cases of exploitation and torture need to be tackled properly. In spite of these hardships majority of migrants have expressed their willingness to migrate in the next season. Migrant workers engaged in different factories like spinning and textile mills, are provided somehow good/ manageable living condition with minimum basic facilities.

6.2.9 So far as the role of labour department of the state is concerned, most of the migrants do not feel its role. In general the role of labour department towards the inter-state migrant is less impressive. This results the dominant role of agents/dalal in the movement of migrant workers. The department comes to the picture in the event of any case of torture or harassment. The department suffers from adequate man power to carry out the task effectively. The MoU signed by the Government of Odisha with its counterparts of Andhra Pradesh and Telengana is likely to improve the condition of inter-state migrant workers of KBK region.

6.3 Statistical Analysis on Migrants' Income

6.3.1 The statistical test on the level of migrants, income before and after migration of the KBK region as a whole shows a significant difference in the income level (as $p=0.00<0.05$). The negative mean income level implies that there is an increase of income of migrants at post-migration period. This is true in all KBK districts except Malkangiri and Nuapada where we find no significant difference between the mean income level of the migrants before and after the migration. Since the general income level of the migrant has increased, the null hypothesis is rejected and it implies that there exists a significant difference in the mean income level of the migrants. When the level of income has increased, it is believed to have increased in their level of expenditure and savings.

6.3.2 The marginal propensity to consume (MPC) for the lower income group is generally high, and it can be applied to these migrants who migrate for their livelihood and any increased in their income will be diverted towards consumption. Under this situation, the marginal propensity to save (MPS) will be low but should be positive in view of the increased income. Saving as a part of income of the migrant arises at the end of the working period and most of the families come to their place of origin with a sum of Rs 10-15 thousand. In other cases they return empty handed. But the general situation of this migration shows that whatever they receive in the form of cash advance at their place of origin forms a major segment of saving which helps them for certain major expenditure in the form of house construction/repair, consumer durables and debt repayment. They manage their life at the working place with weekly maintenance sum provided by the employers. The proportion of saving whatever they accumulate in the process of migration is not substantial enough to manage their family for more than three months. In the next season they become penniless and again they are forced to receive cash advance from the labour agent/ dalal to adopt migration. Thus, migration becomes a part of their livelihood strategy. It may be termed as distress induced migration and it occurs in cyclical manner just like the 'vicious circle of poverty explained by Rogner Nurkse. The cash advance system in the process of migrant labour recruitment from the KBK region has given rise to a type of bonded labour system, which violates the provision of the

Bonded Labour System (Abolition) Act, 1976. However, the rescued bonded labours are rehabilitated by the DRDAs under the Panchayat Raj Department.

6.4 Policy Implications

The research on every socio-economic study points out a set of policy implications which can be considered as a means for the betterment of that section of population for whom the study was undertaken. An attempt has been made towards policy implications in line with the study. Migration as an economic problem cannot be checked altogether, but the harsh conditions of migrants can be minimised. Undoubtedly migrant labours contribute to the process of economic development therefore need the attention of the state for their betterment.

6.4.1 On the study of migration and unemployment Harris and Todaro have drawn a few policy implications. According to them, the payment of minimum wage to the additional industrial worker will induce more rural-urban migration. To solve the problem of an institutional determined wages that is higher than the equilibrium level labour should be employed according to a shadow wage and/or at a payroll subsidy wage. Since the opportunity cost (i.e. shadow wage) of an agricultural worker is lower than the marginal product of an industrial worker, the implementation of shadow wage criterion will have important effects on the level of agricultural output and urban unemployment. (Jhingan; 2008, p. 162 xiii). This implication of rural migration may not hold good in case of distress and seasonal migration although it is also a rural out-migration.

6.4.2 In the present study on internal migration from KBK districts shows a significant presence of inter-state migration which is of seasonal character. It is also a case of distress-induced migration, due to lack of employment and livelihood in the area of origins. Most of the migrants belong to ST and SC community and they are people of resource poor catagory. Majority of them are poor, landless, small and marginal farmers. In the underdeveloped solo crop area, people do not find employment on regular basis for which it becomes difficult on their part to manage their livelihood. In view of this people are forced to adopt migration.

6.4.3 The prevailing distress induced seasonal internal migration is associated with two unhealthy tags namely, bonded labour and child labour which have become a matter of concern. Although there are laws against these labour problems, still it is prevailing in a massive scale. So the complex issue of migration-bonded labour-child labour source out of poverty needs a serious state planning and implementation to curb these socio-economic evils.

6.4.4 To check migration the push factors associated with the locality need to be reduced through generation of large scale employment opportunity in such a way that these groups should get at least 250 days of work in a year. Neither industry nor agriculture can alone achieve this objective. The large scale industries are capital intensive and need skilled workers hence the scope of employment for these illiterate unskilled workers is limited. To make them employable, skill generation among themselves through various technical training programmes is necessary. The scheme like State Bank Rural Self Employment Training should be launched in a more extensive manner to create self-employment opportunity through small employment avenues. To absorb more labour there is the need for the revival of traditional village and cottage industries which is rapidly declining. For example, the demand for country tiles has declined and the potters are facing the problem of unemployment and adopting migration. It is, therefore, necessary to make them employable by reviving their traditional skills according to the need of the hour.

6.4.5 Infrastructure development in the agricultural sector through irrigation, watershed management will promote agricultural development which can absorb the local labour. Irrigation through small irrigation project is advocated but not through large dams because it will create the problem of population displacement and loss of agricultural land. Development of irrigation facility in Kalahandi district has been able to check seasonal migration to some extend, side by side created the Problem of displacement. Odisha is an onion importing state and the KBK region is famous for this crop. But it is a matter of concern that in spite of this situation no proper storage and marketing mechanism has been developed so far for this cash crop. To cite an example, the farming of coitle flower in kandetora Panchayat of Nauapada distristicts has been able to reduce migration/dadan from that area. It is an eye opener for other migrants of the region.

Farmers face distress sale. Unless farm products are provided better remunerative price the farmers can not employ labour for its farm activities. Hence it is necessary to promote such cash crop of this region such as onion, potato, zinger, garlic and cotton with adequate storage and marketing facilities.

6.4.6 In view of potato shortage and political tangle of West Bengal government in 2014 the Odisha government promoted potato cultivation without enhancing the storage capacity and proper marketing as a result the farmers faced distress sale and loss for their product. This also happens in case of cotton cultivation of this area. Cotton cultivation has occupied an important place in this region but the shutting down of spinning mills in the locality of Sonepur, Kalahandi and Bargarh has affected the cultivation of this cash crop. It is necessary to revive such mills and promote cotton cultivation to generate more employment opportunity in agricultural sector. To enlarge employment opportunities in the agricultural sector the cultivation of cash crops should be promoted with proper infrastructure, marketing and storage facilities so as to generate more employment in this sector. In addition to this, there is the need for promotion of food processing industries in an extensive manner to promote employment of local people. The climate of undivided Koraput district is conducive for coffee cultivation. The cultivation of coffee is passing through a declining phase. It is the need of the hour to promote coffee plantation and its processing in the area to absorb more labour in such activities. This area is also known for corn cultivation but lack of processing leads to low income and low employment opportunity. Corn processing industries are also capable of providing large number of jobs to the local people. Vegetables, zinger, onion and garlic production will not only enrich the farmers but also check migration, provided there is better marketing and remunerative price offered to the farmers. These farming can be eco-friendly, organic farming and natural farming. High yield varieties of vegetables and horticulture need to be promoted. The small scale industries, construction works, labour intensive projects, animal husbandry, fishery and the like sectors have better job creation opportunity and labour absorptive capacity to overcome the problem of distress migration to a large extent.

6.4.7 The protection of traditional forest based employment needs to be promoted so as to check the out migration of tribal dependent on minor forest products (MFP). These forest products like kendu leaf, saal seed, mahua etc. can provide better seasonal employment to the tribal during lean agricultural season provided these produced are marketed properly with a remunerative price to the people engaged in such activities. The provision of minimum support price for the minor forest products should be assured to the tribal for their reasonable earning. More of informal employment can be created through a linkage of agriculture and forestry development of the area.

6.4.8 The migrants of KBK region are generally illiterate and education is at a low level and the children of migrant families suffer from the loss of education during their migration. It is a fact that the state of primary education in the state is at a low level. The findings of Pratham an NGO reveals that students of Class – V are not able to read and write properly and unable to do the sum of Class – II. This sorry state of education needs considerable improvement, particularly for the people of poor and backward community/region who cannot afford to private education. The provision of boarding-cum-school activities through seasonal hostels need to be provided extensively. The seasonal hostels should be converted to regular hostels for the children of migrants at the origin and measures can be taken to provide education to the children at destination also. So that it will not only promote education but also prevent child labour. Although a few NGOs are engaged in providing education to the children of migrant families at the destination, it is not sufficient to cover the entire gamut of seasonal migrants working at different places. Provision for hostel facilities at least at the panchayat level will be just to accommodate the children of such migrant families. In addition to proper primary education there is a need to promote employment oriented vocational education and training in different traditional and non-traditional courses to absorb more people in full time and part time job to check migration.

6.4.9 It is observed that the migrants miss opportunity to avail goods under public distribution scheme (PDS) at the place of work. In this regard necessary arrangements should be made at the government level for PDS portability to provide subsidised foodgrains to the migrants at destination so as help in raising their real income. It can be arranged through e-transfer of PDS grains by linking through Aadhar Cards.

6.4.10 From our study it is found that significant proportion of migrants belong to landless, marginal and small farmer categories and they do not process any productive asset. In order to provide self-employment, it is necessary to carry out the land reform measures which is left half way in the implementation of ceiling on land holdings. To provide economic holding, there is need for redistribution of land through the implementation of ceiling on land holding. The forest land should also be provided to the tribal to increase operational holding. Under Forest Right Act, 2006, distribution of land is feasible for the tribal and forest dependent people.[1]

6.4.11 Social security measures, such as insurance coverage should be extended to these migrants. The recently launched Prime Minister Insurance Schemes of May 2015 is a well directed step to cover poor people under insurance protection schemes. As most of the migrants are working in brick kilns and construction sectors, and more than 10 persons are working in these sectors, they need to be covered under Employees Provident Scheme (EPF) so that benefit of EPF can be extended to migrants. This vacuum needs immediate filling through proper action by the labour department in cooperation with the authority of the migrants' destination.

6.4.12 Besides these the needy and helpless people need the protection of the state through proper implementation of different legal provision such as Inter-State Migration Workman Act, Bonded Labour System (Abolition) Act, Child Labour (Abolition) Act, Minimum Wage Act etc, so as to protect the interest of the migrants at the destination and source as well. Unless these acts and other related acts are implemented properly, it will become a simple paper work. The provision of Odisha Building Construction Workers Rules should also be extended to the migrant workers who are working in the brick kilns, because bricks form an important element of construction.

6.4.13 The movement of inter-state migrants should go through a registration process at the panchayat level, so that their detail data will be available with the labour department along with place of work and employer to have an easy access to tackle the problem of any kind of torture or harassment done to the migrant workers.

6.4.14 The employers at the destination need to provide proper living condition so that they can lead a human life. The working condition and working hour need to be monitored periodically by the labour department. The labour department should inspect the working site at regular interval to ensure payment of minimum wages, better working condition and freedom from exploitation. The case of bonded labour and child labour should be dealt strongly by the authority at the destination. For this necessary legal provisions are amended. The ISWM Act should empower the state labour department to take action against the employers at the destination who violate the provisions of the Act.

6.4.15 The left behind old men/women and children of the migrant families need the attention of the community in the absence of the principal earning member of the houses. For this necessary arrangement can be taken up by the NGOs. The NGOs can play certain positive role in the organisation of the migrants; their better working condition, provision of basic amenities and provision of education to the children of migrants. NGOs have a role in improving the general condition of the migrants.

6.4.16 The attitude of the government, people and contractors should change towards the development of the locality and to reduce distress migration. The implementation MGNREGA should be a corruption free and provision of 100 days of work at least to one member of a family need certain amendment in the context of KBK migration infested area. It should have the provision of at least 200 days of work in KBK region as a special provision. The concept of '*labour bank/ pool*' should be considered at the village level to engage them in different public/private works. The women empowerment through self help groups (SHG) should be extended to all the migrant families in an extensive manner to discourage migration.[2]

6.4.17 In the light of above study and policy implications, it may be stated that migration as a socio-economic problem will continue to exist but the nature of distress migration which continues in the KBK region needs to be checked through the above policy implications. Since modern manufacturing industries are capital intensive and limited capacity to absorb labour development of agriculture, afforestation, animal husbandary, fishery, small and medium scale industries, infrastructure, and labour-intensive construction works are the key to the issue. Above all a corruption-free system is necessary for proper development of the region. The multi-programme strategy of development needs further evaluation because of its ineffectiveness in tackling the core issue. The growing population should be checked through massive awareness programme for small family and incentive in different manner to small families. A sustainable development programme along with a special thrust to education and health sector will be the right answer to reduce migration in an effective manner.

6.4.18 The problems of *dadan* or internal migration of labour from KBK districts can be mitigated in a better way if the provisions are made in line with the Maharashtra Mathadi, Hamal and other Manual Workers (Regulation of Employment and Welfare) Act 1969. The Act provisions for the betterment of unprotected workers such as Mathadi (Labour who carries load of goods on his head), Hamal(Labour who carries load of goods on his back) etc engaged in certain unprotected employments. A few such measures may be mention here are; better provision for their terms and conditions of employment, assurance of minimum wage, better welfare measure in the form of free medical facility, housing facility/allowance, accidental benefit, free education for their children, easy access to credit, unemployment allowance, benefit of provident fund and other safety measures. This Act is being implemented through as many as 35 Board. The inclusion of these provisions will definitely show a positive sign of improvement of *dadan* workers of KBK region. The modus operandi of such provision for *dadan* workers needs further deliberation and debate.

References

1. Amin, S. (1974). *Modern Migration in Western Africa,* Oxford University Press, London.
2. Jhingan, M.L. (2008). *The Economics of Development and Planning,* Vrinda Publications (P) Ltd., Delhi.

References and Selected Bibliography

Agarwal, Manmohan and Amit S. Roy (2012)(Eds.). *Globalisation and the Millennium Development Goals,* Social Science Press, Orient Longman.

Agarwala, A.N. and S.P. Singh (1973) (Eds.) *The Economics of Underdevelopment,* Oxford University Press, New York.

Ahluwali, A.S. (2003). *Migrant Labour Section in Unorganised* Sector, in Gopal K. Iyar (ed.) Migrant Labour and Human Rights in India, Kanishka Publication, New Delhi.

Amrith, Sunil, S. (2011). *Migration and Diaspora in Modern Asia,* Cambridge University Press, New Delhi.

Amin, S. (1974). *Modern Migration in Western Africa,* Oxford University Press, London.

Ansari, M. (2009). *Rural Bihar Migrants in Rural Punjabi, 1961-1981.*in K. Gopal Iyer (Ed) Distress Migrant Labour in India, Key Human Rights Issues. Kanishka Publishers and Distributors, New Delhi.

Ariadna Estevez (2012). *Human Rights, Migration and Social Conflict, Towards a Decolonised Global Justice,* Palgrave Macmillan, New York.

Banik, Dan (2007). *Starvation and India's Democracy,* Routledge, Advances in South Asian Studies.

Barik, B.C. (1994). *Rural Migrants in Urban Setting,* Classical Publishing Company, New Delhi.

Bajaj, S.C. (2004). *Inter-State Migrant Labour and the Law* in K. Gopal Iyer (Ed) Distressed Migrant Labour in India Kanishka Publishers Distributors, New Delhi.

Basu, D.D. (2006). *Introduction to the Construction of India,* Wadhwa and Company Law Publishers, New Delhi.

Behera, N.K. (2011). *Displacement, Resettlement and Rehabilitation,* Abhijeet Publications, Delhi

Bhagat, R.M. (2011). *Internal Migration in India: Are the Underclass More Mobile?*in S.I. Rajan(Ed) Migration, Identity and Conflict, India Migration Report 2011, Routledge, New Delhi.

Bhutalia, Urvashi (2007). *Migration/dislocation: A Gendered Perspective*, in Navnita Chadha (Ed.) Gender Conflict and Migration, Sage Publications, New Delhi.

Bookman, Milica, Z. (2002). *Ethnic Groups in Motion,* Frank Cass Publishers, London.

Cai Fang and Wang Dewen (2008). *Impact of Internal Migration on conomic Growth and Urban Development in China.* in J. De. Wind and J. Holdaway (eds) Migration and Development within an Across Boarders! Research and Policy Perspectives on Internal and International Migration, The Social Science Research Council, New York.

Chadha, G.K. (2007). *Globalisation and Informal Sector Employment: The case of India's Unorganised Manufacturing,* in M. Agrawal and A.S. Roy (eds.) Millennium Development Goals, Orient Longman, New Delhi.

Chart, Sylvia (1992). *Gender and Migration in Developing Countries,* Belhaven Press, London.

Chattopadhyay, Asis and Arjun K. Saha (2012). *Demography-Techniques and Analysis,* Viva Books, New Delhi.

Chattopadhyaya, Haraprasad (1987). *Internal Migration in India: A Case Study of Bengal,* K.P. Bagchi and Company, Calcutta.

Chaudhury, Jayasri Ray (1993). *Migration and Remittances,* Sage Publications, New Delhi.

Cherunilam, Francis (1987). *Migration: Causes, Correlated, Consequences, Trend and Policies,* Himalaya Publishing House, Delhi.

Chubayanger, T. (2013). *Migrant and Trafficked Children in Hazardous Employment: The Case of Nagaland,* V.V. Giri National Labour Institute, Noida.

Chatterji, Joya (2010). *Migration Myths and the Mechanics of Assimilation: Two Community Histories from Bengal,* IUC for Humanities and Social Sciences, IIAS, Shimla.

Cohen, Robin (1996) (Ed). *Theories of Migration,* Edward Elger Publishing Limited, Cheltenham, U.K.

Cohen Robin 1996) (Ed) (*The Sociology of Migration,* Edward Elger Publishing Limited, Cheltenham, U.K.

Connel, Johan, Biplab Dasgupta, Roy Laishlly and Micheal Lipton (1976). *Migration from Rural Areas: The Evidence from Village Studies,* Oxford University Press, Delhi.

Desai, Meghnad (2007). *Introductory Remarks, Why India Will Fail to Meet the Millennium Development Goals,* in M. Agrawal and A.S. Ray (Ed) Globalisation and Millennium Development Goals, Orient Longman, New Delhi.

Deshingkar, P. and Johan Farrington (2009). *A Framework of understanding Circular Migration* in Priya Deshingkar and Johan Farrington (Eds) Circular Migration and Multilocational Livelihood Strategies in Rural India, Oxford University Press, New Delhi.

Deshingkar, P. (2008) *Circular Migration and Development in India,* in Wind, J. De. and J.Holdway(Ed) Migrations and Development Within and Across Boarders: Research and Policy Perspectives on Internal and International Migration, Oxford University Press, New Delhi

Deshingkar, P. and et al (2004). *The Evolving Pattern of Circular Migration* in P. Deshingkar and J. Farrington (Ed.) Circular Migration and Multi-locational Livelihood Strategies in Rural India.

Dey, J. Dreze and R. Khera (2006). *Employment Guarantee Act, A Primer,* National Book Trust, India, New Delhi

Fie, John and Gustav Rannis (1961). *A Theory of Economic Development,* in M.L. Jhingan (2008) The Economics of Development and Planning, Vrinda Publications, Delhi.

Estevez, Arianda (2012). *Human Rights, Migration and Social Conflict Towards a Decolonised Global Justice,* Palgrave Macmillan, New York.

Espinosa, Kristin and Douglasa Massey (1977). *Undocumented Migration and the Quantity and Quality of Social Capital*, in Ludger Prices (Ed) Migration and Transnational Social Spaces, Ashgate, Sydney.

Ghosh, Papiya (2007). *Partition and the South Asian Diaspora,* Routledge, New Delhi.

Ghosh, Rama (2004). *Brick Kiln Workers: A Study of Migration, Labour Process and Employment,* V.V. Giri National Labour Institute, Noida.

Giege, Karsten (1999). *Pattern of Migration from Zhejiang to Germany,* in Frank N. Pieke and Hein Mahlee (Ed) Internal and International Migration, Chinese Perspectives, Curzon Press, Richmond, U.K.

Gori, Anantak (2005). *Reflection and Mobilisations*, Sage Publications, New Delhi.

Gunatilleka, Godfrey (1992) (Ed.). *The Impact of Labour Migration on Households, A Comparative Study in Seven Asian Countries.* United Nations University Press, Tokyo.

Gurung, Tejamala (2012). *Migration and Settlement of Nepalese in North-East India,* in D.V. Kumar (Ed.) Social Change and Development, Rawat Publications, Jaipur.

Haan, Aryan De (2006). *What Causes Migration? Poverty or Development? Or is it the Other Way Around?* in Barbara Marshall (Ed.) The Politics of Migration, Routledge, London.

Halfacree, K.H. (1995). *Household Migration and the Structuration of Patriarchy, Evidence from USA,* Progress in Human Geography.

Hugo, G.J. (1983). *"New Conceptual Approaches to Migration in the context of Urbanisation: A Discussion Based on the Indonesian Experience"* In Morrison, P.A. (ed) Population Movements: Their Forms and Functions in Urbanisation and Development, Liege, Belgium: Ordina Editions.

International Labour Organisation (1960). *Why Labour Leaves Land,* ILO, Geneva. International Labour Organisation (2004) *Child Labour*, ILO Genva, International Organisation for Migration (2012) *Migration, Development and Poverty Reduction in Asia,* Academic Foundation, New Delhi.

Jaiswal, G. (2013). *An Inquiry into the Causes and Consequences of Internal Migration in India,* in K.K. Bagchi, (Ed) Internal Migration in India (Part-I) Abhijeet Publications, New Delhi.

Joshi, Y.G. and D.K. Verma (2004). *In Search of Livelihood: Labour Migration from Chhattisgarh,* Manna Publications Pvt. Ltd., New Delhi.

Kaite Willis and Brenda Yeok (2000). *Gender and Migration,* Edward Elger Publishing Cheltenham, U.K.

Kalra, Virendra, S. (2000). *From Textile Mills to Taxi Ranks Experiences of Migration, Labour and Social Change,* Ashgate Publishing Ltd., Alderghot, England.

Kamble, N.D. (1983). *Labour Migration in Indian States,* Asish Publishing House, New Delhi.

Kapoor, Dip and Tejwant Chana (2010). *Adivasi Social Movement in Odisha : Development, Marginalisation and Dispossession,* in Debal K. Singh Roy (Ed.) Dissenting Voices and Transformative Actions, Manohar Publishers & Distributors, New Delhi.

Kasar, D.V. (1992). *Economics of Seasonal Migration,* Classical Publishing Company, New Delhi.

Kaul, Ravender, K. (2005). *Migration and Society*, Rawat Publications, Jaipur.

Khan, Najma (1986). *Pattern of Rural Out Migration,* B.R. Publishing Corporation, Delhi.

Khatana, R.P. (1992). *Tribal Migration in Himalayan Frontiers,* Vintage Books, Gurgaon.

Kosinski, 2 – A and R. Mansell Prothero (1975) (Ed). *People on the Move: Studies on Internal Migration*, Melhuan & Co. Ltd., London.

Korra, V. (2011). *Short-duration Migration in India,* In S.I. Rajan (Ed.) Migration, Identity and Conflict Indian Migration Report 2011, Routledge, New Delhi p. 55.

Kothari, C.R. (2004). *Research Methodology*, New Age International Publishers, New Delhi.

Lahiri, S., B. Paswan and K.C. Das (2011) (Ed.). *Migration, Health and Development,* Rawat Publications, Jaipur.

Lam (2011). *Migration and Development,* in Lahiri et al, Migration, Health and Development, Palgrave Macmillan, New York.

Lee, Everett. (1969). *A Theory of Migration,* in J.A. Jackson (Ed.) Migration Cambridge University Press, Cambridge.

Lewis, A. W. (1954). *Economic Development with Unlimited Supplies of Labour,* in Agarwala, A.N. and S.P. Singh (1973) (Eds.) The Economics of Underdevelopment, Oxford University Press, New York.

Lesher, (2005). *The Millennium Development Goals and Migration IOM Migration Research Series,* International Organisation for Migration, Geneva. Lind, H (1969). *Internal Migration in Britain,* in J.A. Jackson (Ed.) Migration, Cambridge University Press, Cambridge.

Mahamood, R. A. (1992). *Impact of Labour Migration on Households-Bangladesh,* in Godfrey Gunatilleka (Ed) The Impact of Labour Migration on Households A Comparative Study in Seven Asian Countries, United Nations University Press, Tokyo.

Mahato, Kailash (1985). *Population Mobility and Economic Development in Eastern India,* Inter India Publication, New Delhi.

Malhotra, Niki (2013). *Inter-State Migration in India: Nature, Causes, and Consequences* in K.K. Bagchi (ed) Internal Migration in India, Abhijeet Publications, New Delhi.

Mandal, R.B. (1981) (Ed). *Frontiers in Migration Analysis,* Concept Publishing Company, New Delhi.

Mariappan, R. (2013). *Cause of Labour Mobility and Social Job Networks in the Urban Informal Sector Labour Blanket in India.* (Part II)

Malik, P.L. (2008). *Hand Book of Labour and Industrial Law,* Eastern Book Company, Lucknow.

Mathew, K.S. Mahavir Singh and Joy Vaskey (2005) (Eds.). *Migration in South India,* Shipra Publications, New Delhi.

Marshall, Barbara (2006) (Ed). *The Politics of Migration, A Survey,* Routledge, London.

Mehta, G.S. (1991). *Socio-Economic Aspects of Migration,* Deep and Deep Publications, New Delhi.

Menon, N.R.M. (2011). *Can the Licensing-Inspection Mechanism Deliver Justice to Interstate Migrant Workmen?* in S.I. Rajan (Ed) Migration, Identity & Conflict, Routledge, Delhi.

Mishra, P. (2012). *Migration and Mobility in an Eastern U.P. Village,* in Brij Raj Chauhan and A. Satyanarayan (Eds.) Changing village in India. Rawat Publications, Jaipur.

Mishra, R.P. (2011) (Ed.). *Urbanisation in South Asia, Focus on Mega Cities,* Cambridge University Press, New Delhi.

Mishra, S.K. (1981). *Factors and Process of Migration in Developing Economy, A Case Study of Madhya Pradesh,* in R.B. Mandal (Ed.) Frontier in Migration Analysis, Concept Publishing Company, New Delhi.

Meslow, A. (1954). *Motivation and Personality*, NY: Harper, New York.

Mehta, A.K. and Amrita Shah (2003). *Chronic Poverty in India Incidence, Causes and Policies*, World Development 31(3).

Mohanty, M., S. Ray, G.N. Trivedi and N. Sukumar (2011). *Landlessness and the marginalised : A study of Kalahandi, Bhojpur and Chittoor*, inM. Mohanty (ed.) India Social Development Report 2010, Council for Social Development, Oxford University Press, New Delhi.

Mukharjee and Phadke (2011). *Some Facets of Migration to Districts of Maharastra,* in Lahiri et al, Migration, Health and Development, Palgrave Macmillan, New York.

Mukherji, Sekhar (2013). *Migration in India*, Rawat Publications, Jaipur.

Mukherji, Shekhar (2006). *Migration and Urban Decay: Asian Experiences,* Rawat Publications, Jaipur.

Nair (1992). *Impact of Labour Migration on Households-India,* in Godfrey Gunatilleka (Ed) The Impact of Labour Migration on Households A Comparative Study in Seven Asian Countries, United Nations University Press, Tokyo.

Naik, Kshtrabasi (2011). *Dadan* (in Odia), Nabneeta Publications, Balangir.

Oberai, A.S. and H.K. Manmohan Singh (1983). *Causes and Consequences of Internal Migration, A study in Indian Punjab,* Oxford University Press, Delhi.

Oberai, A.S. Pradhan, H.P. and M.G. Sardana (1989). *Determinants and Consequences of Internal Migration in India,* Oxford University Press, Delhi.

Palriwala, Fajni and Patricia Uberoi (2008) (Eds.). *Marriage, Migration and Gender,* Sage Publications, New Delhi.

Pandey, B.K. (2005). *Rural Development: Towards Sustainability,* Vol. I, II and III, Isha Books, New Delhi.

Pankaj, Ashok, (2014)(Ed). *Right to Work and Rural India: Working of the Mahatma Gandhi National Rural Employment Guarantee Scheme,* Sage Publications, New Delhi.

Pattnaik, N. (2005). *Primitive Tribes of Orissa,* D.K. Print World (P) Ltd., New Delhi.

Patnaik, P. and C.P.C. Sekhar (2004). *A Perspective on Migration,* in K. Gopal Iyer (Ed) Distressed Migrant Labour in India Kanishka Publishers Distributors, New Delhi.

Peterson, W. (1970). *A General Typology of Migration,* in Clifford J. Jansen (Ed.) *Reading in the Sociology of Migration.*

Pieka, Frank, N. and Hein Mallee (1999) (Ed.). *Internal and International Migration Chinese Perspectiveness*, Curzon Press, Richmond, U.K.

Pranwell, Mike (1993). *Population Movements and the Third World,* Routledge, London.

Poros, Martisa, V. (2011). *Modern Migration, Gujurati Indian Network in New York and London,* Stanford University Press, Stanford, California.

Pryor, R.J. (1979). *South-East Asia: Migration and Development,* in Robin J. Pryor (Ed) Migration and Development in South-East Asia: A Demographic Perspective, Oxford University Press, Kualalumpur.

Rajan, S.I., V. Kora and R.Chyrmang (2011). *Politics of Conflict and Migration* in S.I. Rajan (Ed) Migration, Identity & Conflict, Routledge, New Delhi.

Ray, T. K, M. Guruswami and P. Arokiasamy (2004). *Population, Health and Development in India,* Rawat Publications, Jaipur Kanishka Publishers and Distributors, New Delhi.

Rajan, S. Irudaya (2011) (Ed.). *Migration, Identity and Conflict India Migration Report, 2011*, Routledge, New Delhi.

Ram, K. (2009). *Inter-State Circular Migration Labour in India,* in K. Gopal Iyer (2009) (Ed) Distress Migrant Labour in India, Key Human Rights Issues. Kanishka Publishers and Distributors, New Delhi.

Rawat, P.S. (1993). *Migration and Structural Change:A Study of Rural Society in Garwal Himalaya,* Sarita Book House, Delhi.

Reddy, N. (2009). *Rural Migrant Labour in Andhra Pradesh,* in K. Gopal Iyer (2009)(Ed.) Distress Migrant Labour in India, Key Human Rights Issues. Kanishka Publishers and Distributors, New Delhi, pp. 186-89

Reddy, D. N. (2007). *Rural Migrant Labour in Andhra Pradesh*, in K. Gopal Iyer(Ed) Distress Migrant Labour in India, Kanishka Publishers and Distributors, New Delhi.

Roy, Archana. K. (2011). *Distress Migration and 'Left Behind' Women,* Rawat Publications, Jaipur.

Sabarwal, Satish (1976). *Mobile Men*, Manohar Publication, New Delhi.

Sjaastad, L.A., (2002). *The Costs and Returns of Human Migration,* in K.F. Zimmerman and T. Baner (Ed) the Economics of Migration (Vol. I) An Elgar Reference Collection, Cheltenham, U.K.

Sah, D.C. (2003). *Involuntary Migration,* Rawat Publications, Jaipur.

Saha, Panchanan (1970). *Emigration of Indian Labour (1834-1900),* Peoples Publishing House, Private Ltd. New Delhi.

Shrestha, Nanda. R. (1996). *A Structural Perspective on Labour Migration in Underdeveloped Countries,* in Vaughan Robinson (Ed) Geography, and Migration (the International Library Studies on Migration) An Elgar Reference Collection Cheltenham, U.K.

Shah, A. (2009). *Brick Kiln Workers from Jharkhand, the Labour of Love,* in P. Deshingkar and J. Farrington (Ed) Circular Migration, Multi-locational Livelihood Strategies in Rural India, Oxford University Press, New York.

Sainath, P. (1996). *Everybody Loves a Good Draught,* Penguin, New Delhi.

Samal Siblal Meher and Srijot Misha (2014). *Migrants in Urban Informal Sector,* SSDN Publishers and Distributors, New Delhi.

Samal, K.C. (2008). *Informal Sector, Concept, Dynamics, Linkages and Migration* Concept Publishing Company, New Delhi.

Samal, K.C. et al (2012). *Migration of Workers to Urban Informal Sector,* Avon Publications, New Delhi.

Samal, K. C. et al (2014). *Migrants in Urban Informal Sector,* SSDN Publishers and Distributors, New Delhi.

Sekhar, T.V. (2011). *Migration and Social Change,* Rawat Publications, Jaipur.

Selier, Frits and Mehtab S. Karim (1986) (Ed). *Migration in Pakistan (Theories and Fact),* Vanguard Books Ltd., Lahore.

Senapati, N.K. (1968). *Odisha Gazetteers, Bolangir.*

Senpati, N. and D.C. Kuanr (1980). *Odisha District Gazetteers – Kalahandi,* Government Press, Cuttack.

Senapati, N. and N.K. Sahu (1968). *Odisha District Gazetteers – Bolangir,* Government Press, Cuttack.

Shah, Mihir (2012). *MGNREGA SAMEEKSHA,* (Ministry of Rural Development, Govt. of India) Orient Blackswan, New Delhi.

Sharma, K.L.(2011) *Culture, Stratification and Development,* Rawat Publications, Jaipur.

Sharma, Ram Naresh, P. and Devendra P. Sharma (1981). *Population of Ranchi Bihar on Move,* in R.B. Mandal (Ed.) Frontier in Migration Analysis, Concept Publishing Company, New Delhi.

Sharma Usha (2006). *Child Labour in India,* Mittal Publications, New Delhi.

———— (2006). *Female Labour in India,* Mittal Publications, New Delhi.

Singh, Manjit (1995). *Uneven Development in Agriculture and Labour Migration*, IIAS, Shimla.

Singh, Sudama (2001). *Migration in the Third World,* Radha Publications, New Delhi.

Sivamurugan, C. (2013). *Rural Out-Migration,* Abhijeet Publications, New Delhi.

Skeldon, R. (1985). *Migration in South Asia: An Overview,* in Kosinski, A and Elaki, K.M. (eds.) Population Redistribution and Development in South Asia, Boston, Reidal.

Sundari, S. (2007). *Migrant Women and Urban Labour Market Concepts and Case Studies of Problems, Gains and Losses,* Deep and Deep Publications Pvt. Ltd., New Delhi.

Sylvia Chant and S. A. Radcliffe (1992). *Migration and Development the Importance of Gender.* in Syliva Chant (1992) (Eds.)Gender and Migration in Developing Countries, Belhaven Press, London, pp. 1-29.

Tadaro, M.P. (1976). *Internal Migration in Developing Countries: A Survey (A. Condensed and Updated Version of a book Entitled "Internal Migration in Developing Nation: Review of Theory, Evidence, Methodology and Research Priorities,* I.L.O., Geneva.

Todaro, M.P. (1980). *Internal Migration in Developing Countries: A Survey*, in R.A. Easterlin (ed) Population and Economic Change in Developing Countries, University of Chicago Press. Access through, http://www.org/chapters/c9668.

Tripathy, S.N. (2005). *Dynamics of Tribal Migration,* Sonali Publication, New Delhi.

Tripathy, S.N. (2013). *Some Reflections on Poverty and Seasonal Migration in Odisha : A Study in KBK Districts* in K.K. Bagchi (ed) Internal Migration in India, Abhijeet Publications, New Delhi.

UNESCO (2013). *Social Inclusion of Internal Migrants in India,* UNESCO, New Delhi.

UNESCO and UNICEF (2012). *Internal Migration in India Initiative,* Workshop Compendium, Vol. 2, UNESCO, New Delhi.(2008) Migration Development and Poverty Reduction in Asia, Academic Foundation, New Delhi.

Verma, Anil Kumar (2011). *Labour Migration in Agriculture Sector,* Discovering Publishing House, New Delhi.

Willis, K. and B. Yeak (2000) (Eds.). *Gender and Migration,* Edward Elgar, Publishing, Cheltenham, U.K.

Zachariah, K.C., E.T. Mathew and S. Irudya Rajan (2003). *Dynamics of Migration in Kerala,* Orient Longman, New Delhi.

Articles

Abbas, Rameez and Divya Varma (2014). *Internal Labour Migration in India raises Integration Challenges for Migrants*, The Online journal of the Migration Policy Initiative 3rd March, 2014.

Bal, C, A. Das and S.C. Kumar (2015). *Silver Lining in Odisha's Organised Manufacturing Sector,* Economic and Political Weekly, Vol. No.15 April 11, pp. 69-79.

Bellak, C., Leibrecht, M. and Libensteiner, M. (2014). *Short-term Labour Migration from the Republic of Armenia to Russian Federation.* The Journal of Development Studies, 2014, Vol. 5, No. 3, 349-367.

Bhattacharya, Prabir (1998). *Informal Sector and Rural-to-Urban-Migration. Some Indian Evidence,* Economic and Political Weekly, Vol. XXXIII, No. 21, May, 23.

Bhowmik, Shartak (2015). *Wages of Tea Plantation Workers, Gap between North and South,* Economic and Political Weekly, Vol. L. No. 19, May 9.

Camelo, (2014). *Migration and Precariousness: Two sides of the Contract Labour Coin,* Economic and Political Weekly, Sept., 6, Vol. XLIX, No. 36. pp. 39-47.

Chopra, Radhika (1995). *Maps of Experiences Narratives of Migration in Indian Villages,* Economic and Political Weekly, Vol. 30 (49) Dec. 9.

Desai, Vandana (1994). *Migration and Labour characteristics of Slum Dwellers in Bombay*, Sociological Bulletin, March, Vol. 43, No. 1.

Editorial (2015). *Let the Children Play,* Economic and Political Weekly, April 18, Vol. L No. 16, p. 8.

Garip, Filiz (2012). *Discovering Diverse Mechanism of Migration: The Mexico – US Stream,* Population and Development Review, Vol. 38, No. 3, Sept, 7.

Grigg, D.G. (1977). *E.G. Ravenstein and the "Laws of Migration"* Journal of Historical Geography, 3, 1(1977) 41-45.

Gill, P.P.S. (2002). *Migrant Labour 'Fear of Social Tension'* The Tribune, Aug., 14.

Golhoskar, Sujato (2013). *The Plight Domestic Workers Confluence of Gender, Class and Hierarchies,* Economic and Political Weekly, Vol. XLVIII, No. 22, June 01.

Gupta,S.K. (1965). *Dandakaranya: A Survey of Rehabilitation, I-The State of Agriculture,* The Economic Weekly, January 2.

Harris, J. and M.P. Todaro (1970). *"Migration Unemployment and Development: A two Sector Analysis,* American Economic Review, 60(1).

Hassankhan, Maurits S. (2013). *Kahe Gaile Bides – Why did you go Overseas? An Introduction in Emotional Aspects of Migration History! A Diaspora Perspective,* Man in India, Jan-March Vol. 93, No. 1.

Halfacree, K.H. (1995). *Household Migration and the Structuration of Patriarchy, Evidence from USA,* Progress in Human Geography 19(2) .

Howie, Emily (2013). *Sri Lankan Boat Migration to Australia,* Economic and Political Weekly, Vol. XLVIII. No. 35, Aug. 13.

Hugo, J.Greeme (1982). *Circular Migration in India*, Population and Development Review, Vol. 8, No. 1, March.

Inbanathan, Anand (1988). *Migration and Adaptation: Lower Caste Tamils in a Delhi Resettlement Colony,* Sociological Bulletin, March-Sept. Vol. 37, Nos. 1 & 2.

Iyer, K. Gopal (2007). *Factors in Inter-State Migration: A Study of Textile Workers in Punjab,* Management and Labour Studies 32(2) May.

Jayaraj, D (2013). *Family Migration 'Push or Pull',* Economic and Political Weekly, Vol. XLV. No. 42, Oct, 19.

Jha, Vikash (2005). *Migration of Odisha's Tribal Women: A New Story of Exploitation,* Economic and Political Weekly, Vol. XL, No. 15, April, 09.

Kalkoti, Gopal (2014). *Status of Rural Migration-Need for Development Initiatives,* Kurukshetra, Vol. 62, No. 11, September.

Kaur. Ravinder (2012). *Marriage and Migration*, Economic and Political Weekly, Vol. XLVII.

Keshari, Kunal, (2012). *Temporary and Seasonal Migration: Regional Pattern, Characteristics and Associated Factors,* Economic and Political Weekly, Vol. XLVII, No. 4, January, 28.

Khwaja, Asim, A. Main and P. Bharadwaj (2008). *The Big March Migratory Flows after the Partition of India,* Economic and Political Weekly, Vol. XLIII, No. 35, Aug. 30.

Kumar, Praveen (2014). *Consequences of Rural Migration*, Kurukshetra, Vol. 62, No. 11, September.

Kundu, Amitabh and L.R. Saraswati (2012). *Migration and Exclusionary Urbanisation in India,* Economic and Political Weekly, Vol. XLVII, No. 26-27, June, 30.No. 43, Oct. 27.

Kundu, Amitabh and Niranjan Sarangi (2007). *Migration, Employment Status and Poverty,* Economic and Political Weekly, Vol. XLII, No. 04, Jan, 27.

Kundu, Amitabh and Shalini Gupta (1996). *Migration, Urbanisation and Regional Inequality,* Economic and Political Weekly, Vol. XXXI, No. 52, Dec, 28.

Korra, Vijay (2011). *Labour Migration in Mehabubnagar, Nature and Characteristics.* Economic and Political Weekly, January 8, Vol. XLVI, No. 2.

Lizhang (2012). *Economic Migration and Urban of Citizenship in China,* Population and Development Review, Vol. 38, No. 3, Sept.

Maharatna, Arup (2003). *Brighter Side of Seasonal Migration,* Economic and Political Weekly, Vol. XXXVIII, No. 35, Aug. 30.

Mahalik, N. (2014). *Cultural Heritage of Undivided Koraput District of Odisha (Origin and Growth of Janajati Culture),* Odisha Review, April-May, pp. 102-105.

Mark Ellis, Dennis Conway and Adrier J. Bailey (2000). *The Circular Migration of Puerto Rican Women towards Gendered Explanation,* in Gender and Migration Edited by Katie Willis and B. Yeak, in International Migration Quarterly Review XXXIV (1).

Manzar, Bashir (2013). *Kashmir: A Tale of Two Communities, Cloven,* Economic and Political Weekly, Vol. XLVIII, No. 30, July 27.

Mazumdar, Indira, N. Neetha and Indira Agrihotri (2013). *Migration and Gender in India,* Economic and Political Weekly, Vol. XLVIII, No. 10, March, 09.

Meher, K. (2015), *Thile Kuli Hele Dadan* (Odiya) Samadrusti, Bhubaneswar.

Mishra, D. and R.S. Rao (1992). *Hunger in Kalahandi, Blinkered Understanding* Economic and Political Weekly, June 13-20.

Nolan, Peter (1993). *Economic Reform, Poverty and Migration in China,* Economic and Political Weekly, Vol. XXVIII, No. 26, June, 26.

Paltasingh, T. and G. Paliwal (2014). *Tribal Population in India: Regional Dimensions and Imperatives,* Journal of Regional Development and Planning, Vol. 3, No. 2.

Pande, Amba (2013). *Conceptualizing Indian Diaspora, Diversity with a Common Identity,* Economic and Political Weekly, Vol. XLVIII, No. 47, Dec. 7.

Papola, T.S. (2011) *Employment in Development: Connection between Indian Strategy and ILO Policy Agenda,* Economic and Political Weekly, March 5, Vol. XLVI, No. 10. Man and Development, March, Vol. XXXV, No. 1.

Pradhan, Jagadish (1993). *Drought in Kalahandi: The Real Story,* Economic and Political Weekly, May 29.

Pruseth, Narayan (2008). *Seasonal Migration in Western Orissa,* Navaratna Journal, Jan-Feb.

Rale, J.R. (1969). *Trends and Significance of Internal Migration in India,* Sankhya: The Indian Journal of Statistics, Series B (1960-2000) Vol. 31, No. 3/4, December.

Rafique, Abdur *et al.,* (2001). *Seasonal Migration, Social Change and Migrating Rights,* Economic and Political Weekly, Vol. XXXVI, No. 49, Dec. 08.

Rodgers, Gerry and Janine Rodgers (2011). *Inclusive Development? Migration, Governance and Social Change in Rural Bihar,* Economic and Political Weekly, Vol. XLVI, No. 23, June 04.

Sainath, P. (2009). *More Migration, New Destinations,* The Hindu, July 11, 2009 URL,http://www.thehindu.com/todaypaper/tpopinion/article 226404.ece, accessed on 17/02/15.

—————— (2011). *Decadal Journeys-Debt and Despire and Spur Urban Growth,* The Hindu, Sept.7, 2011, accessed to website on 17/02/815.

Sen, Sunanda (2016). Indentured Labour from India in the Age of Empire, Social Scientist, Vol. 44/No. 1-2 January-February.

Singh, Abha *et al.,* (2005) *Labour Out Migration, Livelihood of Rice Farming Households and Women Left Behind,* Economic and Political Weekly, XL, No. 25, June 18.

Taylor, Steve and Manjit Singh (2013). *Punjab's Doaban Migration – Development Nexus,* Economic and Political Weekly, Vol. XLVIII, No. 24, June, 15.

Tyner, J.A. (1994). *The Social Construction of Gendered Migration from the Philippines,* Asian and Pacific Migration Journal 3(4). 589-617.

Tripathy, R. (2011). *Migration, Money, Music*, Economic and Political Weekly, November 12, Vol. XLVI, No. 46.

Thapa, Suraj (2013). *Urban Migrants and Electoral Issues in Ludhiana City,* Man and Development, Sept, 13, Vol. XXXV, No. 3.

Upadhya, Carol and Mario Rutten (2012). *Migration, Transnational Flows and Development in India,* Economic and Political Weekly, Vol. XLVII, No. 19, May, 12.

Occasional Papers, Report and News Paper

Bhagat, R.M. (2009). *International Migration in India, Are the Underclass More Mobile,* Paper on the 26th Issue, General Population Conference, Morocco, 27th September – 2nd October.

CRD Report, *Impact Assessment of Externally Aided Project Interventions on Livelihood of the poor and Marginalised in KBK Districts of Orissa, Sponsored by Planning Commission of India*, Centre for Rural Development, Bhubaneswar.

CMLS(2014) *Studies, Stories and a Canvas, Seasonal Labour Migration and Migrant Workers from Odisha*, Aaieevika Bureau, Udaipur.

Dharitri Odia Daily Newspaper, 24th October 2013.

Dharitri Odia Daily Newspaper, 12th December 2013.

Dharitri Odia Daily Newspaper, 14th March 2014.

Dharitri, Odia Daily Newspaper, 27th January, 2014.

Dharitri, Odia Daily Newspaper, 27th March, 2014.

Government of India (2001). *Census of India – 2001,* New Delhi.

Government of India (2011). *Census of India – 2011,* New Delhi

Government of Odisha (2012). *Statistical Abstract of Odisha 2012*, Directorate of Economics and Statistics Odisha, Bhubaneswar.

Government of Odisha (2014). *Odisha Economic Survey, 2013-14,* Planning and Coordination Department, Directorate of Economics and Statistics, Government of Odisha, Bhubaneswar.

Government of Odisha (2014). *Statistical Hand Book of Tribal Sub Plan (TSP) Blocks in Odisha*, Scheduled Castes and Scheduled Tribes Research and Training Institute, Bhubaneswar.

Government of Odisha, *District Statistical Hand Book, Koraput (2009), Malkangiri (2011), Rayagada (2009), Nabarangapur (2009), Kalahandi (2009), Nuapada (2009), Bolangir (2009), and Subarnapur (2009),* Directorate of Economics and Statistics Odisha, Bhubaneswar.

NSSO Report No. 430, Housing Conditions and Migration in India, Ministry of Statistics and Programme Implementation, Govt. of India.

NSSO (2007). *Informal Sector and Conditions of Employment in India 2004-2005*, National Sample Survey Organisation, Ministry of Statistics and Programme Implementation, Government of India.

NSS 64th Round (2010). *Migration in India (2007-08),* Ministry of Statistics and Programme Implementation, Govt. of India.

Haan, A. and A. Dubey (2005). *Extreme deprivation in remote areas in India: social exclusion as an explanatory concept,* Draft paper for Manchester Conference on Chronic Poverty, April, 2003.

Indian Express, English Daily, April, 24, 2012, *No let-up in Migration,* Bhubaneswar.

MiRC (2011). *Children in Brick Kilns*. Aid et. Action, Bhubaneswar.

MiRC. *Debt Migrant Labour, Bondage and Rehabilitation.* Aid et. Action OTV, News, 5th May. 2015.

Parida, N. (2008). *Chronic Poverty and Hunger in KBK Region of Odisha Identifying Causes in the Perspective of a Case Study in Watershed Development Project in Nabarangapur District.* (Research Paper). Institute of Social Studies, The Hague, The Netherlands.

Samaj Odiya Daily 7th October, 2014.

Samaj, Odia Daily 14th January, 2015.

Samaj Odiya Daily 13th Feb. 2015.

Samaj Odiya Daily 13th April, 2015.

Sharma, J. C. (2002). *Inaugural Address in Indian Diaspora, First International Conference on 'Indian Diasporic Experience: History, Culture and Identity'* Organised by Centre for India Diaspora and Cultural Studies, Himachandra-charya North Gujarat University, Patna. During January 22-24, available on http://www.ngu.ac.in/centre/dias/index.htm.

Sinha, B.K.P. and M. Behera (2011). *Changing Socio-Economic Condition and Livelihood of Geographically Isolated Tribal Community in Kandhamal and KBK Districts of Orissa,* A Research Study Report Submitted to the Planning Commission of India, New Delhi.

Times of India, English Daily Newspaper, 18th October 2013.

UNESCO and UNICEF (2012). *Internal Migration in India Initiative Workshop Compendium,* Vol. 2, UNESCO, New Delhi.

Vasundhara (2005). *Development Policies and Rural Poverty in Orissa: Macro Analysis and Case Studies: A Study by Vasundhara,* Bhubaneswar, Supported by Planning Commission of India, New Delhi.

Zacharia, K.C. (1964). *A Historical Study of Internal Migration in the Indian Sub-Continent,* Demographic Training and Research Centre, Bombay, Research Monograph No.1, Asia Publishing House, Bombay.

Khandelwal, R, E. Gilbert and W. Gantt (2009). *Serving Migrants, Reflections on the Aajeevika Bureau Experience*, Aajeeviaka, (NGO).

Workmen's Compensation Act, 1923.

Payment of Wages Act, 1936.

Industrial Employment (Standing Orders) Act, 1946.

Industrial Disputes Act, 1947.

The Minimum Wages Act, 1948.

Employees Provident Fund and Miscellaneous Provisions Act, 1952.

Maternity Benefit Act, 1961.

Payment of Bonus Act, 1965.

Contract Labour (Regulation and Abolition) Act, 1970.

Payment of Gratuity Act, 1972.

Bonded Labour System (Abolition) Act, 1976.

Equal Remuneration Act, 1976.

Inter-State Migration Workmen (Regulation of Employment and Condition of Services) Act, 1979.

Odisha Inter-State Migration (RELS) Rules, 1980.

Child Labour (Prohibition and Regulation) Act, 1986.

The Building and Other Construction Workers (Regulation of Employment and Conditions of Services) Act, 1996.

The Odisha Building and Other Construction Workers (Regulation of Employment and Conditions of Services) Act, 2002.

Mahatma Gandhi National Rural Employment Guarantee Act, 2005, (NREGA, 2005).

Appendix-I

Sample Villages

District			Name of the Block
Kalahandi			
1.	Kegan	.– 27	Golamunda
2.	Chapria	– 53	
3.	Turichhada	– 18	
4.	Sanchargaon	– 06	
		104	
Nuapada			
1.	Khamtarai	– 39	Khariar
2.	Rohanipadar	– 14	
3.	Mahulkhat	– 17	
4.	Podapali	– 30	
		100	
Bolangir			
1.	Debripali	– 50	Belpada
2.	Tentulimunda	– 50	
		100	
Sonepur			
1.	Bahirkhaman	– 50	Sonepur
2.	Godia	– 16	
3.	Lachhipur	– 20*	
4.	Sankara	– 20*	Binka
		106	

Koraput			
1.	Katriguda	– 02	Kundra
2.	Gundal	– 26	
3.	Majhiguda	– 16	
4.	Bhatiguda	– 11	
5.	Baliguda	– 10	Baipariguda
6.	Debtaguda	– 10	
7.	Polla	– 18	
8.	Umriguda	– 14	
9.	Hakaguda	–	
		107	
Nabarangpur			
1.	Gopalguda	– 16	Jharigaon
2.	Itchapur	– 12	
3.	Tarakandi	– 12	
4.	Dengaguda	– 14	
5.	Pulsagaon	– 08	
6.	Basudevguda	– 12	
		74	
Rayagada			
1.	Deokhupali	– 36	Muriguda
2.	Dhubagudi	– 16	
3.	Gudiakhata	– 13	Bisamkatak
4.	Papikhal	– 08	
5.	Patpadar	– 05	
6.	Mirgundi	– 05	
7.	Munda	– 06	
8.	Godaba	– 06	
9.	Ajingpadar	– 06	
10.	Kuntabadi	– 05	
11.	Daragadi	– 04	
12.	Dedipada	– 10	
		120	

Malkangiri

1.	Pujariguda	– 42	Mathali
2.	Talagadiali	– 20	
		62	

Appendix-II

Benefits under Odisha Building and Other Construction Workers' Welfare Board

Sl. No.	*Nature and Provision of Assistant*	*Amount (Rs.)*
1.	**Assistant in case of Accident**	
	a. Permanent total disability due to accident	1,50,000/-
	b. Loss of one limb/eye	80,000/-
	c. Permanent disability without loss of two limbs/eyes	40,000/-
2.	**Death Benefit**	
	a. Normal death	1,00,000/-
	b. Accidental death	2,00,000/-
3.	**Assistance for Funeral Expenses**	5,000/-
4.	**Medical Expenses for Treatment of Major Ailments** (On completion of one Year)	Benefit as per Rastrya Swasta Bima Yojana
5.	**Education Assistance** (On completion of one Year)	
	a. For Class-11th/12th	5,000/- Per Annum
	b. For Classes of B.A./B.Sc/B.Com./P.G Studies	7,000/- Per Annum
	c. For ITI	7,000/- Per Annum
	d. For Diploma/ Polytechnic	10,000/-
	e. B.Tech/B.Arch/B.Pharm/MCA/MBA/M.Arch/ M.Tech/M.Pharm/Medical/ Hotel Management and Catering Services	40,000/-
6.	**Marriage Assistance** (On completion of one Year)	25,000/-
7.	**Maternity Benefit** (On completion of one Year)	8,000/-
8.	**Assistance for Purchase of Working Tools**	4,000/-
9.	**Assistance for Purchase of Bicycle**	4,000/-

(Contd...)

10.	**Assistance for Purchase of Safety Equipment** (Helmet, Safety Shoe and Gloves)	1,000/-
11.	**Financial Assistance for Skill Up-gradation, Training** a. Through CSTI, Gopalpur, Cuttack and Odisha State Employment Mission. b. Through RPL Scheme	2,000/- P.M. for six months 200/- per day as daily wage compensation during training period.
12.	**Construction of Rest Shed and Drinking Water Outlets**	At labour congregation places (As per Requisition)

Source: Odisha Labour Welfare Board, Bhubaneswar.

Index

L

M

S

U

V

W

Z